INSIGHT GUIDE

MADEIRA

Discovery CHANNEL

APA PUBLICATIONS
Part of the Langenscheidt Publishing Group

ABOUT THIS BOOK

Editorial

Editor
Melissa de Villiers
Managing Editor
Emily Hatchwell
Editorial Director
Brian Bell

Distribution

UK & Ireland
GeoCenter International Ltd
The Viables Centre, Harrow Way
Basingstoke, Hants RG22 4BJ
Fax: (44) 1256 817988

United States
Langenscheidt Publishers, Inc.
46–35 54th Road, Maspeth, NY 11378
Fax: (718) 784 0640

Canada
Thomas Allen & Son Ltd
390 Steelcase Road East
Markham, Ontario L3R 1G2
Fax: (1) 905 475 6747

Australia
Universal Press
1 Waterloo Road
Macquarie Park, NSW 2113
Fax: (61) 2 9888 9074

New Zealand
Hema Maps New Zealand Ltd (HNZ)
Unit D, 24 Ra ORA Drive
East Tamaki, Auckland
Fax: (64) 9 273 6479

Worldwide
Apa Publications GmbH & Co.
Verlag KG (Singapore branch)
38 Joo Koon Road, Singapore 628990
Tel: (65) 6865 1600. Fax: (65) 6861 6438

Printing

Insight Print Services (Pte) Ltd
38 Joo Koon Road, Singapore 628990
Tel: (65) 6865 1600. Fax: (65) 6861 6438

©2002 **Apa Publications GmbH & Co.**
Verlag KG (Singapore branch)
All Rights Reserved
First Edition 1991
Second Edition 2000. Updated 2002

CONTACTING THE EDITORS

We would appreciate it if readers
would alert us to errors or out-
dated information by writing to:
Insight Guides, P.O. Box 7910,
London SE1 1WE, England.
Fax: (44) 20 7403 0290.
insight@apaguide.demon.co.uk

www.insightguides.com

This guidebook combines the interests and enthusiasms of two of the world's best-known infor-mation providers: Insight Guides, whose titles have set the standard for visual travel guides since 1970, and Discovery Channel, the world's premier source of nonfiction televi-sion programming.

The editors of Insight Guides pro-vide practical advice and general understanding about a destina-tion's history, culture, insti-tutions and people. Discovery Channel and its Web site, www.discovery.com, help mil-lions of viewers to explore their world from the com-fort of their own home and also encourage them to explore it first hand.

This fully updated edition of *Insight: Madeira* is carefully struc-tured to convey an understanding of the island and its culture as well as to guide readers through its sights and activities:

♦ The **Features** section, indicated by a yellow bar at the top of each page, covers the history and culture of the island in a series of lively and informative essays.

♦ The main **Places** section, which is indicated by a blue bar, is a complete guide to all the sights and areas that are worth seeing on the island. Places of spe-cial interest are coor-dinated by number with the maps.

EXPLORE YOUR WORLD

◆ The **Travel Tips** section, with an orange bar, provides a handy point of reference for information on travel, hotels, shops, restaurants and more. Information can be found quickly using the index on the back cover flap, which can also serve as a bookmark.

The contributors

This revision of *Insight: Madeira* was supervised by **Melissa de Villiers**, a London-based travel journalist who also introduced new chapters on east, west and central Madeira, and on excursions from Funchal.

Two people proved invaluable to the updating process. Prolific travel writer **Christopher Catling** substantially reworked the essay section, and brought the text on Porto Santo

and the Ilhas Desertas up to date. Catling also updated the guide in 2002. The new chapter on Island Walks was the contribution of **Chris Hawksworth**, a travel broadcaster (and keen hiker) who lives in Yorkshire; he also efficiently updated the Travel Tips.

The current edition builds on the foundations created by the editors and writers of previous editions of the book, most notably **Ute York**, editor of the original *Insight: Madeira*, who also wrote the original essays on The Home of Columbus and Distinguished Visitors.

Cornelia von Schelling recounted the history of the celebrated Reid's Hotel, along with Madeira's traditionally tense relationship with Portugal and its traditionally good relationship with Britain.

Martina Emonts contributed the original chapters on Porto Santo and the Ilhas Desertas, as well as the articles on the local crafts of embroidery and wickerwork.

Dieter Clarius documented the parts played by both slavery and piracy in the island's history.

The original chapters on the island's food and wine were by **Christa Eder**, while **Gerhard H. Oberzil** wrote about Funchal. Other contributors to previous editions include **Günther Heubl, Paul Otto Schultz, Petra Deimer** and **Susanne Lipps**.

Many of the photographs in this book are the work of **Glyn Genin**, a regular Insight Guide contributor, along with **Phil Hall, Terry Harris** and **Bill Wassman**.

Thanks also go to **Bryony Coleman** for proofreading and **Caroline Wilding** for indexing this latest edition, and to **Siân Lezard** for editing the Travel Tips listings sections.

Map Legend

─ ·· ─	International Boundary
─ · ─	National Park/Reserve
─ ─ ─	Ferry Route
✈ ✈	Airport: International/Regional
🚌	Bus Station
P	Parking
ℹ	Tourist Information
✉	Post Office
🕈 † ✝	Church/Ruins
†	Monastery
☾	Mosque
✡	Synagogue
🏰 🏛	Castle/Ruins
∴	Archaeological Site
∩	Cave
1	Statue/Monument
★	Place of Interest

The main places of interest in the Places section are coordinated by number with a full-colour map (e.g. ❶), and a symbol at the top of every right-hand page tells you where to find the map.

CONTENTS

Maps

Boats and their
skippers in
Câmara de Lobos

Travel Tips

◆ **Full Travel Tips index
is on page 249**

Insight on ...

Information panels

Places

BEMVINDO A MADEIRA

With its warm climate, exotic scenery and friendly people,
Madeira's a restful retreat from the hectic pace of modern life

The "Island of Eternal Springtime", "Pearl of the Atlantic", "the Floating Flowerpot": just a few of the descriptions of Madeira dreamed up down the centuries by visitors from around the world. The island's natural charms are still as alluring as they were when it was first settled by the Portuguese in the 15th century. Back then, it was as a supplier of sugar – "white gold" – that Madeira first came to Europe's attention, although the sweet local wines soon became its major claim to fame. Today, it's the dramatic landscape, the friendly people, the exotic splendour of the vegetation and the mild climate that make the place such a favourite with holiday-makers who want to relax in style and comfort – at any time of year.

Younger travellers (clubbers and party animals, particularly) may bemoan the lack of beaches and lively nightlife, but, for hikers and nature lovers, few destinations can offer such a varied landscape within such a small area. At just 58 km by 23 km (36 by 14 miles), Madeira's volcanic mountainous interior offers ever-changing views of misty gorges, green valleys and deserted plateaux, while along the coast, towering cliffs plunge precipitously into the foaming surf. Keen walkers rejoice in the hundreds of miles of pathways lining the drainage channels (*levadas*) which feed the fields and vineyards, penetrating deep into the island's rural heart.

Also justly celebrated are the island's public parks and gardens. Rich volcanic soil and a subtropical climate provide ideal conditions for a huge range of flowering plants, introduced from as far afield as South America, South Africa and Asia. There's something to see all year round, but the flowers are at their best in spring, when the scent of blossom mingles with the sharp tang of sea breezes.

Porto Santo, Madeira's smaller neighbour some 40 km (25 miles) to the northeast, has far less greenery; but that is more than compensated for by the excellent long, sandy beaches and wild desert-like countryside. Two further groups of islands, both barren and uninhabited – the three Desertas 30 km (17 miles) southeast of Madeira and the two remote Selvagens 250 km (155 miles) further south – complete the picture.

In addition to its beauty, the little archipelago has a lively history spiced with romantic legends about its discovery, controversy regarding relations with Portugal (the mother country) and an intriguing "British connection". It isn't a place to be rushed but to be sipped slowly and savoured, like its famous fortified wines. For those who appreciate a warm climate, striking scenery, exotic greenery, rich cultural heritage and friendly people, it is a place to return to again and again. ❑

PRECEDING PAGES: Funchal cathedral's 16th-century choir stalls, which were carved in Flanders; codfish drying in the sun to make *bacalhau*; making friends in Funchal Old Town; breaktime for island fishermen.
LEFT: a Monte toboggan-driver in traditional straw boater.

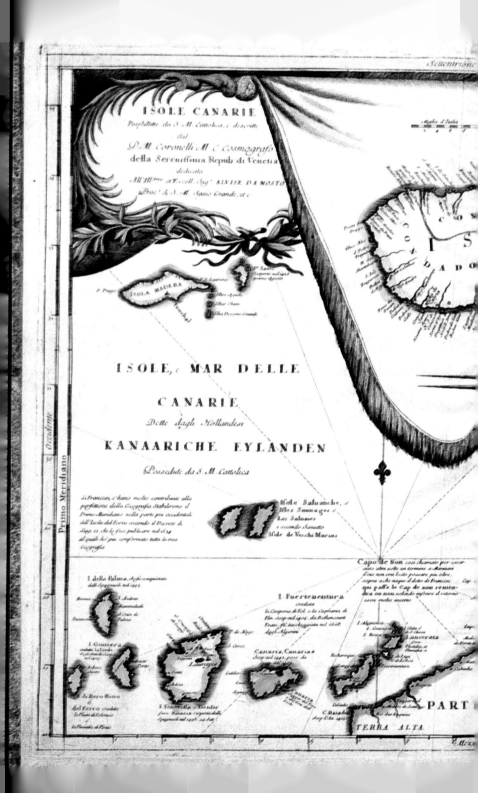

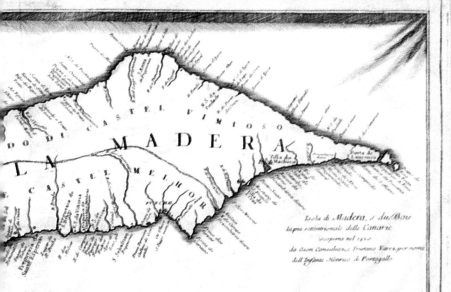

Isola di Madera, è du Bois
la piu settentrionale delle Canarie
scoperta nel 1420
da Gion Consaluez, e Tristano Varez, per nome
dell'Infante Henrico di Portogallo

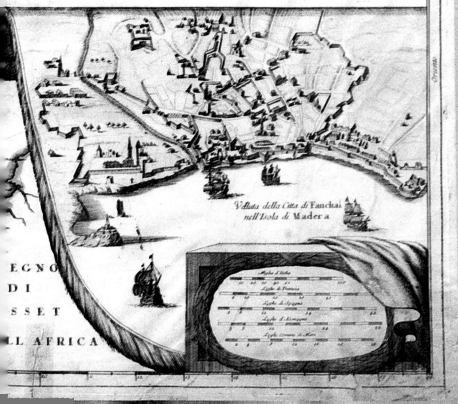

Veduta della Città di Fanchai
nell'Isola di Madera

Decisive Dates

20 million years ago Massive submarine volcanic eruptions force the island of Madeira up through the surface of the Atlantic.

1.7 million years ago Madeira's volcanoes cool and finally die. The landscape slowly takes shape as – lashed by wind and rain – the soft volcanic rock is carved into jagged mountains, deep ravines and sheer cliffs that plunge down into the sea.

2,000 years ago Although known to Phoenician, Roman and Carthaginian sailors, Madeira remains uncolonised and without indigenous inhabitants.

COLONISATION AND CONTROL

1351 A Genoese map – now displayed in Florence's Laurentian Library – depicts Madeira for the first time. Titled *Isola di Lolegname* ("wooded isle"), it appears alongside its island neighbours now known as Porto Santo and the Desertas.

1373 A Treaty of Friendship is signed between England and Portugal upon the marriage of Philippa of Lancaster to the Portuguese King John I. They give birth to a son, later known as Prince Henry the Navigator.

1418 Prince Henry sponsors two of his naval commanders, João Gonçalves Zarco and Tristão Vaz Teixeira, to explore the Guinea Coast of Africa. Blown off course, they seek shelter on Porto Santo

and return to Lisbon to report sightings of a much larger wooded island nearby.

1419 Henry sends a second fleet, again headed by Zarco, to explore the archipelago further. A Portuguese base is established on Porto Santo.

1420 Zarco claims Madeira for Portugal.

1440–50 Zarco and Teixeira are given half-shares in Madeira and divide it up among their friends and relatives, many of whom begin cultivating sugar.

THE RISE OF THE SUGAR TRADE

1452 The first consignment of slaves – Guanches from the Canary Islands, and West Africans – is shipped out to Madeira to work in the sugar-cane plantations. The construction of the island's vast network of irrigation channels (*levadas*) begins. Madeira soon becomes Europe's most important supplier of sugar; grapevines and grain are also cultivated.

1478 Christopher Columbus sails into Funchal harbour on a trading mission to buy sugar. Later in the year he marries Felipa Moniz, daughter of Porto Santo's governor, and briefly settles on the island.

1480 onwards Various contingents of settlers arrive from Europe. Many are merchants who invest in the sugar plantations and the ever-expanding irrigation systems. Maintaining their connections with the world of high finance in Europe's commercial centres, the newcomers often perform the triple role of landowner-merchant-financier.

A PLAGUE OF PIRATES

1514 The island's first census states that the population of Madeira has reached 5,000 (excluding slaves). Funchal's cathedral is completed, building having begun in 1485.

1530 onwards The importance of the sugar trade begins to decline in the face of fiercer competition from Brazil and Central America. By the mid-16th century, many of the sugar plantations have been replaced by vines from Cyprus and Crete.

1542 A defensive wall with ramparts is built around Funchal to protect it from pirate attacks.

1566 One of the worst pirate raids in Madeira's history takes place. Funchal's defences prove totally inadequate as 1,000 French pirates attack, killing the governor and 250 islanders and ransacking the monasteries and convents and the homes of the wealthy.

1569 King Sebastião grants permission for the founding of a Jesuit college in Funchal.

1580 Philip II of Spain occupies Portugal; Madeira consequently comes under Spanish rule and is drawn into the conflict between Spain and England. The coast is subject to repeated raids by English corsairs.

1640 The Portuguese regain their kingdom from Spanish rule (1 June is still celebrated annually on Madeira as Independence Day).

BRITAIN AND THE WINE TRADE

1662 The marriage of the English king, Charles II, to Catherine of Braganza, daughter of João IV of Portugal.

1703 Anglo-Portuguese trade relations are normalised under the terms of the Methuen Treaty. Britain, which has supported Portugal's struggle for independence from Spain, demands (and is granted) numerous trade concessions in return. As a result, a good many British merchants settle on Madeira, and soon dominate the wine trade.

1761 Madeira begins the drawn-out process of abolishing slavery with a ban on the purchase of slaves in Africa.

1768 Captain Cook anchors at Madeira on his first voyage in his ship, the *Endeavour*.

1807–14 In response to the French occupation of mainland Portugal during the Napoleonic Wars, the British station 2,000 soldiers on Madeira. Many remain once the war is over.

1856 Elizabeth Phelps, daughter of a local British wine merchant, introduces a lucrative commercial aspect to Madeira's traditional art of embroidery.

1872 *Phylloxera*, a parasitic insect imported by accident from America, destroys most of the vines on Madeira. Although new, more resilient vine varieties are planted, the wine industry never really recovers from this blow, and a wave of emigration ensues. Bananas now replace the vine as the main cash crop, becoming the most important branch of the island's economy.

INTO THE MODERN AGE

Mid-19th century onwards Exiled aristocrats, well-heeled consumptives, writers, artists and politicians from all over Europe "discover" the island as a place to escape the rigours of the northern winter. Tourism begins to grow into one of Madeira's major sources of income.

1891 Reid's Hotel opens.

1916 In response to a request by the British, Portugal confiscates all German possessions on Madeira. A German submarine promptly surfaces off the coast and sinks three ships anchored in Funchal harbour before shelling the town itself.

1939–45 World War II causes the temporary closure of Reid's Hotel. Some 2,000 refugees from Gibraltar are accommodated on the island.

1960 An airport is opened on Porto Santo; four years later, Santa Caterina airport opens on Madeira, ending the island's isolation.

1974–75 Portugal's 1974 revolution overthrows its post-war dictatorship and paves the way for future democracy.

1976 Madeira becomes an autonomous region, with its own parliament.

1986 Portugal joins the European Union. Membership means that funds are released to improve Madeira's infrastructure, bringing roads, electricity and sanitation to remote communities.

1997 The *Rapide* motorway opens, transforming island transport; journeys from Funchal to Ribeira Brava now take 15 minutes instead of an hour.

2001 The island's new airport opens, allowing jumbo jets to land there and heralding a large increase in visitor numbers. In the same year, the Funchal to Monte cable car opens, providing new ways to explore the island.

2002 Several new luxury hotels open around the island, offering an alternative to the hotels of the capital, Funchal. ❑

PRECEDING PAGES: a 17th-century chart of the islands.
LEFT: a memorial to the explorer Zarco, Funchal.
RIGHT: Portuguese and Madeiran flags, Vila Baleira.

TALES OF DISCOVERY

History books recount that Madeira was first discovered in the early
15th century, but the island's legends tell a different tale

My determinate voyage is mere extravagancy
– Shakespeare: Twelfth Night.

Theories about exactly when Madeira was discovered abound. Most are based on legend rather than historical evidence, though the fact that they have common elements suggests they may contain grains of truth. One of the most interesting is the tragic love story of an exiled English nobleman written by the medieval chronicler Valentine Ferdinand (alias Fernandes), a printer from Bohemia who lived in Lisbon between 1495 and 1561. The tale he wrote (in Latin) refers to what is thought to be the oldest account of the archipelago.

His sources are a matter for speculation. It seems likely that, since the industrious Fernandes also worked as an interpreter and agent for European trading companies, he first heard the story of the unfortunate Englishman and the discovery of Madeira in a Lisbon harbour inn, where he would have consorted with captains, shipowners and merchants. In that era, vessels would sail into port with crews of cabin-fevered adventurers who could scarcely wait to share their experiences – and wildest fantasies – with an astonished world.

The legend

Fernandes, like Shakespeare, was well aware that the common folk of his time enjoyed a good yarn, and he was quick to pick up on interesting material for his work. We may assume, therefore, that the facts of Madeira's discovery are mixed with a generous portion of fiction, and that the tellers of the tale – who would have added their own embellishments, of course – were Christian seafarers.

According to the story, the nobleman, Sir Robert Machin (or Machyn), was exiled from England – although we are not told exactly

why. In any event, he purchased a small ship and had his goods and chattels taken on board, together with several goats to provide milk and meat for the journey. He was accompanied by his crew and his concubine – a mistress of lower social standing. He was hoping to reach Portugal, but the travellers were caught in a

storm near the island of Berlenga, and this swept them southwards until they suddenly sighted land. Machin and his crew went ashore, taking the goats with them.

The land is thought to have been Porto Santo, because when visibility improved "they saw more land across the sea and sailed over there to see what sort of a country it was." The ship anchored in a bay, which they called "Machin". (Later, the theory goes, the Castilians "Iberianised" the name of the bay, calling it Machico; a small port on the east coast of Madeira still bears this name today.)

Machin, assuming control of their misfortune, instructed his crew to set up camp on the

---

LEFT: when Portuguese explorers first landed on Porto Santo in 1418, they reported sightings of a mysterious mist-covered island to the southwest...
RIGHT: Henry the Navigator, prince of discoverers.

shores of the bay and went off alone to explore the island. On returning from his foray three days later, he found that the crew had mutinied and disappeared with his ship, leaving only his page and mistress behind. The treacherous crew had tried to talk them into going with them, but, loyal to the last, they refused, saying: "God would not want us to desert our master."

Life on the desert island could not have been sweet, even for the lovers. Distressed by the hopelessness of their situation, Machin's mistress gave up hope and died "of grief". Accordingly, Sir Robert built a small chapel to serve as her last resting place and called it Santa Cruz.

However, the tale doesn't end there. As in all good stories, the evil crew were punished for their treachery. Their plans for escape were thwarted when another violent storm blew up and drove their ship on to Morocco's Barbary Coast. There they were captured by Arabs and thrown into prison.

Machin and his page were determined to return to civilisation. Managing to build a raft, they put out to sea but they, too, ran into a savage storm and were tossed on to the very same beach where the crew had been captured.

The two castaways were duly captured by the Moors and imprisoned with the traitors. It

LISBONA.

VARIATIONS ON A THEME

One of the best-known variations on Fernandes' Madeiran tale is the *Epanáfora Amorosa*, written in 1654 by Francisco Manuel de Melo. This version is enhanced by a lavish baroque setting: Machin's martyrdom in the infidels' dungeons is a motif El Greco would have been proud to immortalise on canvas. Melo also makes Machin's lady love an aristocrat, the toast of Edward III's court. It is in order to escape an arranged marriage between Ana and a high-ranking nobleman that the lovers flee and board a ship for France. However, their plans are disrupted by a tempest, which blows them off course and propels them on to a strange island...

was Sir Robert's opportunity to avenge the treachery that he believed had ruined their best chance of escape from the island. In fury, he jumped on the first seaman he could lay his hands on, ready to kill him.

It was this which, according to the tale, led to the wider discovery of Madeira. The Arabs were so surprised at such violence among countrymen and co-religionists that they reported it to the King of Fez. He summoned them to appear before him, and thus came to learn of Madeira. However, "since he could gain no profit from the island", he magnanimously dispatched Sir Robert Machin to King John I of Castile to report on the island's existence and ask the Castilian monarch if *he* would like to benefit from its discovery. King John, however, was far too busy waging war to be greatly interested in taking Madeira.

The historical version

Fantasy isn't left out of the historians' version of events, either. They attribute Madeira's discovery to the Phoenicians, the influential traders and seafarers who from about 3000 BC dominated the Mediterranean and beyond, heading out into the Atlantic on their trading ventures and frequently stopping off at such islands as Madeira for shelter and water.

Madeira itself is clearly visible and reachable from there (especially with a little help from one of the Atlantic's frequent storms).

The facts are few but undisputed. At the beginning of the century – some historians set the date at 1312 – a Genoese, called Lancelotto Malocelo, tried to establish a colony on Lanzarote, one of the Canary Islands. Twenty years later, however, he was driven away by the original inhabitants, a Stone-Age tribe with only primitive weapons. A succession of expeditions to the Canary Islands followed, involving not only the Italians, but also the Catalonians and the Portuguese.

Although the island was known to Roman and North African sailors as well, it was never colonised, and its earliest known appearance on a map is only in 1351. The cartographers of the so-called Medici Map (which is now kept in Florence) described Madeira as the *Isola di Lolegname* ("Wooded Island").

It is known that there was considerable shipping traffic in these waters during the first half of the 14th century. Madeira's neighbours, the Canary Islands, were certainly visited, and

LEFT: Madeira's distant capital: a 17th-century depiction of Lisbon.

ABOVE: a Madeiran replica of a 15th-century caravel.

In 1342, the Castilians also took part in expeditions to the Canary Islands, and, in 1344, Luis La Cerda, a descendant of King Alfonso X of Castile, drew up a bold plan to conquer a large group of legendary islands, among them the Canary Islands. The pope proclaimed La Cerda ruler of this fictional principality and appealed to the kings and princes of Christianity to join him in a crusade against the heathen islanders. But, with more tangible affairs of state to attend to, they left La Cerda to day-dream on his own.

Alfonso IV of Portugal (1325–57) also called upon the pope to validate him as ruler of the Canary Islands. He claimed that he had been sending sailing ships to the Canaries for many years, and that Portugal was the European kingdom closest to these islands. Madeira is only a short distance away from the direct Canary Islands route, and on this wooded island his vassals were able to obtain timber and fresh water, as well as fresh meat – presumably from the descendants of poor Robert Machin's goats.

The Age of Discovery

In 1415, Portugal managed to establish a foothold on the African continent. Morocco's seaport of Ceuta was besieged and taken – an event that marked the start of a new era of Portuguese expansion worldwide.

But the lands he "discovered" were not all desolate or even unknown to others. "There is some misunderstanding over the two words 'discover' and 'discovery'," writes Salvador de Madariaga, Christopher Columbus' Spanish biographer. "They are interpreted far too narrowly, as though a seafarer or cosmographer speaking of discovering a certain country necessarily means wild and unexplored territory. That is not so. For people in the 15th and 16th centuries, 'discovery' meant nothing less than 'integration into the Christian community'."

Nonetheless Henry the Navigator was a driving force in the discovery of the world beyond

It was at the siege of Ceuta that Dom João I of Portugal's youngest son first made a name for himself: Infante Dom Henrique, known in our history books as Henry the Navigator (1394 –1460). He was an avid collector of all the latest information on sea maps and shipping, newly discovered countries and coastal regions, navigation and cosmography, all of which he had evaluated at his "documentation centre" in Sagres in the western Algarve.

He designed a brand-new type of ship, too, the caravel, which could sail against the wind, and commissioned seafarers to discover new routes to India and China. His main aim, of course, was to exploit their rich resources.

the established trade routes. Seafarers cautiously nosed their vessels southwards along the West African coast. Cape Juby (Cape Bojador) was navigated in 1434, but even the most seasoned seafarers did not dare to venture further, believing that the bottomless depths of the "Dark Sea" lurked beyond. Time and time again, an impatient Henry the Navigator tried to dispel their fears by producing hard facts. He finally managed to cajole his sea-captains into sailing south beyond the latitude of the Canary Islands with bribes and promises of land.

Reports of their discoveries gradually aroused interest in Africa and its riches. Portuguese trade relations were established, with forts and trading companies springing up all along the West African coast. The most coveted commodities were gold, ivory, pepper, sugar cane – and slaves.

Claimed for Portugal

In his *Crónica dos Feitos da Guiné*, one Gomes Eanes de Azurara tells in the chapter "How Madeira and the other islands were settled" of two veteran Portuguese knights, João Gonçalves (known as "Zarco") and Tristão Vaz Teixeira, who were employed in 1418 by Henry

Henry's response was to order a return voyage back to the islands so that the explorers could investigate further.

Consequently, in 1419 a ship commanded by the navigator Bartolomeu Perestrelo set off to colonise Porto Santo, while two more under Zarco and Vaz were dispatched to explore its mysterious mist-covered neighbour. Early in 1420 they found what they were looking for: a densely wooded, mountainous island Zarco named Ilha da Madeira, after the Portuguese word for wood.

the Navigator to explore the coast of Guinea. Their sailing ship never reached West Africa, for they, too, ran into one of the region's ferocious storms and were swept away on to an island they called Porto Santo ("Blessed Port") in gratitude for their safe landing. After exploring for a few days, they decided the island was suitable for settlement and headed back to Lisbon to report back to the Prince. They also claimed to have seen a much larger island to the southwest, covered in a dark shroud of mist.

LEFT: Porto Santo was the first part of the archipelago to be "discovered" by Prince Henry's explorers.
ABOVE: the Discoverers' Monument, Belém, Portugal.

Settlement begins

In 1425, King João I pronounced Madeira an official province of Portugal, and presented it as a gift to Prince Henry. He, in turn, confirmed the land ownership rights of the archipelago's discoverers.

Northeastern Madeira was given to Teixeira, who made his base at Machico. Zarco got the southwestern part, including Funchal; he also became the island's senior governor. The boundary line between the two territories ran from Ponta da Oliveira in the south to Ponta do Tristão in the north. Porto Santo, meanwhile, fell under Perestrelo's jurisdiction.

A number of aristocratic families set sail

from Lisbon to help colonise this brave new land for Portugal: in such surnames as Ornelas, Bettencourt and Almeida, their legacy lives on.

The discoverers, known as *capitães* (naval captains) now set about investing trustworthy subordinates or other applicants with special rights – for instance the right to operate sugar mills, to bake bread or produce salt – for which charges were naturally made. Part of these payments flowed back into the coffers of the donors Henry used to finance his expeditions, and to support the Order of the Knights Templar, of which he was Grand Master. Naturally, the king also imposed taxes.

Trustworthy settlers were given land to cultivate, which after five years became their own property, assuming that the *capitães* were satisfied with the state of their plantations. Alfonso V "The African" (1432–82) ultimately confirmed the legal situation in the archipelago, much to the delight of the *capitães,* in 1450.

Early boom

One of the settlers' very first acts was to burn down most of Madeira's vast, ancient woodlands to clear the land for cultivation. Early chroniclers report that the fires soon developed into an inferno, which began to rage wildly out

of control. Not only did the blistering heat of the flames drive the Portuguese back to their ships for two days, but some parts of the island continued to smoulder for seven years. Those hapless souls that were cut off by the fires and unable to reach their vessels only managed to escape by taking refuge in the Ribeira dos Socorridos valley near Câmara de Lobos, a few miles' west of Funchal.

Nonetheless, their efforts were eventually rewarded with large expanses of arable land, well-fertilised by the ashes of the burnt trees. Soon the settlers began to build the *poios*, or cultivated terraces that still fringe the steep flanks of the mountains like a covering of fine

A QUESTION OF PATRONAGE

When Henry the Navigator died in 1460, he was succeeded in office by his adopted son and then by his widow, who acted as guardian to the Duke Diogo, her youngest son. Diogo was, however, executed some years later for allegedly conspiring against King João II (1455–95), and Henry's office passed to the Duke of Beja. Following Beja's accession to the throne as Manuel I in 1495, it was decided that patronage of Madeira should pass to the Portuguese Crown. This put an end to the frequent outbreaks of open resistance to the Crown by Madeira's noble families, whose loyalties had more often been to the *capitães* and their heirs rather than the king.

green lace, and Madeira's unique irrigation channels, the *levadas*.

Grapes (for wine), grain and sugar cane were grown on the island from the very beginning. A local document dated 1461 emphasises the importance of these products as export commodities, along with "dragon's blood", the sap of the *dracaena* tree, and *orseille*, a red lichen-based dye. But in those early days, it was grain that proved to be vital for colonisation.

The early settlers brought not just plants, farming know-how and implements with them, but sweated labour as well. In 1452, the first consignment of slaves – West Africans, and Guanches from the Canaries – was shipped over to work in the sugar-cane plantations.

Economic prosperity on the islands was astonishing. Funchal and Machico soon developed into flourishing towns, the former becoming Portugal's third city after Lisbon and Porto, and the major trading centre in the Atlantic.

The basis of the boom was the highly fertile soil. According to the historian Gaspar Frutuoso, at least 60 bushels of grain were grown from one bushel of seed, compared with a maximum of 40 bushels in Europe. Nevertheless, by 1466 the islands were already importing grain; in 1478, there was only enough grain for two months, and eventually in 1485 famine broke out.

The reason is simple: it was far more profitable to grow sugar, and the wheat fields gradually gave way to prolific sugar plantations. The Azores became the region's granary, while Madeira itself concentrated on producing the "white gold" for which there was an insatiable appetite in the Mediterranean and northern Europe. The sugar production curve soared between 1450 and 1506 before plummeting downwards. A cheaper variety grown in colonial Brazil had flooded the international market, and from 1530 onwards, sugar cane was replaced by vines from Cyprus and Greece.

Merchants and noblemen

Initially, Madeira's upper class consisted solely of aristocratic landowners, predominantly the families of the *capitãoes* and the minor landowners dependent on them. From 1480

LEFT: chapel on Machico, the oldest settlement on Madeira. RIGHT: this seafarer's compass dates back to the late 16th century.

onwards, various contingents of settlers arrived from Castile, Italy, Flanders and France. Many of them were merchants, who invested in the sugar plantations and the extensive irrigation systems. They maintained connections with the world of high finance and the commercial centres of Europe.

The newcomers often performed the triple role of landowner, merchant and financier. It was hardly surprising, therefore, that these enterprising gentlemen soon attracted the attention of the island's aristocracy and upper middle class. In other words, a well-arranged marriage with a substantial dowry was a very

reliable way of increasing your land and improving your social standing into the bargain. A resourceful and ambitious merchant might even manage to capture the heart of a wealthy *capitão*'s daughter.

The population grew rapidly, with further waves of emigrants from Europe flooding the quays. The small group of settlers that in the 1420s had accompanied the three founding fathers – Teixeira, Zarco and Perestrelo – had already grown into 150 leading families by the 1440s, and had multiplied to no less than 800 families by 1450. According to the population census of 1514, the island already had 5,000 inhabitants. ❏

THE HOME OF COLUMBUS

Many myths surround the time Columbus spent on Madeira,

yet the island's influence on the great explorer was strong

Until recently, there were few reliable facts about the life of Christopher Columbus. He was familiar enough from schoolbooks as the visionary captain of the *Santa Maria*, the man who "discovered" the New World in 1492 – but of the man behind the myth, precious little was known.

By 1992, the 500th anniversary of Columbus's first voyage to the Americas, all this began to change. Historians went back for another look at the evidence. By now, the trend amongst historians was to debunk old myths and reveal all the weaknesses and foibles of people whom a previous generation had counted as flawless heroes. Columbus emerged as a quarrelsome social climber, an inveterate liar, a despotic tyrant so full of exaggeration and self-importance that nobody believed him when he returned from his first pioneering voyage claiming to have discovered the eastern sea route to the Indies.

Madeiran marriage

That does not mean that Columbus lacked friends. When he first arrived in Madeira in 1478, as an ambitious 27-year-old, working as a sugar-buyer for a Lisbon-based merchant, he was received courteously at the house of Bartolomeu Perestrelo. Both men – Columbus and Perestrelo – had been born in Genova, so they shared a common bond. But Columbus was also motivated to make the acquaintance by the fact that Perestrelo was very wealthy: as the hereditary feudal governor of the island of Porto Santo he was monarch of all he surveyed (albeit of a very small and remote island).

What is more, he had an unmarried daughter, Dona Felipa Moniz. The way the Columbus Museum on Porto Santo tells the story, after what must have been a whirlwind courtship, the pair were wed.

LEFT: this statue of Columbus as a young man stands in Funchal's Parque de Santa Catarina.

RIGHT: the great explorer in dashing mode, depicted setting foot on American soil for the first time.

Biographers have made much of the contrast between her aristocratic status and the lowly social standing of Columbus, the son of a humble weaver and little more than a penniless adventurer himself. They have speculated that Dona Felipa might have been spectacularly ugly, or disgraced by a previous affair – but

whatever the truth, they married and their first child, Diego, was born in 1479. Then, tragically, first Dona Felipa died, and then Diego. In a few months Columbus went from being a proud husband and father to a childless widower.

Dreaming of distant lands

Porto Santo is the sort of place that encourages musing: there is not a lot to do here, even today, and Columbus must have spent much of his time on the island wandering along the lonely shores lost in his thoughts. Local legend has it that the strange and exotic vegetation he found washed up on the beach convinced him that there were other islands to explore out there in the Atlantic.

Another theory has it that the existence of America was revealed to Columbus by a shipwrecked seafarer who – caught in a violent Atlantic storm – had been swept westwards and discovered new land.

Stories like this belong to the old discredited version of history, in which myth has no place. The sober facts are that Columbus probably learned a lot about seamanship from his time in Madeira, not least from his father-in-law, who was an experienced sea-captain and owned a large library of navigation

SWEET ATTRACTION

The renovated remains of Esmerandt's house in Funchal, where Columbus stayed in 1498, now form the core of the intriguing "City of Sugar" Museum (*see page 148*).

charts. In 1480, his imagination fed, Columbus headed back to mainland Europe to raise the funds he needed to follow up his hunch. But before leaving he paid a last visit to another friend, the young Jennin Esmerandt, who, like Columbus, was a sugar merchant, working for a Flemish consortium.

Revisiting old haunts

He was not to return until 1498, some 18 years later. This time he stayed for six days as a guest in the splendid new house that Esmerandt had built on one of Funchal's finest squares.

Columbus regaled the stay-at-home Esmerandt with tales of his adventures, as they sat chewing nuts and drinking wine. It had taken Columbus the best part of 10 years to find a patron, but eventually he had persuaded Ferdinand and Isabella of Castille to give him the money to fit out three ships and hire a crew of 120.

Seventy days after setting sail, Columbus sighted the Bahamas, going on to visit Cuba and Haiti in 1492. In 1493 he crossed the Atlantic again to visit the Dominican Republic and Puerto Rico. Now he was returning to America for the third time – when he would discover the South American mainland – but he would also suffer the humiliation of being sent home in chains and rejected by his fellow adventurers, who revolted against his tyrannical governorship.

For all his vision and courage, Columbus was a man of despotic temperament. The same determination that enabled him to undertake risky voyages, and compel his mutinous crew to sail on into uncharted waters also led to his downfall. Forbidden to return to the Americas, he disobeyed, and made a final voyage, discovering the Gulf of Mexico, in 1502.

Columbus eclipsed

By this time, many other adventurers were crossing the Atlantic to check out Columbus's claims and to grab territory for Dutch, Italian, Spanish, French and Portuguese concerns. One of these was Amerigo Vespucci, a Florentine, whose observations led to the first maps of the New World, and the realisation that Columbus had discovered an entirely new continent.

By the time of his death in 1506, poor old Columbus was forgotten and discredited: Italian cartographers honoured their compatriot by naming the new land America, and Vasco da Gama became the hero of the day by pioneering a new route to the Indies, via the Cape of Good Hope. Columbus would become a myth, and it would be several centuries before archaeologists, excavating the remains of Esmerandt's Funchal house, would find a few discarded nut shells and animal bones – the remains, perhaps, of a dinner party held in honour of the great explorer, and a reminder of the happier times that Columbus once spent on Madeira. ❑

LEFT: Columbus's Porto Santo home.
RIGHT: an astrolabe, a nautical aid of bygone days.

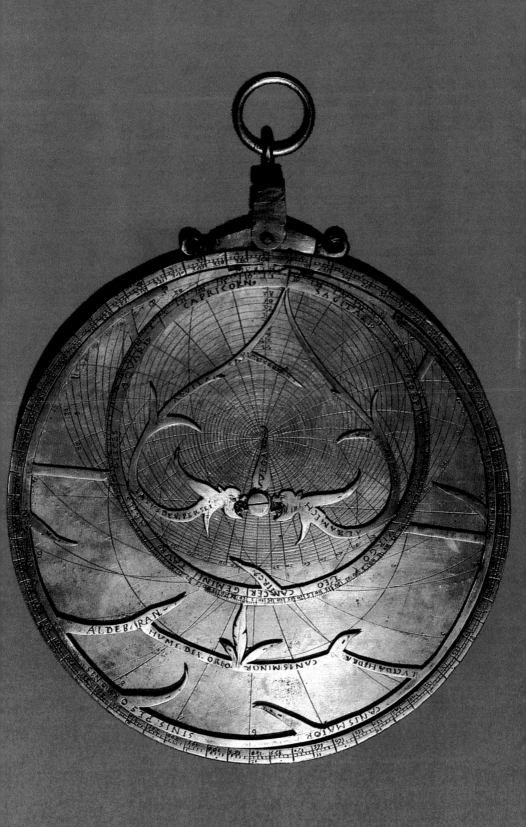

SLAVERY

*Slave labour built Madeira's celebrated irrigation system,
along with the sugar trade that generated much of its early wealth*

Slaves were being shipped to Madeira as early as the mid-15th century. Today, the only thing that reminds visitors of this dark episode in the island's history are a few streets in Funchal with names such as Rua das Pretas (Street of the Negresses), Rua da Mouraria (Street of the Moorish Quarter), or Lombo do Mouro (Hill of the Moors).

Without slavery, Madeira would certainly not have flourished as the supplier of sugar to Europe that it did in the late Middle Ages. The very first settlers were quick to recognise that it would be impossible to cultivate the land on their own, and hence labour was imported in the form of slaves. By 1552, there were 3,000 slaves on Madeira.

During the first part of the colonial era, they worked the fields and sugar plantations, where their main task was to build the famous *levadas*, the island's vast network of artificial irrigation channels. The slaves often had to hew these out of precipitous walls of rock while suspended in baskets above sheer drops. It was this backbreaking, dangerous work that created the basis of the island's present network of over 2,100 km (1,300 miles) of *levada* channels and 40 km (25 miles) of underground tunnels.

Cultural legacy

Most of the slaves on Madeira were captive Berbers from North Africa, but there were also West Africans, natives of the Canary Islands and even Indians. They have all left their mark on the island, on its music and dance, costumes and folk tales, and on the local cuisine.

Of the West African slaves, those from Guinea were prized most for their strength and robust constitution, and were generally assigned to work in the fields.

The trade in captive Africans was regulated by a contract drawn up by Madeira's leading

families and the governors of the African colonial regions. A letter written by an African chieftain, D. Manuel, condemning the abduction of helpless human beings, describes this practice. The natives of the Canary Islands, the Guanches, were also hunted down; they were imported mainly from the island of Gomera.

Records show that in 1582, Tristão Vaz de Veiga, the then-governor of the Madeiran archipelago, had 12 Indian servants in his residence.

Slaves were often auctioned. In many cases a contract was made guaranteeing them freedom on the death of their master. A certain Dona Branca de Atouguia gave clear instructions in her will for two of her slaves to be admitted to the convent of São Bernadino after her death.

The business of buying a slave was treated with great seriousness by Madeiran landowners. Conde Giulio Landi, who paid a visit to the island at that time, reports as follows: "Trading with slaves calls for great care because it is by no means sufficient to merely

LEFT: slave drivers thought nothing of using neck braces to restrain their hapless charges and discourage them from trying to escape.
RIGHT: slaves were generally sold by weight.

parade the slave back and forth. A careful physical examination must be carried out to establish if the body has any flaws, such as missing teeth, which would make the slave physically weaker than a healthy one still in possession of all his teeth."

A law passed on Madeira in 1470 decreed that any slave seen on the streets after the evening curfew would be treated as a fugitive; that rule applied even if they were carrying messages or running errands for their masters. The curfew bell was still rung regularly in Machico right up until 1906, and traces of the corresponding law can still be found in Ponta

them. Some were allowed to learn a handicraft, many were treated like children of the family and were often set free to marry farm labourers." However, as early as 1473, a law was passed forbidding slaves to own houses; only after they had been set free could they do so.

Slaves were sometimes used as confidential agents by the island's gentry; the aforementioned Dona Branca de Atouguia had one such named Damião. She came to rely on his intelligence and discretion, and upon the death of her first husband, made him manager of her estate. His appointment was made official when she had it recorded in the public notary's office,

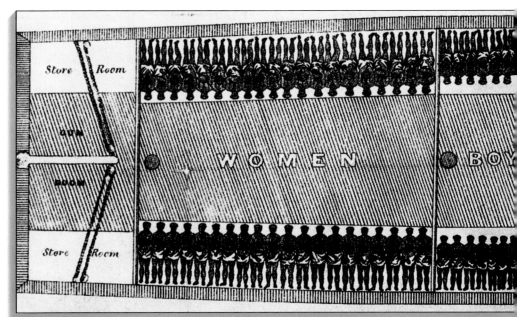

do Sol, where street-doors are inscribed with instructions forbidding slaves to cross the mountain ridge after the bell had been tolled.

If a slave fled, he could be sold by any person who managed to catch him if his master had failed to find the fugitive within four months of his escape. According to a decree issued by King Manuel, the owner of a disobedient slave was allowed to cut off one of his ears. Later, during 1481, slaves had to bear a visible mark on their breast or arm as a public symbol of their bondage.

Apparently, the slaves were not treated as badly on Madeira as in other parts of the world. According to the records, "People were kind to

UNHOLY ORDERS

Madeira's clergy also had their say on the slavery issue, although no one was moved to condemn the practice outright. In the 16th century, a certain Bishop D. Luis de Figueiredo, the official representative of the Catholic Church on the island, went so far as to order all local slave-owners to ensure their slaves – of both sexes – received religious instruction. In 1505 the Bishopric of Funchal also decreed that every slave "living in sin" should marry, while clergy themselves were forbidden to keep female slaves under the age of 50. Indeed, there appears to have been more concern about the virtue of the island's professedly celibate clergymen than the moral issue of slavery itself.

which is how we know this controversial arrangement came about.

However, it was not until 1537 that Pope Paul III was moved to criticise the conditions under which slaves were kept. And a further 200 years were to expire before Madeira was to begin the process of abolishing slavery, with a ban on the purchase of slaves in Africa in 1761 (when a slave-ship anchored off the island that year, the sale of its human cargo was prohibited by an injunction issued by the district court). What's more, the total abolition of slavery in Portugal was not finally achieved until 1858, when a ban was introduced on the initiative of

evident in Madeiran music and dance. For instance, the tradition of dancing in a circle is reminiscent of the African round dance, while the custom of bowing the head while dancing is another African influence.

Some reflect the harsh living conditions endured: the *baile pesado* ("strenuous dance") comes from Ponta do Sol and Canhas, where many slaves were quartered. Others symbolise the laborious work carried out by slaves on the land and in the sugar plantations, depicting complete work sequences graphically mimed in dance form.

The West Africans instilled songs with a

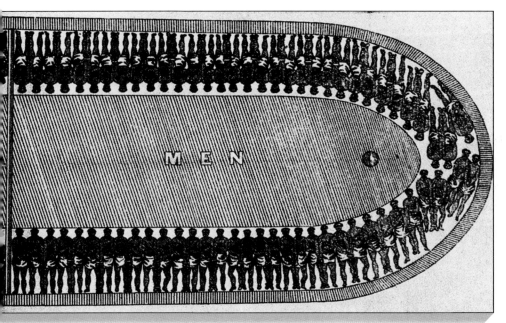

the Marqués Sá da Bandeira prohibiting both the selling and the keeping of slaves.

Into the melting pot

By this time, marriages between liberated slaves and farm labourers had been common for centuries. Assimilation was rapid; the observant visitor to the island today will detect in the Madeiran population many handsome faces with the dark complexion and full lips characteristic of their forebears.

Traces of the slave's ethnic origins are also

ABOVE: slaves were packed for shipment from Africa like sardines; many did not survive the journey.

vibrant undertone of sentimentality and melancholy. *Berço*, an old lullaby passed down from those early days of slavery on Madeira, goes like this: *Imbala, preta, imbala / menino do teu Senhor / canta-lhe bem amoroso / aninalo com Amor* (Rock your master's son in your arms, slave woman / Sing him a song that is sweet / Embrace him with your love).

And this jaunty old song – full of romantic sexuality – is still popular among Madeirans today: *Dei um beijo numa preta / cheirou-me a café torrado / Nunca na minha Vida dei um beijo tao bem dado* (I gave a black girl a kiss / It smelt of black coffee /The most wonderful kiss of my life). ❏

PIRATE SHIPS AHOY!

*For centuries, the Madeirans were subject to brutal raids
from the buccaneers who roamed the high seas in search of gold*

Pirates spread fear and terror all over the world's oceans well into the 19th century. Motley crews of ne'er-do-wells from Morocco, Algeria, England and France invaded coastal settlements and sailed up rivers, plundering villages and leaving behind them a trail of death and destruction.

Madeira and Porto Santo suffered many brutal attacks. It was not easy for the islands' inhabitants to protect themselves against these ocean brigands, skilled in handling their ship's cannons and fearing nothing and no one. For centuries, locals lived in permanent fear of pirate forays.

The archipelago also plays a part in the story of Captain Kidd, one of the most colourful of all the outlaws and the man said to have inspired Stevenson to write *Treasure Island*.

Born a minister's son in Greenock, Scotland, circa 1645, Kidd began his career as a legitimate privateer, guarding English ships in the Red Sea and Indian Ocean. Commissioned to suppress piracy and equipped with a powerful armed vessel, he soon gave into temptation and turned to piracy himself, preying on heavily laden pilgrim ships on their way to Mecca. For almost ten years, he was the scourge of the high seas, before being arrested in 1699 and expedited to London. Tried for piracy and murder and hanged, his body was chained to a post in the Thames for three tides, then tarred and hung for several more years as a gruesome warning to others tempted to take up the pirate life.

But what became of Kidd's considerable pile of loot – including the spoils from his sacking of Lima Cathedral? Legend has it that the treasure is buried somewhere on the Ilhas Desertas, although all searches so far have proved unsuccessful *(see page 245)*.

Warning fires

The islanders did at least succeed in building up a reasonably efficient early-warning system against the pirate threat. Since the buccaneers almost invariably sailed in from the north or west, the fishermen of Porto Santo were able to recognise the approaching vessels, with the dreaded "Jolly Roger" flying from their masts, earlier than the inhabitants of Madeira.

Huge bonfires were then lit to warn the Madeirans of an advancing pirate fleet. Sentinels, posted round the clock on Pico do Facho mountain above the port of Machico, kept a close watch on Porto Santo in case danger was signalled. When it was, the inhabitants would flee into the interior of the island, taking with them as many of their belongings as they could carry. When they returned, they invariably found their houses destroyed by fire.

Pico do Facho ("Torch Mountain") owes its name to the fires and torches lit to warn the inhabitants of the next valley down of the approaching corsairs. Climb up on a clear day for magnificent views of Porto Santo from its 329-metre (1,080-ft) peak.

Despite being a relatively small town, Machico had three fortresses – testimony to the locals' determination to defend themselves against the pirates. Only two survive today: São João Baptista fort on the eastern side of Zarco Bay, and the triangular Forte do Amparo, which straddles the beach in front of the town.

Two fortresses were built in Funchal as well, but these were also almost entirely ineffectual.

Island catastrophe

In the days of João Gonçalves Zarco, Madeira's "discoverer" and first governor, pirates had been only a minor problem. People on the island still proudly tell the tale of the day when three pirate ships anchored in the bay at Funchal, and Zarco, already somewhat advanced

pirate raid in Madeira's history – the island had no Zarco and no heroic figure to appear on the scene and strike fear into the hearts of a fierce band of brigands. Nor was the early-warning system at Porto Santo and Machico of any help either. This time, the pirates had assembled a huge armada that was simply too powerful for the island's defences.

Madeiran chronicles and several Portuguese historical records describe the event in detail. They report that the island's governor, the 5th Commander of Funchal, Simão Gonçalves da Câmara, happened to be on furlough at the royal court in Lisbon at the time, but had

in years, boldly saddled his horse and, brandishing his mighty sword, rode down to the beach with a handful of faithful comrades. There, he struck an awe-inspiring pose, threatening the would-be intruders with his sword. News of Zarco's bravery and legendary skill in combat must have spread through the entire pirate community, because the three vessels promptly weighed anchor and speedily turned tail for the open sea.

In 1566, however – the year of the worst

PRECEDING PAGES: repelling the buccaneers.
LEFT: Captain Kidd: where does his treasure lie?
ABOVE: a vanquished town surrenders.

THE NUNS' RETREAT

Stay on Madeira and you'll notice the beauty spot of Curral das Freiras ("the Nuns' Hideaway") listed on every tour operator's itinerary. The place is so called because it was here that the sisters from the Santa Clara Convent in Funchal fled in 1566, in an effort to escape the French pirates' attack. The hamlet they founded some 20 km (12 miles) northwest of Funchal – in a secret valley which looks like a giant crater, surrounded by towering peaks – successfully kept out not just pirates, but the rest of the world, too, for only in 1959 was a modern road built. The nuns, however, are no longer there – they returned to Funchal once the pirates had left.

appointed his uncle Francisco Gonçalves da Câmara to act as his deputy during his absence. Knowledge of this fact reached a certain Gaspar Caldeira, a Portuguese intent on wreaking revenge on the Madeirans.

Caldeira had been one of the biggest timber merchants on the African Gold Coast, but he had abused his rights, and his property was confiscated by the Portuguese government. He fled to France to ponder on how to avenge himself, no matter how or on whom. He knew, of course, that there were very wealthy merchants on Madeira, and he had just learned that in the absence of the 5th Commander the island's

defences against an attack from the sea were even more vulnerable. The Madeirans would be easy prey for ships bristling with cannon and brigands armed to the teeth.

So Caldeira hatched an evil plot and in Bertrand de Montluc he found a shady accomplice to sponsor him. A nobleman at the court of King Charles IX, Montluc bore what in those days was a most prestigious name, for the Marshall de Montluc, his father, had made history for France on the battlefield. Why Bertrand de Montluc became involved in what was to be a risky and brutal act of piracy is unclear. Probably Caldeira had beguiled him with tales of the rich booty waiting on Madeira for the taking

and, with the cost of court living as high as it was at that time, the young French aristocrat could hardly resist the temptation to take a share of those riches.

At any rate, Montluc managed under false pretences to obtain the support of King Charles IX for this "expedition", without divulging the real aims of the voyage. Then, during early September 1566, he and Caldeira put to sea with a formidable armada of 11 ships manned by a crew of 1,300 buccaneers.

Propelled by powerful autumn winds, the pirate fleet landed on Funchal's Formosa Beach at 9 o'clock on the morning of 3 October, and attempted to invade the town from two different directions. Despite desperate resistance by the townspeople at the gates of São Paulo, they were finally overrun, leaving the way free for the pirates to storm the fortress of São Lourenço, where the acting governor of Funchal had retreated with his troops. The fortress fell, and although there were still brave pockets of resistance, Funchal finally succumbed to the ferocious attacks of the invaders.

Madeiran troops had assembled at various points on the island but, as the old chronicles tell us, their commanders decided not to march to the rescue of Funchal because they considered their own forces to be too weak.

Bloody slaughter

The onslaught lasted 16 days, and what the pirates could not stow away on board ship they destroyed. Thousands of wine casks were split open and left to run dry, and the entire sugar stocks destroyed. The ships' holds were crammed with costly furnishings plundered from the homes of wealthy islanders, together with silver stolen from Madeira's cathedral and the stocks of the big mercantile houses. Worse still, more than 250 people were massacred by the invaders. Bertrand de Montluc's triumph was, however, short-lived – he died within a few days from a wound received in the attack on São Lourenço.

The worst of the many invasions suffered by the Madeirans in the course of their history, the attack is still remembered today in schools all over the island. ❑

LEFT: death by hanging was the usual fate for a captured pirate.
RIGHT: the solid São Lourenço fortress in Funchal.

RELATIONS WITH BRITAIN

British links with Madeira go back a long way,
thanks in no small measure to the island's wine trade

Britain's connections with Madeira are many and various: the fair-haired children who play around in the streets of Funchal's *Zona Velha* are the genetic legacy of the island's occupation by British soldiers during the Napoleonic wars, evidence that relations between the islanders and their protectors were especially cordial at that time.

Anglo-Portuguese firms continue to dominate the Madeira wine trade and British people predominate amongst the island's visitors – indeed, it was Sir Winston Churchill who put Madeira on the map by taking regular holidays here in the 1950s, and where Churchill led, others followed.

In more recent times, other northern European visitors have swelled the island's transient population, striding around the island's volcanic slopes with slim blue books in their hands. But there again, Madeira's reputation as one of the best walking destinations in Europe has been led by a British enterprise (albeit headed by the American travel writer, Pat Underwood) called Sunflower Guides. The company's pioneering *Landscapes of Madeira* walking guide has done so much to boost the island's tourist economy since its publication in 1980 that Underwood is now treated like a demi-god whenever she visits.

An English mother

Women have always played a pivotal role the development of close relations between Britain and Madeira. Indeed, a popular 14th-century legend relates that the island was discovered because the Bristol-based merchant, Robert Machin, eloped with his lover, Ana de Erfert (or Anne of Hereford). Fleeing from her tyrannical father, the couple got caught in a mid-Atlantic storm and were driven to the shores of this hitherto unknown island (*see page 22*).

Romantic as the legend is, recorded facts tell us that the Madeira was known to sailors at least as far back as the Phoenician era, and that its colonisation by Portugal in 1420 was down to Henry the Navigator's desire to secure a source of fresh water and food in the eastern Atlantic. This could then serve as a base for his

country's daring series of exploratory voyages along the African coast. Henry's mother, a guiding influence and always an important source of ideas and inspiration, was Philippa of Lancaster, daughter of the wealthy and aristocratic John of Gaunt. In a marriage that laid the foundation for an Anglo-Portuguese alliance that has lasted 600 years (and still remains strong), the English Philippa wedded Portugal's King João (John) I in 1373.

In the 17th century relations between the two islands were bolstered by another royal alliance – this time the marriage of England's Charles II to Catherine of Braganza, the Portuguese noblewoman. As part of the marriage settlement,

LEFT: an *azulejo* frieze adorning Funchal's former Chamber of Commerce, depicting a British tourist taking a toboggan ride.
RIGHT: Philippa of Lancaster, British wife of João I.

Madeira came very close to becoming an English possession. Catherine's dowry provided for the surrender of the Portuguese colonies of Tangier and Bombay to the English: Madeira was kept in reserve and would have been offered to Charles II as a final inducement, had he not accepted the dowry as it stood.

Madeiran trade privileges

In fact, Madeira was virtually an English territory already. When the island was first settled in the 1420s, adventurers came from all over Europe. Initially, Flemish merchants from Antwerp were predominant, buying up all the

already thriving Madeira wine trade. Under the new laws, British colonies in the New World were only permitted to import British goods, carried in British ships. The aim was to undermine the strong grip of the Dutch on trans-Atlantic trade, and to boost British exports. Within the policy lay the seeds of the antagonism that would lead, a century later, to the Boston Tea Party and the American Revolution.

For 100 years, however, wine merchants in Madeira, who were treated as "British" for the purposes of Charles II's law, enjoyed a virtual monopoly on wine sales to America. With wine exports from France, Spain and Italy banned,

sugar that the island could produce. Their portraits can be seen carved into the choir stalls in Funchal cathedral, clad in heavy woollen cloaks entirely inappropriate to the Madeiran climate.

In time, wine replaced sugar as the island's main crop. English merchants, already well-established at Oporto in central Portugal (the source of port wine), in Xerex (Jerez) in southern Spain (the source of sherry) and in the Canary Islands (the source of the dry white wine known as "sack", Falstaff's favourite tipple) soon came to dominate the commercial life of the island.

Protectionist measures introduced by King Charles II in 1665 did much to boost the

American colonists developed a taste for Madeira – so much so that when the fledgling American Congress ratified the Declaration of Independence, it was Madeiran wine that they used to toast the success of their enterprise.

Support in times of trouble

Another important historical date in the history of the British connection is the year 1801. Combining bold opportunism with a genuine commitment to the defeat of the dictator Napoleon, the British government dispatched ships full of troops to Funchal to "prevent Madeira from being invaded by France".

Whether or not France had any intention of

invading Madeira, this provided the British with the perfect opportunity to establish a military garrison on the island. Once the Napoleonic Wars came to an end, the British were in no hurry to take down the British flag from the mast of Madeira's fortresses.

Many of the 4,000 British soldiers who were stationed on the island in the early decades of the 19th century married local women and settled in Madeira after their retirement from active service. The old water fountain at Santo da Serra is inscribed with the names of members of some of the original British expeditionary force sent to defend the

when the *Northumberland*, the ship carrying the defeated emperor to exile in St Helena, moored in Funchal harbour.

Admiral Sir George Cockburn anchored well out to sea, and the only islander allowed to board the vessel was Henry Veitch, the British Consul. He was rowed over to pay his respects to the vanquished emperor, and to take him books, fruit and a barrel of Madeira wine.

Veitch was subsequently dismissed from his post because he was overheard addressing Napoleon as "Your Majesty", though Prime Minister Palmerston soon reinstated him after receiving a petition from influential members

island (Taylor, Hardy, Turner, etc). In this village, and in the regions of Monte and Camacha, where sections of the British garrison were stationed, it is easy to spot the descendants of British soldiers and their Portuguese wives because of the unusually large number of blue-eyed, fair-haired inhabitants.

Napoleon's souvenir

The British and the Madeirans had their final encounter with Napoleon on 23 August 1815,

of the expatriate community on Madeira – Veitch was a popular figure on the island.

Napoleon paid for the wine with some gold coins that the consul saved as a souvenir. These were buried under the foundation wall of the island's first Anglican church when construction began in 1822. That elegant Neo-classical church, the centre of English expatriate life in Madeira to this day, was also designed by Veitch, a gifted and enthusiastic amateur architect on top of everything else.

Blandy, Leacock & Co

Peace in Europe after the end of the Napoleonic Wars brought new trading opportunities. Some

LEFT: King João I holds a banquet for his father-in-law, John of Gaunt, the Duke of Lancaster.
ABOVE: 18th-century British resident in a sedan chair.

of the British merchants who arrived at this time established dynasties that continue to play an important role in Madeiran commercial life. Two names predominate: the Blandys and the Leacocks. Charles Blandy and Thomas Slap Leacock were originally partners – one a shipping agent and the other a wine exporter. Later, the Leacocks founded their own commercial firm which still operates under the name of Leacock & Co.

It was these two families who, in 1852 and 1873, rescued the island's wine industry after it had been devastated by *phylloxera*. They replanted the island's vineyards with vines

Madeira continues to provide rural employment to this day is down to the energetic efforts of Miss Elizabeth Phelps, an Englishwoman, who, from 1860, established the export of Madeira's embroidered tablecloths, pillowcases, bedspreads and other items to Victorian England. Miss Phelps also got the Madeiran women to adapt their embroidery to English tastes, without spoiling the unique character of their needlework.

British tourism

The settlement of Madeira by British merchants was part of the last flowering of the British

imported from the United States and Mauritius. Thanks to them, Madeira's wine-growing industry recovered and was able to produce bumper harvests again by 1900.

Other British settlers also had a profound philanthropic effect on the island community. Second only to wine, Madeira is renowned for its lacework and embroidery. In the 19th century, no self-respecting middle-class home in England was without its Madeiran tablecloths and napkins, its antimacassars laid across the backs of chairs to prevent hair oil from marking the upholstery, its elaborately embroidered blouse collars and cuffs.

The fact that the embroidery industry on

colonial culture. Similar trading colonies established in Hong Kong, Singapore, China, Japan, India and Indonesia created a demand for company servants (employed by the East India Company) and administrators, employed by the government. Many would call at Madeira on their way to and from the colonies, and Madeira became a favourite rest and recuperation centre for colonial civil servants on leave from duties in the Far East.

Living costs and travel expenses on Madeira were far lower than in Britain, and, for people used to the enervating tropical heat of India, China or Brazil, the island had a far more equable climate.

By the middle of the 19th century, this kind of tourism began to grow into one of Madeira's major sources of income. In the wake of the British, affluent travellers from other European countries came to discover Madeira: sun-worshippers, business people eager to exploit aspects of the island's agriculture, tuberculosis patients hoping Madeira's subtropical climate would provide some relief. Famous writers, politicians, heads of state and other people of note travelled to the island to enjoy a life of luxury in the hotels on the Bay of Funchal.

Churchill's influence

Madeiran tourism remained resolutely upper-middle class well into the 20th century, characterised by that certain kind of British stuffiness and superiority that takes pride in precise etiquette. Luxury hotels, such as Reid's, try to perpetuate this side of Madeira while the rest of the island has moved on.

Winston Churchill was one of the first to breeze through the island, chiselling away at Victorian values. He came not to sit on a terrace drinking tea, but to paint the coastal scenery around Câmara de Lobos. So grateful are the Madeirans to Sir Winston for helping to promote the island that they have erected a reverential plaque on the spot where he used to set up his easel, on the eastern side of Câmara de Lobos harbour, and local shops sell postcards of the former British Prime minister in battered hat, smoking one of his trademark cigars.

Winston was also fond of his drink, and the greatest honour that the island could pay him was to present him with a bottle of the Napoleon Madeira – the very same vintage that had been given to Napoleon by Henry Veitch in 1815. Sharing the bottle with fellow guests at a dinner given in his honour, Churchill was enraptured by the idea that the wine "had something of the scent and fragrance of the era of Marie Antoinette".

Shortly after Churchill's visit, the British transport line, Aquila Airways, began to operate a flying-boat service to the island, transporting passengers between Southampton and Funchal and back. The experiment ended with a disastrous air crash in 1958, after which air traffic to

and from the island ceased. Flights were not resumed until 1964, when Madeira's airport opened, marking the start of the first mass-market holiday packages to the island.

Today, what remains of British influence on the island is rapidly being eroded as other nationalities (German, Austrian and Scandinavian, in particular) discover the delights of the island, and as the people of Madeira grow in confidence as an autonomous region. Once a virtual British colony, Madeira is now proudly Madeiran first, Portuguese second and European third – with perhaps just a touch of British eccentricity surviving here and there. ❑

A STICKY MOMENT

Relations between the Madeirans and the resident British community have generally been cordial, although there have been a few sticky moments. The worst of these occurred in the 1840s, when a wealthy medical doctor and part-time pastor named Robert Kalley – a fanatical Scottish Calvinist – launched a campaign to convert the island's Roman Catholics to Protestantism. Despite warnings from the governor, Kalley persisted with his prayer-meetings, landing himself briefly in jail in 1843 on charges of blasphemy and heresy. In 1846, after a series of Protestant meetings were attacked, Kalley fled the island disguised as a woman. He was never to return.

LEFT: perhaps Madeira's most famous British fan (and the most instantly recognisable): Winston Churchill.
RIGHT: still very British: guests at Reid's Palace Hotel.

DISTINGUISHED VISITORS

A multitude of colourful characters from around the world

has played a role in Madeira's development over the centuries

The first visitors to risk the Atlantic sea trip from mainland Europe to Madeira – a long and dangerous voyage, full of privation – did so largely for commercial reasons, though some also came as an escape from their past.

The little church of Madalena do Mar, in western Madeira, is the burial place of King Wladislaw III of Poland, who chose self-imposed exile on the island after losing the Battle of Varna in 1414. Here, under the name of Henrique Alemão (Henry the German) he became a prosperous farmer. Some years later, he was recognised by two visiting friars from Poland, and summoned to Lisbon for an audience with the Portuguese monarch. Tragically, he drowned off Cabo Girão when his ship hit the rocks at the very start of his journey.

Wladislaw was a rare exception to the rule: most of those who were attracted to Madeira in the 50 years following the island's colonisation by Portugal were footloose adventurers and soldiers of fortune, attracted by tales of the prosperity already prevailing on this once-uninhabited island. One of the earliest visitors was Captain Kidd, the most notorious buccaneer of his time. We are told that he did no harm to the Madeirans, however, and that he buried his legendary treasure on one of the islands of the Desertas (*see page 245*).

A Cook's tour

Another famous seafarer to visit Madeira was Captain James Cook. He set sail from Britain in August 1768 in the *Endeavour*, and took 17 days to reach Madeira, where he anchored for six days to take on supplies. On board were members of a Royal Society expedition, travelling with Cook on a historic voyage to Tahiti, where a team of Royal Society scientists was to record the transit of Venus across the face of the sun.

PRECEDING PAGES: 19th-century view of Quinta Vigia.
LEFT: Captain Cook made two brief visits on his historic voyage to Tahiti and New Zealand in 1768.
ABOVE: Empress Elisabeth ("Sissi") of Austria.

On the return voyage, Cook and his companions circumnavigated New Zealand for the first time, charting its coastal waters and mapping the eastern coast of Australia. Stopping off again at Madeira on the way home, the crew handed over several species of Australian flora that went on to flourish in the island's rich soil.

Ships carrying the merchants of the East and West India Companies to exotic far-off shores frequently used Madeira as a fuelling station en route, Many of those that stopped off here were captivated by the beauty of the island and gave glowing accounts of its attractions on returning home.

Thanks to its wonderfully mild climate, Madeira became a popular destination for well-heeled British travellers, and by the middle of the 19th century, they had helped make it a fashionable holiday destination throughout Europe. Emperors and kings, politicians, painters and writers – in short, everybody who could afford it – came in search of relaxation and to escape from the rigours of the northern European winter.

The small island was anything but prepared for this sudden invasion of sophisticated travellers. In 1840, Funchal had just two hotels, and 45 years later there were still only six of them. As a result, it became the practice for distinguished travellers and their entourages to rent a *quinta*, (a country villa), which came complete with servants and furnishings.

Birth of a legend

William Reid, founder of Reid's Hotel, was one of the rental agents who made a fortune out of

this embryonic travel industry. One of twelve children of an impoverished Scottish crofter, Reid ran away to sea in 1836 and worked his passage to Madeira, where he eventually set up an agency finding suitable accommodation for Madeira's wealthy foreign visitors.

From renting *quintas*, Reid soon made enough money to start buying property. Eventually, a fine plot of land on a promontory above Funchal came his way, and he was able to launch the project most dear to his heart: to build the world's best luxury hotel. Sadly, he died in 1888, aged 66, before seeing the completion of his vision. His sons took over the business, however, and the hotel finally opened

its doors to paying guests in 1891. It is still going strong today (*see page 160*).

In sickness and in health

Many of those who came to Madeira in the 19th century did so on the recommendation of their doctor. Madeira's mild and humid climate was considered good for respiratory conditions and weak hearts, as well as "nervous conditions" – a catch-all phrase that covered a multitude of problems, many of them psychological rather than physical.

Some of the patients who came to Madeira were no doubt genuinely ill, and silent testimony to their suffering can be found in the British Cemetery in Funchal. This beautiful spot, opened in 1887, was used as the burial ground for Protestants of all nations, not just the British, and the moving memorials tell the story of many a young life was prematurely ended by consumption – that is, tuberculosis.

All was not sickness and gloom, however, as Isabella de França recorded in the humorous diaries she kept during a visit she made to Madeira in 1853. She was merciless in her scrutiny of sickly English spinsters "polking around the dance floor like clockwork automatons, as if they ran on wheels", and describes their habit of sitting on the balcony, ostensibly for fresh air, and using their telescopes not to admire the view of the harbour but to spy on each other whilst exchanging catty remarks.

She also hints that suppressed sexuality is at the root of their problems, and records how often they were ready to faint in to the arms of the "swarthy and half-naked fellows" employed to take them on trips round the island. Visitors travelled by hammock, palanquin, bullock-cart or by means of the famous Monte toboggan run (which Ernest Hemingway is said to have described as one of the most exhilarating rides of his life – but he was probably being ironic).

She also records the fact that these same piratical natives deliberately swung their hammocks out over ravines in order to frighten their obese passengers, and talked amongst themselves (in Portuguese), swapping uncomplimentary jokes about the physical defects of their customers.

Isabella, whose diaries, together with her own watercolour illustrations, now part of the collection of the Museu Frederico de Freitas (*see page 155*), was scathing in her comments about many aspects of Madeiran life. She reserved particular scorn for the fat and self-satisfied Catholic priests that she encountered, and described the island's religious paintings and gilded altars as "disgraceful daubs", and "all painted in a style that would disgrace a sign-post". In this, Isabella was echoing the popular Protestant view of Catholic Europe as corrupt and hypocritical.

This fascination with Catholic excess threw up an unlikely tourist attraction on Madeira. Funchal's Santa Clara convent was home to a cloistered beauty called Maria Clementina. Maria was held to be the most beautiful girl on the island, but she was forced to enter the convent on her 18th birthday because her parents could not afford a dowry. A year later, the newly established liberal government in Lisbon ordered convents to release all those inmates who had been forced to take the veil against their will.

Maria was released and fell in love with a handsome army officer. Before they could marry, however, Portugal's absolutist monarch revoked the new law, forcing Maria to return to the convent where she spent the remainder of her life. Visitors to the convent would come to buy the legendary almond sweetmeats made by the nuns, but also hoping to catch sight of the legendary Maria, tragically cut off from the delights of the world, who lived here until her death at the age of 65.

The last emperor

Among the many compelled to spend time on Madeira – whether through exile or ill health – were several members of the imperial Hapsburg family, rulers of the Austro-Hungarian empire. One of the first and most celebrated visitors to the island was the Empress Elisabeth, known as "Sissi". Her striking beauty is documented by photographs on permanent display in the foyer of the Carlton Park hotel, which stands on the site of the Quinta Vigia *(see page 153)*, where Sissi and her family used to stay.

It was on Madeira that the consumptive Austrian empress at last managed to recuperate

> ### CLOISTERED STAR
>
> Maria Clementina's glamourous looks thrilled Isabella de França, who found her dressed "in the most elegant and recherché style that the garb of a Nun will admit".

from the illness that had been plaguing her – although Sissi's biographer, Brigitte Hamann, suggests that this was a mere pretext. The true source of her anguish was her failing marriage and the crushing boredom of life at the imperial court in Vienna, aggravated by constant disputes with her mother-in-law, who acted as the real confidante of Sissi's husband, the Emperor Franz Joseph.

A generation later, Emperor Karl I was to choose Madeira as his place of exile, following the collapse of the Austro-

Hungarian empire at the end of the First World War. Crowned emperor in 1916, Karl (or Charles) was deposed in 1918. He sought refuge first in Switzerland, then came to Madeira, at his own request, in 1921.

Sadly, however, the quiet peace he found here and the respect that he had gained from the local population for his humility were both to be short-lived. He died in 1922 at the age of 35 from a sudden attack of pneumonia, and now lies buried in a sombre black coffin in a side-chapel in Monte's Nossa Senhora church. The *quinta* in Monte where he spent his final years still stands crumbling and empty, its ownership subject to a long-standing dispute. ❑

LEFT: the 19th-century diarist, Isabella de Franca.
RIGHT: the deposed Austrian emperor, Karl I, who went into exile on Madeira in 1921.

WAR AND TYRANNY

After hundreds of years of authoritarian rule, the 20th century and modernisation brought few political changes to Madeira

Madeira approached the end of the 19th century via a string of disasters. The island's vines, some of them planted way back in the 15th century, were devastated by *phylloxera*, a destructive little aphid that weakens the plant and leaves it vulnerable to fungal attack. The island's entire stock of vines had to be uprooted and replaced by modern strains, the result of crossing local varieties with blight-resistant stock from America and Mauritius.

The potato crop was the next to be struck, leading to such famine on the island that food ships were sent from Portugal to relieve the starving population. As if this were not enough, cholera carried off over 7,000 people. The island's administrators simply ran away from the problem: Portuguese officials, fearing disease, left the island in chaos as they took the first available boat home.

Politically, Portugal and Madeira were in the throes of a long-running battle between right-wing monarchists and landowners, who supported the status quo in Portugal with its antiquated feudal laws, and liberal-minded reformers, determined to forge a new and democratic constitution for Portugal – and for Brazil, its vast South American colony. Madeira's problems were simply exacerbated by constant political friction between the island's conservative and liberal factions.

Positive growth

A succession of right-wing governors had, in each of their brief three-year terms of office, managed to change little in Madeira's rigid feudal structures. One admirable exception was José Silvestre Ribeiro, a governor with progressive ideas who greatly improved the educational system and social facilities, and modernised the infrastructure.

LEFT AND RIGHT: 19th-century *portadores*, or porters. While the rest of Europe was undergoing rapid modernisation during this period, the mills of change ground much more slowly on Madeira.

All was not doom and gloom, however. The much-needed modernisation of the island's vine stock was so successful that record harvests were achieved in 1900. The planting of bananas on the island was stepped up as part of a diversification scheme that has reaped ample rewards: bananas remain, to this day, one of the

island's most important agricultural exports. Of even greater importance for the future, the island was developing a healthy high-class tourist trade. Reid's Hotel opened in 1891, the first of several luxury hotels designed to cater for wealthy winter visitors.

The island's potential as a holiday paradise was appreciated well beyond Madeira's shores. In 1905, a German company, headed by Prince Frederick Karl Höhenlohe, offered to build a string of hospitals and sanatoria on the island, and to develop a chain of modern holiday resorts. Benign as this sounds, there was a sting in the tail. In return for this magnanimity, the German company wanted to take over all the island's business concerns – making them, in other words, Madeira's *de facto* rulers.

Such an outrageous proposal could not succeed in normal times, but the inept and anachronistic Portuguese government saw Madeira as more a problem than an opportunity and agreed to the scheme. But they had not reckoned on British reaction. The British, after all, had long seen themselves as the unofficial fount of authority on the island, and they succeeded in persuading the Lisbon-based government to reject this form of back-door colonisation. Revenge was sweet in 1914, when, at the outbreak of World War I, the Madeiran governor announced the confiscation of all German property on the island.

> ### A STRONG BOND
>
> The monument at Terreiro da Luta is surrounded by a symbolic rosary made from anchor chains. The chains were salvaged from ships sunk in Funchal harbour by a German submarine.

for Atlantic shipping. The submarine sank three Allied ships moored in Funchal harbour, and then it began to bombard the city itself. Several people were killed and devout Madeirans turned to the Virgin for help; they vowed to erect a statue in her honour if the shelling would end.

The bombardment promptly ceased, and Funchal survived the rest of the war without further casualties. In fulfilment of their vow, Madeirans built the huge monument to the Virgin that now stands high on the hill

government to reject this form of back-door colonisation. Revenge was sweet in 1914, when, at the outbreak of World War I, the Madeiran governor announced the confiscation of all German property on the island.

World War I

Madeira was a long way from the fighting during World War I, but it did not entirely escape enemy action. In 1916, Portugal officially entered the war on the Allied side and immediately set about impounding German war ships moored in Lisbon harbour. A few weeks later, Germany sent a submarine to Funchal in an attempt to end Madeira's use as a supply base

at Terreiro da Luta, above Funchal. Hung with a rosary made from anchor-chains and illuminated at night, it is a beacon visible from afar.

In other respects the war was disastrous for Madeira: after achieving record wine shipments at the turn of the century, the island now saw her export markets collapse. To the inevitable decline in trade that occurred because of wartime blockades, Madeira next faced the end of its lucrative trade with Russia because of the war and revolution. In America, Prohibition (lasting from 1920 to 1933) then dealt a mortal blow to the all-important US market. In Britain, changing tastes and social attitudes meant that fewer people were indulging in the rituals of after-dinner drinking. The Madeira wine trade had reached the lowest point in its long and honourable history.

The road to a republic

Meanwhile, Portugal was undergoing its own minor revolution. Little by little, more sections of Portuguese society were given the right to vote in elections. This extension of the franchise posed no threat to the corrupt and inefficient Portuguese government so long as popular discontent continued to be fragmented. Voters faced a plethora of nationalist, progressive, liberal and reformist parties, all promising various degrees of reform.

It took two decades – from the 1890s to the 1910, for the ascendant Republican party to gather the mass support it needed to win real power. Whenever it finally threatened to do so, the Portuguese monarch, still endowed with absolute power, intervened to impose his own choice of government upon Portugal, which only had the effect of strengthening popular support for the Republican cause.

Matters came to a head in 1908, when Dom Carlos, the ruling monarch, was assassinated. His successor, Dom Manuel II, attempted to appease the Republicans, but he was overthrown in 1910 by a coalition of Republican military and naval personnel. Portugal was declared a republic on 5 October 1910.

On Madeira, the government made determined efforts to establish democracy, and to grant the "District of Madeira" considerable autonomy. Nevertheless, the mills of change continued to grind slowly on the island; the republic altered neither the conservative attitudes ingrained in most of the inhabitants nor their deferential behaviour towards those they considered their betters. Far from bringing an end to the Portugal's woes, republicanism simply led to a series of short-lived governments, and little progress was made towards achieving much-needed social reform.

Life under Salazar

In 1924, the military again took matters into its own hands. The civil government of the First Republic was toppled by a coup, led by General Oscar Carmona, who eventually became president in 1928. Carmona appointed António de Oliveira Salazar, an economics professor from the University of Coimbra, to the powerful post of Finance Minister, with a mandate to do whatever was necessary to stabilise the Portuguese economy. Salazar was so successful at controlling inflation, reducing the national debt and balancing the national budget that many hailed him as a hero. He was appointed prime minister of Portugal in 1932, and, under the new ultra-conservative constitution of 1933, effectively became dictator for life.

Portugal was officially neutral during World

War II, but it performed a careful balancing act. On the one hand, Salazar was a strong supporter of Franco and the Nationalist regime in Spain, and Portugal continued to trade with Nazi Germany right up to 1944. On the other, Portugal was sympathetic to the Allied cause and allowed its islands to be used as a supply base for Atlantic shipping.

Like Franco in Spain, Salazar succeeded in clinging on to power after the war while the rest of Europe was undergoing rapid modernisation. The man who had done so much to resolve Portugal's problems in the 1930s was to prove disastrous for Portugal's economy and international standing in the longer term. ❏

FAR LEFT: an allegory of Portugal's 1908 elections
LEFT: a republic is declared in 1910.
RIGHT: António Salazar, Portugal's dictator.

A KIND OF AUTONOMY

The revolution which ushered in democracy for Portugal in 1974
was to have far-reaching consequences for Madeira and its islands

I n 1931 a rare event took place on Madeira that says much about Salazar's ruthless approach to dissent, and for the island's growing desire for autonomy. In 1930, Lisbon had shipped several hundreds of political prisoners to Madeira, the Azores and Cape Verde, hoping to isolate them from their mainland sphere of influence. The 300 political prisoners deported to Madeira included some highly placed military opponents of Salazar, including General Sousa Dias. In 1931, Dias and his fellow deportees were instrumental in fomenting the island's first ever general strike in protest at the high price of bread and the collapse of two local banks, where the majority of Madeirans held their savings.

Lisbon sent troops to Madeira, but they promptly defected to the rebel cause. With General Dias at their head, they formed a rebel government on the island. More troops were sent from Lisbon, this time with the aim of blockading Madeira to starve out the rebels. The situation became so serious that British troops were despatched from Gibraltar to throw up a cordon around the hotel zone, offering sanctuary to the island's foreign residents.

In April, Portuguese soldiers landed on the island and drove the rebels out of the eastern part of the island. In May, most of the rebel leaders gave themselves up to the British, who granted them asylum and took them off the island. General Dias had no choice but to surrender, and he spent the remainder of his life in a Portuguese prison.

For the first *and last time in their history*, however, the normally quiescent population of Madeira had taken action against their Lisbon-based rulers, and they had lost. Never again was dissent to be expressed so openly. Instead, underlying dissatisfaction with the political situation in Madeira was expressed by the

increasing number of islanders who chose to emigrate in search of a better life overseas.

A wish for more control

In the post-war period, Portugal struggled to hang on to its colonies, long after other nations had bowed to the inevitable and granted their

former subjects independence. At vast cost in terms of military expenditure and human lives, Portugal fought a losing war against guerrillas in Angola, Guinea-Bissau and Mozambique.

Though the Madeirans would never have compared their situation to that of Portugal's African colonies, they nevertheless still harboured the desire for a greater degree of control over their own affairs – not least because some accused Portugal of ransacking Madeira's relatively buoyant economy to finance shortfalls on the mainland.

Whether this is true or not is difficult to prove, because of the secrecy and censorship that characterised Salazar's 48 long years of

LEFT: after the war, dissatisfaction with Portugal grew: many Madeirans felt their buoyant economy was being ransacked to feed mainland shortfalls.
RIGHT: Salazar remained in power for 48 years.

dictatorial rule, and because of the strongly centralised administration. Portugal's 11 inhabited islands were divided into four completely separate administrative districts, governed directly from Lisbon. This rendered the islands incapable of co-operating with one another, and neatly prevented them from developing any feeling of joint identity, strength and mutual responsibility.

The Salazar regime deliberately fostered the view that the islands were economically dependent on Portugal, and that they would be lost without the succour of the mother country. Schoolchildren started every day by saluting the Portuguese flag and repeating the slogan: *A nação é tudo; tudo pela nação* (the nation is all; all to the nation). Today, there are many on Madeira who claim that this was the direct opposite of the truth, and that Madeira's income from tourism and the export of wine and fruit would have been sufficient to make the island self-sufficient and prosperous, had these revenues not been appropriated by the mainland.

Some money was reinvested in the island's infrastructure: Santa Caterina airport opened to commercial flights in 1964, marking a change in the type of visitor coming to the island. Previously, only the wealthy had been able to

THE MADEIRAN CHARACTER

During 48 years of dictatorial rule, the Madeirans did little publicly to oppose Salazar's authoritarian regime. The British author Francis Rogers attempts to explain the main features of the Madeiran character which gave rise to this mentality in his book, *Atlantic Islanders of the Azores and Madeira*. He points to an innate sense of political powerlessness among the islanders – especially those in the lowest income brackets – and a strongly fatalistic attitude to life. He claims this is typical of the inhabitants of small islands, especially where the government is a faraway assembly on a remote mainland which few locals have visited or can even count on visiting in their lifetime.

afford the sea journey from Southampton to Funchal, or the even more expensive flying boat service. Now, Madeira was to benefit from the package-tour boom, and new hotels began to spring up around Funchal and Machico to cater for the increasing number of visitors.

Few of the British tourists who flocked to this exotic semi-tropical hideaway realised that there were plenty of people in the remoter rural parts of the island who had yet to benefit from modern health care or even electricity, or that Madeira suffered privation on a scale that put many of its people throughout the 1960s and 1970s right at the bottom of the European poverty league tables.

The end of dictatorial rule

Madeirans did little publicly to oppose the authoritarian regime of Salazar, nor did they benefit very much from the rule of his marginally more liberal successor, Prime Minister Marcello Caetano, who took over from Salazar when the dictator suffered a stroke in 1968.

Caetano was finally ousted by the military coup of 25 April 1974 – an event that has gone down in history as the Carnation Revolution. This bloodless coup gained its name because supporters of the revolution placed carnations in the barrels of the soldiers' guns as a spontaneous gesture of goodwill. The soldiers carried these carnations with them when they occupied the Portuguese parliament buildings to symbolise their desire for peaceful change.

Overnight, Portugal's long-delayed modernisation got under way, and the speed with which people reacted to the situation bears witness to the pent-up desire for change that had long existed just below the surface in Portugal. Madeirans greeted the Revolution with enthusiasm, even though it had the effect, temporarily, of deterring tourists from visiting the island.

Some politically active islanders reacted by demanding outright independence from the mainland. They were chiefly motivated by a fear that Portugal would fall to Communism in forthcoming democratic elections, as people reacted to centuries of feudal repression by swinging to the opposite extreme.

Such fears were especially prevalent in rural areas, both on the mainland and on Madeira itself. To the smallholders, dependent as they were on the local oligarchy and the conservative clergy, Communism represented a threat to their traditional existence on the land. The principles to which they felt bound, notably the Catholic faith, the right to own land, the rural way of life, their traditional attitudes and moral values, all seemed to be endangered by the growing force of Communist ideology on the Portuguese mainland.

Winds of change

For the first time since the settlement of Madeira, a growing number of conservative elements on the island began to agitate against

LEFT: grinding poverty was a byproduct of the policies of Salazar in Madeira.

RIGHT: parading military pomp in Belém, Portugal.

the government in Lisbon. In summer 1975, they founded the right-wing separatist movement, Frente de Libertao Madeirense (FLAMA), which fought for total secession from the mother country. Various acts of sabotage, including the destruction of the radio station in Funchal, were ascribed to FLAMA. But the organisation's activities were short-lived: by the end of the same year it was clear that the Communist danger had already been averted.

Instead, Madeirans were more inclined to listen to the more moderate voice of Dr Alberto João Jardim, owner of the island's newspaper, the *Jornal da Madeira*. Jardim urged a more

cautious approach, while the island's representatives hammered out a deal with Lisbon that gave them a kind of autonomy.

In recognition that Madeira was too small to stand alone in the world, it was agreed in 1976 that the island should become an Autonomous Political Region. In elections to the newly created island parliament later that year, Jardim swept to victory as the island's first President and head of state. His PSD (Popular Social Democratic) Party won an impressive 65 per cent of the poll; the widely feared Communists managed to muster just 0.6 percent.

With the creation of an island parliament, hostility between Madeira and the mainland drew to a close. Jardim's centrist party ruled by cautious consensus and did as little as possible to upset the island's status quo. Madeira did not witness the Marxist-inspired confiscation of property and land that characterised the situation on the mainland at the end of the 1970s and beginning of the 1980s. Instead landowners, hoteliers and entrepreneurs were encouraged to continue with the task of making the island economically stable and prosperous.

New autonomy

So what did Madeira actually gain from the 1974 revolution and the democratic constitu-
tion that was given to the island in 1976? Compared to the previous situation, quite a lot in fact. Madeira, Porto Santo and the other islands of the Madeiran archipelago now make up an autonomous political region. All decision-making at grass-roots level is in the hands of town councils. The islands are represented by 50 members of the regional parliament, which meets in Funchal.

In practice, most decisions are taken by the cabinet, which consists of the President and Vice President and six Secretaries of State. The Madeiran parliament possesses the authority to deal with all issues directly affecting the island,

THE PORTUGUESE REVOLUTION

The coup carried out in Lisbon in 1974 by the officers' organisation, the MFA, ushered in an extraordinary period in Portuguese history. While in many ways the two years that followed were a time of virtual anarchy, with no clear political programme, decisions of enormous importance were nonetheless made, including the granting of independence to the overseas territories and political autonomy to Madeira. Above all, it was a time of extraordinary idealism that manifested itself in changes both large and small: while peasants cheerfully seized land from its wealthy owners, for example, it was also pronounced that it was no longer an offence for lovers to kiss in public.

including economic affairs, taxation and customs duties. That is why, for example, Madeira has been able to establish a tax-free zone – the *Zona Franca Industrial* – near Caniçal, designed to attract manufacturers and distributors to use Madeira as a base, paying no taxes on the materials they import and export. By the same token, the island's finance industry has developed a lucrative and substantial offshore banking service, whereby overseas investors pay far less in taxation on the interest they earn here than they would on the Portuguese mainland.

Madeira elects five members to sit in the Lisbon-based Portuguese parliament. The mainland still looks after matters relating to foreign affairs and defence policy, and the military presence on the island is evident in the large barracks in the middle of Funchal, in the 16th-century Palaçio de São Lourenço. This is just the largest of several ancient fortifications around the city that are still used by the military. Most are out of bounds to the public, despite being protected historic monuments.

Although many of Madeira's brightest students still elect to study in Lisbon, Coimbra or Evora, a growing number are choosing to study at the University of Madeira, housed in a former Jesuit College, to the north of Madeira's main square, the Praça do Município.

hardly fail to shine after the appalling poverty and grinding repression of the Salazar era. This is only part of the story. Jardim placed a very high priority on providing for the islanders' basic social needs. Every village was given a health clinic and a school. Electricity was carried across difficult terrain to the remotest communities. Road links were built to ensure that islanders had easy access to the capital, and a means of earning cash by selling their produce in Funchal's bustling Farmer's Market. Most recently, the airport runway has been extended to take jumbo jets, and moves are afoot to name the new airport terminal after

Jardim's legacy

Dr Alberto João Jardim has served as Madeira's head of state for over 25 years. He is viewed with almost god-like awe as a result of the transformation that he has worked on the island, and he has presided over a period of quite unprecedented economic growth, during which the living standards of most of Madeirans have risen beyond their own wildest dreams.

Critics from the PS (socialist) party and the CDS (centre-right) party say that Jardim could

---

LEFT: Portuguese prime minister Mario Soares signs Portugal into the EC in 1988.
ABOVE: for young Madeirans, the future looks bright.

Jardim as a tribute to his achievements across the island.

Today the issues facing Madeira's politicians are a legacy of that success – not how to raise living standards, but how to cope with problems arising from growing prosperity, such as the abandonment of the land in favour of city-based service industry jobs, the pollution from factories and wide-scale car ownership, and the untrammelled development that has scarred the island's face. Tourism, which accounts for a large share of the island's net income, has flourished, and restricting the industry's disturbingly obvious side-effects may prove to be one of the biggest challenges of the 21st century. ❏

TITANIC FORCES

No visitor to Madeira can fail to be struck by the island's

extraordinary landscape – but what made it this way?

Despite all the clichés about "God's Greenhouse" and the "Floating Flowerpot", the most striking feature of Madeira is not the semi-tropical vegetation, but the sheer drama of its landscapes. For those who love the thrill of mountains but without the discomfort of snow and mountain huts, the island is sheer heaven, for within 30 minutes of leaving the comfort of a luxury hotel, you can be walking amongst some of the most enthralling scenery to be found anywhere in Europe.

Asked to describe Jamaica, Columbus famously took a sheet of paper, crumpled it into a ball and placed it on the table saying: "this will give you a better idea of the island's appearance than any of my words." The same image perfectly describes Madeira, with its sheer cliffs rising straight out of the Atlantic waves (the island's cliffs are among the highest in Europe) and the high mountain ridges that dominate the island's interior.

Madeira's deep valleys and ravines, cloaked in green, are reminiscent of Bali or the Philippines, especially where the steep mountain sides have been carved into tier upon tier of fertile terraces. Roads have to navigate a tortuous zig-zagging course, making journeys around the island slow (and unpleasant if you happen to suffer vertigo or car sickness). Modern roads, such as the new south coast highway, tunnel through mountains or soar across valleys on bridges and causeways. The old north coast highway (now bypassed by tunnels) is simply a ledge, scarcely wide enough for two cars to pass, cut into the cliff face above the pounding sea and constantly showered by waterfalls that plunge from the rock face above.

Violent beginnings

This tiny but dramatic island was born of violent volcanic forces some 20 million years

PRECEDING PAGES: picnics are a favourite Madeiran pastime; Porto Santo has the only white sand beach.
LEFT: volcanic forces created the Curral das Freiras.
RIGHT: bands of ancient lava on the Ilhas Desertas.

ago. If you could drain the Atlantic Ocean you would see that Madeira and her neighbouring islands represent the peak of a massive oceanic ridge. Below the water line, Madeira's sheer cliffs continue to plunge for a further 1,000 metres (3,280 ft) before reaching the bottom of the sea and a leaky crack in the earth's crust.

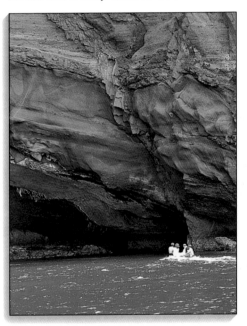

Layers of lava have been erupting upwards from the ocean floor here for millions of years, building up layer upon layer of igneous rock. When the lava eventually broke through the surface of the ocean, it formed a small conical island. Further eruptions then spilled lava down the eastern and western flanks of the central cone, to create the elongated ridges that run like a spine down the centre of Madeira.

Most of this island-forming activity came to an end some 1.8 million years ago, but hot lava continued to flow through weak points in the rock to create a liquorice all-sorts mixture of black, brown, grey, purple and orange rocks. Massive earth movements then squeezed the layers of solid rock to form dramatic concertina-like folds that are visible in road cuttings – for example along the new road to Punta de São Lourenço, where bulldozers have cut slices out of the mountain sides to create the highway and tunnels that serve Madeira's free-port industrial zone.

A stunning rock show

All this volcanic activity ceased about 400,000 years ago, but there are plenty of places on Madeira where the landscape looks as if it were

still fresh from the bowels of the earth. The cinder-like soil that greets visitors to Pico do Arieiro looks more like the surface of Mars than a semi-tropical island in the Atlantic. Swirling clouds lend a primeval feel to a panorama of craggy pinnacles, where few plants have managed to gain a hold.

The sense of being present at the dawn of time is even more pronounced when the red, orange and brown rocks are lit by the fiery rays of the setting sun or bathed in the gentle pink of the light at dawn. Thoughtfully, the Portuguese authorities have built a *pousada* (a government-run hotel) on Pico do Arieiro's summit, just so that visitors can enjoy this magical experience.

> **WATERWORLD**
>
> Some historians speculate that Madeira is the remains of Atlantis, that fabled civilisation lying somewhere west of Gibraltar and flooded 80,000 years ago.

Another spot that still bears the scars of the island's violent volcanic origins can be found at the Grutas de São Vicente, the newly opened cave system that lies above the pretty village of São Vicente. Here you can visit the spot where one of the last eruptions took place. The caves consist of a series of tubes in the rock that were created not by water erosion, but by white-hot lava, melting a pathway through joints and weak spots in the surrounding strata.

Stalactites hanging from the ceiling look like the classic calcium carbonate formations, but are, in fact, formed from drips of molten rock. In those tunnels where the lava flows survive, they look like molten chocolate: it is disconcerting to touch a substance that looks liquid, but that is really solid stone.

Sculpted by nature

If some parts of the island resemble sun-baked deserts, there are other spots where the dense vegetation has colonised the fertile soil to create the appearance of a virgin rain forest. Rain and river erosion has carved the already contorted island into ever-more dramatic shapes, washing away the softest rocks, and cutting deep into joints and cracks in the rock to create the deep valleys and the spectacular ravines of the island's interior.

One of the most celebrated examples is the so-called "Nun's Refuge", the Curral das Freiras, where majestic peaks encircle the little village that sits at the bottom of the cauldron-shaped valley. H. N. Coleridge (nephew of the poet) was moved to describe the view into this secret spot as "one of the great sights of the world."

Madeira has many such magical spots, but, fortunately, few are as accessible as the Curral das Freiras, which heaves with visitors. Walkers who use *levada* paths to seek out such vividly named beauty spots as the Caldeiro do Inferno (Hell's Cauldron) or the Caldeiro Verde (Green Cauldron) can enjoy a private vision of earthly paradise, where vertiginous cliffs clothed in jungle-like vegetation drop down to ferny glens, and waterfalls splash on to the rocks to create a series of dancing rainbows.❑

LEFT: lush vegetation cloaks the cliffs at Rabaçal.
RIGHT: splendid views greet visitors to Pico do Arieiro.

A FLOATING GARDEN

A subtropical climate and fertile volcanic soil provide
ideal conditions for a vast range of colourful plant species

The very first thing visitors notice as their plane touches down on Madeiran soil is the rich patchwork of terraced fields covering the island's vertiginous hillsides. Concentrated mainly in the south, these giant green "steps" testify to the industriousness of local farmers, who have spent millions of labo-

rious hours converting the island's rocky, unpromising slopes into arable plots of land.

Naturally, the landscape did not always look so well cultivated. In fact, in 1419, when João Gonçalves Zarco and his crew first discovered the archipelago, Madeira was covered in a dense cloak of virgin woodland.

Clearing operations

Nowadays, only about 15,000 hectares (37,000 acres) of the original forests survive – roughly 20 per cent of Madeira's total land area. Spread across the higher regions of the north, these woods have been declared a World Heritage Site because they are home to a rich variety of indigenous plant species, the remains of a Mediterranean flora which, millions of years ago, flourished throughout central and southern Europe. Stable climatic conditions – mild temperatures and an abundance of sun, along with regular doses of mist and rain – have enabled Madeira to preserve this lush world, one it shares with its north Atlantic island neighbours, the Canaries and the Azores.

Today, the woods are protected by Madeiran law, but the first settlers were less considerate of their welfare and quickly set to work burning most of them down to clear the land for cultivation. While such efforts were rewarded with large expanses of arable land, a good deal of the fauna and flora inhabiting it also perished in the blaze. The loss of the protective carpet of vegetation also eventually resulted in serious soil erosion.

Nonetheless, there are now three main types of island vegetation: that of the intensely cultivated lowland and coastal region (also called the subtropical bush region), growing up to a height of 700 metres (2,300 ft) above sea level; of the warm, temperate zone of the indigenous woodlands (700–1,200 metres, or 2,300–3,900 ft); and of the cool, temperate moorlands in the land above 1,200 metres (3,900 ft).

Cultivating the land

Once the fires had subsided, the early settlers began to build the terraces, or *poios,* that we see today. Beginning at sea level they rise to a height of about 800 metres (2,500 ft), the maximum height at which crops can be grown on the island. Supporting walls were built to prevent the erosion of the rich reddish-brown soil and narrow channels installed to carry irrigation water from the main *levadas (see pages 87–88).* To ensure that the precious water runs off from one terrace to the plot below, each terrace was designed to slope gently downwards.

PRECEDING PAGES: it's easy to see why Madeira is nicknamed "the Floating Flowerpot".
LEFT: no shortage of orchids on this stall in Funchal.
RIGHT: the south coast is patched with terraced fields.

For Madeiran farmers, every scrap of land on their little island counts. As you explore, you'll come across vineyards and vegetable patches tucked into clefts in steep cliffs, or in remote bays that can only be reached by boat. This partition of the land into tiny plots might seem to indicate that it is owned by many smallholders, but in fact the government wants the land to belong to those who farm it, and promotes private ownership with loans and other means of support. However, about one-third of arable land is still farmed on a *latifundia* basis – large estates belonging to single landowners and worked by tenant farmers.

When the Portuguese arrived on Madeira, the *fidalgos* – "sons of someone important" – were rewarded by the Crown with gifts of land, just as they might have been under the northern European feudal system. The land was cultivated by the *colonos*, tenants, who in turn had to give the landowners 50 per cent of the so-called *culturas ricas*, the valuable export crops: sugar cane, grapes and later bananas. Since the tenants could hardly subsist on what was left over they soon began to cultivate their own fruits and vegetables, and were permitted to keep this excess produce for themselves.

Even today, landowners possess not only the

WHITE GOLD

Sugar cane was introduced to Madeira around 1425, when Henry the Navigator had plants imported from Sicily. The crops flourished, and by the beginning of the 1500s Madeira was exporting 1,500 tons a year to Europe. The sugar merchants built lavish houses in Funchal and the city prospered. However, by 1530 the first sugar plantations had appeared in Spain and Portugal's South American colonies. The tiny island could not compete with its larger rivals, and by the mid-16th century many plantations had been replanted with vines. The boom in "white gold" was over. Funchal's coat-of-arms, however, still bears five sugar-cones – testimony to the industry that launched it.

land, but also a share of the island's water. This is allocated to them according to a system of quotas. Tenants, on the other hand, own all the structures they build themselves, retaining walls, buildings, stables etc, and any trees they plant. If the landowner sells the land, a sum of money must be paid to the tenant to reimburse the cost of the improvements made to the estate.

Low returns

You will notice that many farmers still work the land equipped only with a simple hoe and carry in the harvested crops on their backs. Contrary to what many outsiders think, on Madeira this is not a sign of backward farming methods, but a necessity dictated by the island's topography: most terraced fields are far too small and inaccessible for modern machinery or draught animals to be used effectively. The result is a heavy reliance on manual labour.

Historically the resulting low level of productivity in the agricultural sector eventually rendered its produce uncompetitive on the European market. For instance, demand for Madeiran sugar, once the leading industry on the island, plummeted when a cheaper variety grown in the Portuguese colony of Brazil flooded the international market (*see box, page 75*).

It is a difficulty that, unfortunately, has still not been overcome. Since becoming a member of the European Community in 1986, Madeira has been facing the very same problem with respect to its major export products, wine and bananas. Due to the low level of income in the agricultural sector, farmers are being forced to earn supplementary income or abandon farming activities altogether. Tourism, in any case, is fast displacing the island's reliance on agriculture, but it is sad to think that when there are no longer enough young people willing to follow their parents and seek their living tilling the island's terraces, this unique agricultural landscape is doomed to disappear.

GRAPE EXPECTATIONS

The wine produced from Malvasia grapes is the same "Malmsey" savoured to excess by Falstaff and his boisterous companions in Shakespeare's *Henry IV*.

Vintage harvests

Vines originally came to Madeira from Greece. At the beginning of the 15th century, Henry the Navigator had the famous *Malvasia* grapes – said to have taken their name from the town of Monemvasía in the Peloponnese – shipped to Madeira for planting purposes. During the 16th and 17th centuries, Jesuit monks

introduced other high-quality vine species, including *Verdelho*, *Boal* and *Sercial*.

In 1852, a mildew fungus befell the island's vines, destroying the harvest. Twenty years later, another disaster struck. Nearly all the vines on the island succumbed to *phylloxera* bugs, which had been accidentally imported from Europe. In their place, new and more resilient vines imported from America were planted, crossed with each other or with European vines; these hybrids still occupy much of Madeira's wine-growing area. However, they are now being supplanted by high-quality grape varieties in an effort to improve the standard of wine produced.

The island's volcanic geology, with its bed of rock and fertile soil, and the climate (main rainfall in spring, long warm summers) offer optimum conditions for the cultivation of vines. On the other hand, such advantages are countered by other considerations – for example, too much sun makes the grapes over-sweet at the expense of their aroma. In order to prevent fungal disease, the vines are often trained to grow up frames. On the north coast, high hedges serve to protect them against adverse winds. After planting, the vines need six to eight years before they produce grapes for harvesting, but from then on they can produce grapes for several decades.

The wine harvest takes place from late August to early October, depending on the variety of grape and the location of the vineyard. After the vegetables have been gathered in as well, green animal fodder is planted; its roots are worked into the vineyard soil the following year to act as natural fertiliser.

Tropical crop

The *phylloxera* disaster of 1872 was a blow from which Madeira's wine industry never fully recovered. From then on, bananas replaced the vine as the main cash crop, becoming the most important branch of the island's economy.

Vineyards need intensive care all the year round. Work begins in winter (February, March) when the vines are pruned back. The soil is then ploughed and prepared for the planting of new vines during the autumn. As soon as leaves and flowers appear on the vines, the vintner sprays them with sulphur and copper sulphate to ward off pests.

Vegetables, French beans, haricot beans, potatoes, pumpkin, sweet potatoes, marrows, and so on are also planted between the rows.

LEFT: grapes and their growers at Arco de São Jorge.
ABOVE: on Madeira, the banana grove has just as much importance as the vegetable patch.

Of course, the cultivation of bananas had begun here long before that. Originally indigenous to South-East Asia, the plants were introduced to Africa by Arab seafarers, where they were given the name by which we still know them: the word *banana* probably comes from one of the African languages. The fruit was introduced to Europe by the Portuguese, reaching the Atlantic islands at the beginning of the 16th century and South America a little later.

Most of the crops you see growing on Madeira today are the so-called Canary banana or miniature banana *(Musa cavendishii)*, a tallish tree bearing relatively small fruit which are golden-yellow in colour and aromatic in flavour. There are also isolated plantations of other banana tree varieties, which are even taller and bear far more fruit.

Used to tropical climates, bananas don't flourish along the north coast of the island, and even in the south they seldom grow above a height of 20 metres (65 ft). Their ideal habitat is the wind-protected bay of Funchal, though they are being squeezed out by the capital's ever-expanding suburbs. The once extensive plantations on the fringes of town are gradually being devoured by new housing and hotels.

Because the cultivated form of the banana plant yields seedless fruits, called "berries" by

botanists, they are propagated by seedlings, which sprout up next to the parent plant. After only 12 months, the new plants are capable of producing a bunch of approximately 200 bananas, or "paradise figs", as they are also called locally.

They make an extraordinary sight, these huge bunches of fruit (hanging in the "wrong" direction, too, due to their considerable weight). At the very bottom (that is, the tip) the reddish-blue supporting leaves have male flowers, followed by underdeveloped hermaphrodite flowers and then the bananas themselves, which grow from the female flowers without being pollinated.

Due to their form, the individual fruit are known as "fingers", and a row of fruit is called a "hand". Following the harvest, the involuted sheath of the tree stem is cut down and used as animal fodder.

A hut for every cow

On such a small island, there is not much room for livestock production. The only large expanse of grazing land is on the high plateau of the Paúl da Serra in west Madeira. Few goats and cattle can be seen grazing in the open; most of the island's farm animals "live" in *palheiros*, thatched-roof huts. These shelters constitute another attractive feature of Madeira's terraced landscape, though those with animal welfare in mind might disagree. The cows are shut up in their small *palheiros* for days on end. The green fodder required for these "incarcerated" animals is cut and gathered along the side of paths and other unfarmed terrain.

Island blossom

It is, of course, to see Madeira's flowers in full bloom that so many people visit the place. Isabella de França, an Englishwoman who honeymooned on Madeira in 1853 with her Portuguese husband, described in her diary the magnificent island gardens "now flowering with oleander, heliotrope, blue hydrangea, the white blossom of the coffee tree, and a thousand other flowers new to an English eye, and more brilliant in colour than can be described."

Few of today's visitors realise that much of this sweetly-scented luxuriance only arrived in Madeira in the 18th century, when the British wine merchants – many of whom, fortuitously, also happened to be keen gardeners – settled

---

A TASTE OF THE TROPICS

It's not just bananas that flourish in Madeira's richly fertile soil. Some of the more exotic fruits include the *loquat,* or Japanese medlar, an East Asian species which reached Madeira about 150 years ago. The round canary-yellow fruits have a large, shiny, brown pip, covered by a layer of sweet-smelling but surprisingly piquant flesh. Also look out for the *anona*, a Caribbean tree whose magnolia-type blossoms produce fist-sized fruits like light-green hand grenades; the pulp (mushy and very sweet) conceals long black seeds. Cucumber-shaped Mexican *bread-fruits* are another curiosity; finally, there's the *tomarillo* (tree tomato), a delicious egg-shaped fruit – but beware the sour skin.

here. They brought plants from all over the world to adorn their brand-new *quinta* gardens, and regularly held competitions to see who possessed the most striking botanical rarity.

During the winter, the most noticeable plants are the enormous poinsettia bushes; at the beginning of the year, the camel's foot trees with their delicate pink blossoms and the camellias begin to flower in the Quinta Palheiro Ferreiro public gardens in Funchal and elsewhere on the island.

At the end of April, the capital's main avenues turn an electric-blue colour when the jacarandas bloom. Riverbeds and walls are sud-

Coastal and lowland vegetation

Away from Funchal's carefully cultivated gardens and along the coast, the island presents a different picture entirely. The most striking plants in this zone are the colonies of prickly pears *(Opuntia tuna)*, a cactus introduced from Central America in 1826 for the cultivation of the cochineal insect.

Amid the many different grasses and annual herbs introduced from the Mediterranean grow species such as spear-leaved spurge *(Euphorbia piscatoria)*, a bush with gnarled branches and a poisonous milky sap, once used by fishermen to stun large fish.

denly lush with magenta bougainvillaea, in dazzling contrast to the African flame trees ablaze with bright red flowers.

Unlike most Mediterranean countries, Madeira has no dry season in summer, so blossom continues to grow in profusion. In the autumn the enormous kapok, or silk-cotton, trees *(Chorisia speciosa)* produce their violet blooms (it is their seedcases, which resemble cotton – hence the name – which can be seen flying through the streets in spring).

LEFT: angel's trumpet tree, Quinta Palheiro gardens.
ABOVE: camellias grow to huge sizes on Madeira
RIGHT: this flowering agave is from South America.

Other varieties include the tree houseleek) (Aeonium arboreum) with yellow blossoms, the shrubby globe flower *(Globularia salicina)*, with its small, white flowers and the splendid "Pride of Madeira" *(Echium nervosum)*, with its imposing steel-blue blossoms.

The fissures of the basalt cliffs and the streaky lava rocks are a home to the ice plant (Mesembryanthemum crystallinum), whose leaves glisten like ice crystal, the fleshy-leaved Hottentot fig *(Carpobrotus edulis)*, and the Madeiran sea stock *(Matthiola maderensis)* with its lilac flowers.

Of special floral interest are the moist areas flanking the *levadas*, where the soil contains a wealth of nutritional substances. Particularly rich in plant life on the southern side of the island are the Levada dos Tornos, Levada do Norte, Levada do Curral et Castelejo and the Levada Calheta at Ponta do Pargo. They support a wide range of flora, from the wild chrysanthemum *(Argyranthemum pinnatifidum)*, the eupatorium (Ageratina adenophora) and the Mauritius nightshade *(Solanum mauritianum)* to the service tree *(Sorbus maderensis)* and the Canary ivy, which clings to the trunk of the sweet pittosporum *(Pittosporum undulatum)*.

Water-splashed rock faces, with a thick covering of moss and ferns – some of which

gum *(Eucalyptus globulus)*, whose skinny trunks are surrounded by swathes of belladonna lilies in the autumn. In addition, small groups of Douglas fir *(Pseudotsuga taxifolia)*, Lawson cypress *(Chamaecyparis lawsoniana)*, Japanese red cedar *(Cryptomeria japonica)* and Indian silver fir *(Abies spectabilis)* have also been planted for commercial timber.

Laurel woods

The north of the island around Faial and Portela is where you'll find extensive stands of indigenous laurel wood, the last survivors of those ancient forests burnt down by Madeira's early

are so tall that they look more like trees – alternate with dense thickets of shrubs, consisting of honeysuckle *(Lonicera etrusca)*, the elm-leaved blackberry *(Rubus ulmifolius)* the climbing ground set *(Senecio mikanioides)*, the morning glory vine (Ipomoea acuminata), and the butcher's broom (Semele androgyna). Places where land cultivation has been neglected for many years form a refuge for many plant species, which compete for control of the ground at their disposal.

Sections of the island's south-facing slopes have been planted with pine *(Pinus pineaster)*, used to make the pergolas and trellis-work upon which the vines are trained, and Tasmanian blue

settlers. These trees form the nucleus of an enormous national park created in 1982. They flourish at an altitude of 700–1,200 metres (2,300–3,900 ft) and enjoy an average annual rainfall of 1,500 mm (60 inches), with high humidity and steady, moderate temperatures.

Along with the *Laurus nobilis*, or Mediterranean laurel, you'll also come across the *Laurus azorica* whose dried "bay leaves" are used for flavouring in cooking: both species are tall, dense evergreens with leathery, aromatic-smelling leaves.

Other trees to look out for include the "Til" *(Ocotea foetens)*, the Madeira mahogany or "Vinhático" *(Persea indica)*, a tropical tree of the mimosa family, and finally the ironwood *(Apollonias barbujana).*

Before electricity arrived on Madeira, the islanders used to extract oil from the *Laurus azorica* to burn in their lamps. Some of Madeira's other plants are still put to good use. Dye is still obtained from the Mediterranean laurel, as well as from the yellow flowers of the sow-thistle *(Sonchus fruticosus),* the purple of the Madeira geranium *(Geranium maderense)* and the blossoms of the yellow foxglove *(Isoplexis sceptrum),* which colour the shady forest floor.

One impressive feature of these jungly laurel woods is their wealth of ferns. There are over 70 varieties, including the curious liverwort *(Adiantum reniforme),* whose rounded kidney-shaped fronds are quite untypical of a fern.

In several places – on the Encumeada Pass, for example – the laurel woods give way to a bush landscape reminiscent of the *macchia* found in Corsica. Typical plants include tree heath *(Erica arborea),* heather *(Erica scoparia),* and the wax myrtle *(Myrica faya).* Interspersed with these colonies is the Madeira bilberry *(Vaccinium padifolium),* which grows to a height of 60 cm (2 ft) and yields copious quantities of tasty berries.

Less than a tenth of this surviving indigenous woodland is considered to be in perfect condition. To see the ferns, mosses and lichens at their best, try walking along the Levada do Furado from Ribeiro Frio to Portela, or doing the shorter route from Ribeiro Frio to Balcões (see Central Madeira, page 187). Alternatively, ramblers could try the scenic route from Queimadas to the Caldeirão Verde – the "Green Cauldron" – with its magnificent waterfall *(see Island Walks, page 226).*

Mountain flora

The moorland region found up at 1,200 metres (3,900 ft) is reminiscent of the Scottish highlands. With its bed of basaltic lava rock covered with streaky brown layers of tufa, this zone is dominated by heaths *(Erica arborea)* and heather *(Erica scoparia).*

Up here, winter nights are always freezing but daytime temperatures can get quite warm, creating extreme, near-Alpine conditions. Most alluringly, the fissured rocks, scree and small patches of grass at these heights form ideal habitats for many rare species of plants that are indigenous to Madeira.

Among them are the celebrated Madeira violet *(Viola maderensis)* with its lovely lemon-coloured flowers, the white-flowered Madeira saxifrage *(Saxifraga maderensis)* and stonecrop *(Aichryson villosum),* the giant buttercup *(Ranunculus cortusifolius),* with its characteristic waxy yellow flowers, and the navelwort *(Umbilicus horizontalis),* which has fleshy rounded leaves.   ❑

LEFT: thick ferns line the Levada do Furado between Ribeiro Frio and Portela.
RIGHT: the indigenous Madeiran geranium.

FLOWERS IN SEASON

● SPRING: Agapanthus, Angel's Trumpet, Arum Lily, Broom, Camellia, Canna, African Coral Tree, Jacaranda, Madeiran Orchid, Magnolia, King Protea, Passion Flower, Red Hot Poker, Snowball Tree, Tibouchina, Wisteria.

● SUMMER: Agapanthus, Angel's Trumpet, Broom, Canna, Coral Tree, Dragon Tree, Flame Tree, Frangipani, Golden Trumpet, Pride of Madeira, Red Hot Poker.

● AUTUMN: Belladonna Lily, Frangipani, Golden Trumpet, Passion Flower, Poinsettia, Tibouchina.

● WINTER: Arum Lily, Camellia, Camel's Foot Tree, Frangipani, Golden Shower, Mimosa, Poinsettia, Pride of Madeira, Tibouchina, Tree Rhododendron.

MARVELS OF THE FLORAL KINGDOM

Thanks to its volcanic soil and long summers, Madeira is a botanist's feast, rich in exotic imported blooms and rare indigenous species

For many visitors it is Madeira's amazing range of flora that is one of the island's chief attractions, just as it has been for centuries.

However, few people realise that the majority of the tropical and sub-tropical plant species which they see in the parks and gardens arrived on the island as recently as the 18th and 19th centuries.

A RICH LEGACY

As Madeira's wine industry grew, it came to be dominated by British merchants, who moved into large *quintas* on the island and created splendid gardens, importing exotic seeds and bulbs from all around the world. Over the years, their creations became nurseries for the rest of the island, too.

Their legacy is a rich one. During the winter, the grand old *quinta* gardens are full of flowering camellias and vivid poinsettia bushes. At the end of April, Funchal's avenues turn a gentle mauve as the jacaranda trees blossom, while magenta bougainvillea streaks the dry riverbeds and walls. Look out, too, for the yellow flowers of the Pride of Bolivia (*Tipuana tipu*) and the magnificent orange blooms of the Australian Tulip Tree.

▽ **CROWNING GLORY**
The dramatic pink-shelled king protea (*Protea cynaroides*) is a South African import. Its natural habitat ranges from sea level to the high mountain slopes.

▷ **HERE BE DRAGONS**
Indigenous to Madeira, the distinctive Dragon Tree (*Dracaena draco*) is now rarely found in the wild. The early settlers tapped trees for the bright red resin, used for dyes and medicines.

△ **LUSH LANDS**
Wide swathes of indigenous forest cloak northern Madeira, where tree heathers drape evergreens such as the laurel (*Laurus azorica*).

▽ **BLUE NOTE**
The stately agapanthus is another South African import. Growing wild along the verges, it makes a fine summer display.

MADEIRA'S INDIGENOUS FLORA

△ ISLAND PRIDE
You have to search hard for a glimpse of a wild Madeira orchid (*Dactylorhiza foliosa*); it grows deep in the indigenous laurel woods.

△ PEAK PRACTICE
Up in the mountain zone, winter nights are freezing but daytime temperatures get quite warm, creating extreme conditions ideal for alpine flora.

▷ CASH CROP
Orchids are big business in Madeira, with many thousands of plants exported every year – mainly to Germany.

◁ SOUTHERN TIP
Favouring river banks and moist, rocky slopes, the flamboyant red-hot poker (*Kniphofia uvana*) is yet another immigrant from South Africa.

Of all the floral species growing wild on the island, approximately 200 are Macaronesian – that is, indigenous to Madeira, the Canaries, the Azores and the Cape Verde islands. What is truly impressive, though, is that around 120 of these are endemic to Madeira itself.

The mountain forests in the north are where you'll find the indigenous species at their most prolific. Look out here for the imposing purple brush-shaped blooms of the Pride of Madeira shrub (*Echium candicans*) and the bright yellow sow thistle (*Sonchus futicosus*), along with the shrubby yellow foxglove (*Isoplexis sceptrum*).

Tree ferns like the one depicted above are another striking feature of the forests; over 70 varieties of fern grow wild on the island, some reaching huge sizes. By contrast, the rocky zone at the top of the central mountain range seems bereft of any vegetation apart from a few wind-battered briar-forests, yet these shelter rarities like the shy Madeira violet (*Viola maderensis*), a beauty that takes quite a bit of finding.

TAMING THE WILDERNESS

An innovative irrigation scheme built by Madeira's
early settlers now benefits the tourist industry

Madeira's early settlers were faced with a simple problem: how to combine the rainwater that falls on the north side of the island with the sunshine that warms the southern slopes so as to create ideal growing conditions for sugar cane and grapes. The ingenuity with which this problem was solved has left the island with a unique legacy: an elaborate system of irrigation canals extending for some 2,150 km (1,335 miles) that encircle the island and penetrate some of Madeira's most secretive and inaccessible valleys.

Madeira has a very stable and predictable weather pattern: moist rain-bearing-clouds scud across the Atlantic at between 700 and 1,000 metres (2,300 and 3,300 ft) above sea level, picking up moisture as they go. Once they hit the tree-clad slopes of northern Madeira, the clouds are forced upwards. Cooling as they climb, they shed copious amounts of rain – over 2 metres (78 inches) annually. Some of this rainfall is soaked up by Madeira's sponge-like volcanic rock, and vast amounts also run off to create spectacular waterfalls ribboning and crashing down to the sea.

High up on the bleak tops of Madeira, reservoirs and storage tanks are now used to collect this abundant supply of water and distribute it to the sunny south side of the island, where rain rarely disturbs the bodies turning bronze beside the hotel swimming pools.

A unique system

To get from the wild and uninhabited north to the intensively farmed south, the water is carried by a series of aqueducts, called *levadas* (from the Portuguese word *levar*, meaning "to carry"). Little more than a concrete-lined ditch, the *levada* is nonetheless the means by which Madeira's economy was (and is) nurtured and sustained.

PRECEDING PAGES: lush vineyards at Estreito do Câmara de Lobos.
LEFT: a complex canal system keeps Madeira green.
RIGHT: *levadas* irrigate the south coast fields.

From the earliest times, the *levadas* performed several functions. As well as irrigating the fields, *levadas* supplied the water power that drove the sugar mills. Blasting tunnels through impenetrable granite and digging channels through dense forest, the slaves who constructed the *levadas* opened up new areas

of virgin land, providing an access route to slopes that could be terraced and turned into productive fields. Only within the past 50 years have roads supplanted *levada* paths as the island's main transport network.

Today, water from the *levadas* is put to work driving the turbines of electricity-generating power stations, as well as irrigating the fields. *Levadas* are also responsible for the capital's entire water supply. *Levada* paths have taken on a new role as an important source of foreign currency earnings as walkers from all over the world come to enjoy the pleasures of a leisurely stroll while viewing the island's spectacular scenery.

Levada law

So critical were the *levadas* to the colonisation and exploitation of Madeira that their construction and maintenance was (and is) subject to government control. The island's governors passed laws to guarantee that water was distributed as fairly as possible, employing civil servants to patrol the *levadas* and ensure that laws were observed.

In the second half of the 19th century, the *levada* system was privatised, with disastrous consequences: the water's flow was

> ### THE LONGEST WAY
>
> The last major *levada* to be built was the Levada dos Tornos, near Monte and overlooking Funchal. Dating back to the 1960s, it is over 100 km (60 miles) long.

now controlled or modified to suit the new owner's purposes. Bands of speculators bought water holes and then sold access to the water at whatever price they pleased. Farmers could be left high and dry if they refused to co-operate. The *levadas* are now back under strict government control and, since the end of World War II, a public water commission has been concentrating on modernising and expanding the canal system.

Maintaining Madeira's *levadas* is an important occupation, entrusted to the *levadeiro*, whose job is to patrol his allotted stretch of canal, and carry out constant repairs. *Levadas* run through dense woodland and are easily blocked by falling leaves; landslides frequently interrupt the waters flow, and can damage the water channel, causing the precious water to run away. Ignorant tourists, unaware of the important role played by sluices, grilles and watergates, can interfere with the delicate system by which water is diverted and distributed to properties along the *levada's* route. Resolving problems such as these is the *levadeiro's* full-time job, and one that requires dedication amounting almost to a labour of love.

Even so, the clients will often complain; at the height of summer, any delay in the delivery of water can have disastrous consequences for certain crops. If the water is not available when needed, disputes inevitably occur, with neighbours blaming each other for diverting the supply or taking more than their allotted share. In theory, the distribution of water is carried out according to a carefully worked-out schedule, but in reality the *levadas* of Madeira provide constant ammunition for old and new feuds.

Rambler's delight

Visitors to Madeira are seldom aware of such disputes. To them, the *levadas* are simply a marvellous resource, offering the perfect combination of easy walking and stunning scenery. For running alongside every *levada* is the *passeios*, a footpath created in order to facilitate the regular maintenance of the canals.

Though built for purely functional reasons, they offer a series of walks that follow the island's contours, gently meandering through the beautifully varied Madeiran countryside. One moment the paths slice through ancient woodlands hung with lichens; the next they pass houses where children paddle and women wring out their washing in the canal-water.

Until 1980, the very existence of these *levada* paths was known only to a handful of regular island visitors. Today, following the publication of *The Landscapes of Madeira*, John and Pat Underwood's pioneering guidebook, they have become a major tourist resource, whose value is well understood by the island's tourist authorities. ❑

LEFT: the *levadas* are a hit with walkers, too.
RIGHT: sugar is just one of the crops fed by the canals.

STAYING HOME

Island society is changing fast, with the young and old

increasingly inhabiting very different worlds

A Madeiran grandmother called Av sits on the ground in front of her small cottage keeping a watchful eye on her three youngest grandchildren. Their mother, Celina, travels to Funchal every day, where she works long hours as a hotel chambermaid. In the evening, she is driven back home, where she cooks and cleans for her family.

Celina's husband, a mechanic, also works hard, but he at least has time for relaxation. After leaving work, he heads for the local bar. At that time of day only men are to be found in these island institutions. Traditonally, they spend a couple of hours drinking with their friends before heading home for supper.

Av is illiterate. Celina, on the other hand, attended primary school and her husband runs a car. Maria, Celina's 19-year-old daughter, is the first female member of the family to benefit from vocational training. She plans to become a beautician, and has no intention of getting married until she has obtained her diploma.

Maria's fiancé, who works in a bank, fully supports her career ambitions. Whereas Celina had her first child at the age of 20, Maria wants to buy and furnish a flat in Funchal first, and will delay having children until she is sure she can afford it.

Social change

Av, Celina and Maria are fictitious, but their stories typify the way that people's lives have changed on Madeira over three generations, as the island's economy has evolved from a peasant-based economy to one based on tourism, banking and services.

Av raised her family without the benefit of electricity, television or telephone. She cooked on a wood fire and the family ate whatever they could grow – not a bad diet, given that it was

---

PRECEDING PAGES: even nowadays Madeira remains very much a male-dominated society.

LEFT AND RIGHT: times were often hard for Madeira's older generation, a large number of whom grew up in a peasant economy.

possible to win three crops a year from the fertile soil and frost-free climate. Any surplus would be bartered with the blacksmith for tools, or sold in Funchal market.

The fields that Av's husband rented and tilled have been seriously neglected since his death. The landlord eventually hopes to sell the land to a rich emigrant who is returning home wealthy after a lifetime working overseas and is looking for somewhere to build a villa in which he can live after he retires.

Av's hands are constantly busy as she works away at her embroidery. This traditional craft was developed as an industry in the 1850s by Elizabeth Phelps, the British philanthropist, as a practical means of helping impoverished islanders to earn much-needed cash. Av is one of a diminishing band of outworkers on the island who are still paid per stitch to produce fine collars, cuffs and table linen.

Embroidery is a dying craft, but not because the market has been undermined by cheap machine-made imports from the Far Fast. Genuine Madeira lace is as much in demand as ever – especially from Parisian couturiers – but the grinding poverty that once drove women like Av to work deep into the night, ruining their eyesight, in order to supplement the family income, is no longer such a prevalent force on the island. Av herself now does the work more out of habit than necessity.

When Av was young, Funchal was a day's journey away. Sometimes her husband would let her come with him when he went to sell their potatoes, carrots or cabbages in the Farmers' Market. He would ride on his donkey and she would walk behind. They would set out early on the Thursday and arrive at dusk, snatching some sleep beneath the stars before the market began at dawn. If they were lucky, they would sell their produce quickly and be home that same day. If not, it was difficult for Av to persuade her husband not to spend the little cash they earned in the busy bars around the market.

Madeira's roads have improved to the extent that Celina now goes there every day. She travels with a group of other young women in the back of an open truck, and she enjoys the camaraderie of the journey, sharing gossip with

CONSERVATIVE VALUES

Madeiran society is changing, but it is still dominated by men. Mothers are still largely responsible for looking after the children and running the house, even when they go out to work. Although the constitution of 1976 proclaimed the equality of men and women as a basic right, few women seem to question this division of labour. Used to submitting themselves to parental control, they find it easier to fit in than to risk provoking potentially hostile criticism. What's more, since the family is still so important, the lifestyle gap between the generations is far less marked than it is in northern Europe. Punks, goths, skinheads and crusties – you won't see any of these colourful sub-cults on Madeira.

the other girls. She earns enough to keep her family well clothed and fed. Her brother has gone to work in Venezuela, and the money he sends home at Christmas and on birthdays pays for special treats.

They would be a little more prosperous if her husband were not so fond of spending all his time in the village bar. Every week without fail the parish priest preaches to the men: "respect your families and say no to the demon drink" – but the men do not listen. They slouch at the back of the church, waiting for the mass to end and then go straight back to the bar, spending what little money they earn drinking and playing cards.

Maria is a great help to her mother when her father comes home drunk and depressed. She is an honest girl and works hard, but Celina doesn't understand her. When she was a teenager in the 1970s, no decent girl would go out unaccompanied after dark. Some girls never left their home unless accompanied by a father, brother, uncle or cousin.

Until just a few years ago, parents even chose marriage partners for their daughters, in consultation with the parish priest. Maria has been brought up to help in the house and look after her younger brothers and sisters, but she is not like some of the other girls in the village, who, once they get married, cling to the role that earned them the recognition and approval of their parents.

As *donas de casa* – quite literally "mistresses of the house" – most of these housewives live according to the strict rules of their own traditional family upbringing. Maria is different: like many female students and women with jobs, she values her independence and is beginning to rebel.

Bright future

Maria learned all about sex and birth control at school, although her mother is still too embarrassed to talk about it. It was also at school that she learned English – the language providing the key to a career and economic wellbeing on Madeira. She is good at putting people at ease, and she hopes to deploy this skill to earn good money as a beautician in a top hotel salon. João, her fiancé, also has a promising career ahead – working as a bank clerk, he is already better paid than many Madeirans of his age. She is very fond of João, but she still insisted on an engagement ring before they had sex. A ring serves to reassure a man that his future wife remains absolutely faithful, and a woman knows where she stands.

Even so, Maria will not throw aside all that she has inherited from the past. She goes to church, even though she doesn't agree with all that the priest says. She remains very close to her family – and not just to her parents.

Family ties play an important role on Madeira, and embrace what can be a truly huge

family clan. The extended family includes second and third cousins – all of them treated as if they were first cousins, *primos* and *primas*. Considerable influence in family matters is also wielded by Maria's godparents, the *padrinhos*, who take their role extremely seriously.

Strong family affiliations tie down Madeira's womenfolk, but they also offer security and ensure that no one becomes lonely and neglected. Unmarried women, for example, along with widowed aunts and grandparents, all enjoy the guardianship of the extended family. Single people, living alone in flats and pursuing an independent life, are virtually non-

existent on Madeira. If Maria leaves home to take a job, she will live with relations. Aunts and uncles in Funchal will keep a sharp eye on her comings and goings.

Madeira is still a small enough place for most people to know each other – at least by sight. Living here can be insular, stifling and claustrophobic, and some of Maria's friends could not wait to do national service or escape to a mainland university. For the time being, however, Maria herself is content to stay on the island of her birth – for her, as an educated and self-confident Madeiran, the future certainly looks a lot brighter than it has done for any previous generation.   ❑

LEFT: the look of emancipation.
RIGHT: there are more opportunities than ever before for educated and self-confident young Madeirans.

THE WANDERERS RETURN

Increasingly, the Madeirans who went abroad in the 1970s
are coming home – causing more than a few problems for the locals

Poverty and an appetite for adventure has traditionally driven hundreds of thousands of Madeiran farmers and city dwellers to seek their fortunes overseas. This was a particular feature of the post-war era, when the economic policies of the Salazar regime deprived plenty of hard-working nationals the chance to give free reign to their entrepreneurial instincts.

Young people who saw no prospects for themselves locally simply left for far-off countries. No strangers to physically demanding work, they found a niche in many countries doing the menial labour-intensive jobs that nobody else would do.

Jersey and Guernsey today still have a large population of expatriate Madeirans, recruited as migrant labour for the back-breaking tasks of planting and harvesting Jersey Royal potatoes and Channel Island tomatoes. Some of them have prospered and now own shops and hotels on the islands.

In Venezuela and Brazil, armies of fit Madeirans have sacrificed their youth to the punishing work of timber extraction and oil production. In South Africa and the USA, Madeirans have opened convenience stores, fast-food shops and off-licences in some of the poorest neighbourhoods, eking a living by staying open all hours of the day and night. Their travails in these foreign climes – suffering attacks by armed gangs of robbers who do not hesitate to use violence, for example – are all duly written up in all the local newspapers back on the island.

New money

The newspapers are also fond of "rags-to-riches" tales – stories about "emigrants" (as they are called by the people back home on the island) who have left Madeira in poverty and returned as millionaires.

LEFT: a rash of new villas now line the south coast.
RIGHT: having made their fortunes abroad, many emigrants have returned from South Africa and South America to open small businesses on the island.

However, every emigrant claims to be prospering simply in order to save face – having gone abroad to seek work, nobody wants to admit to failure. Letters home are full of plans and promises, and the money that emigrants send home to their families is a very significant element in the island's invisible economy.

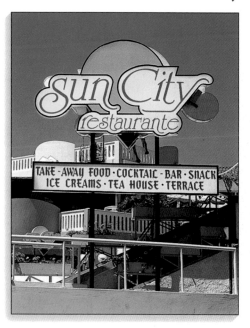

This also explains why there are so many banks in Funchal offering competitive rates for rand deposits, and why illiterate grandmothers are nevertheless adept at calculating exchange rates in various South American currencies.

Some emigrants have genuinely prospered, even if not all of them are as successful as José "Joe Gold" Berardo, the gold prospector who is now one of the richest men in the world *(see page 165).*

Having made their fortunes abroad, many emigrants have returned to invest considerable sums in the island, building hotels and restaurants, creating employment and livelihoods, thereby saving their fellow Madeirans from the fate of having to emigrate themselves. Those who choose to emigrate nowadays, however, are finding that they face competition for low-paid jobs from floods of economic migrants from Turkey, Eastern Europe and the Balkans.

The relationship between islanders and returning emigrants has always been ambivalent. A strong emotional bond exists within Madeiran families, continuing into the second and third generation, and remaining firm even when the emigrants have long since acquired the nationality of their adopted country. Some reinforce this bond by making large and generous donations to the church or village of their

birth. The spectacular fireworks that accompany many a Madeiran saint's day festival (and especially the Feast of the Assumption on 15 August) are often paid for with emigrant money.

On the other hand, such largesse can be interpreted as a calculated snub to those who stayed at home, highlighting their lack of self-confidence and achievement – their lack of masculine ambition and drive. For this reason, some of those returning home are regarded with envy and mistrust.

There are other reasons for questioning whether Madeira's emigrants are, in fact, an unmitigated benefit. For one thing, their wealth has contributed to a rapid increase in the island's cost of living. More visibly, they have escalated the pace of development on the island, and are largely to blame for the rash of ugly modern villas that now scar the south coast and even the island's interior.

Better roads

Yet the rapid pace of change on the island is not, of course, entirely down to the emigrants. Road building has been a government priority since the 1980s, and, thanks to Portugal's entry into the European Union in 1986, a flood of development funds has been released. As a result, an ambitious programme of road building has been implemented.

To this day, there are isolated communities in the remoter island valleys cut off from the rest of the island by steep mountains. The inhabitants are forced to make long journeys on foot in order to reach the nearest road. Agricultural produce has to be carried great distances from the fields to the roadside, where it is collected and sold to a local co-operative or to a middle-man who pays a lower price than could be obtained in the market.

All this changes wherever bulldozers create straight new roads. Local people benefit from faster access to the markets where they sell their agricultural produce direct. The community now has access to emergency medical services and to remunerative town-based jobs.

By the same token, town dwellers now have access to beautiful countryside within commuting distance of their jobs. Wherever roads go, it is not long before the newly accessible valley is noisy with the sound of concrete mixers and transistor radios.

Local farmers are only too eager to sell their land to developers and retire from a life of toil. Soon the island's new highways are lined by large modern houses, their terracotta roofs glaring in the sunshine and a gleaming silver Mercedes on the forecourt.

A changing environment

By this means the landscape of Madeira is rapidly changing. Where visitors once looked down on a green valley sculpted into tiny terraced fields, they now see building sites, rubbish tips, neglected terraces choked with weeds, whitewashed villas with bright orange roofs, and all the trappings of suburbia.

To turn the clock back is impossible, and

nobody would wish Madeirans to live in rural poverty just to look picturesque for the tourists. On the other hand, precious little control has been exercised over the scale, quality and appearance of these developments, and one wonders how much longer free-spending foreign visitors will continue to come to Madeira if the beauty that attracts them is destroyed.

Locals blame the emigrants for the ugliness of the most ostentatious villas. Returning home after decades of hard work in Venezuela or South Africa, they can afford to

A CROWDED ISLAND

Space is another problem where returnees are concerned. Finding room for another 100,000 or even 10,000 residents would be a real headache for the government.

stone are frequently the only ornamentation.

A clue to ownership is the garishly-coloured statue or saint's portrait in tiles above the front door. Islanders honour their family patron saints less publicly, with a little altar inside the house. Doubtless the returnees intend to thank their guardian saint for their patronage and the prosperity they earned abroad, but they are not averse to impressing their neighbours at the same time.

For many small businessmen, returnees can bring unwelcome competition. Witness an

build houses that symbolise their wealth and achievements – houses that say "I made a success of my life".

There is a marked contrast between the architectural styles of the houses built by returning emigrants and those of families who have never left the island. The houses of the former reflect tastes and aspirations acquired abroad, and are often very ornate indeed – especially compared to the simple four-square Madeiran vernacular style, where window-edgings of dark basalt

---

LEFT: it's often emigrant money that pays for the grand firework displays at saint's day festivals.
ABOVE: this north coast hotel typifies the modern style.

argument between taxi-drivers touting for clients and the chances are that one of the participants will be an emigrant, and the other will not. The emigrants are the ones that can afford the expensive new limousines that impress the tourists, while the others must pay off their less-flashy vehicle in instalments.

What's more, many an emigrant's new house incorporates an enormous garage, giving the owner the option of converting it into a business at a later date. The past few years have seen a mushrooming of small rural shops and restaurants all over the island, even though there are not really enough customers to go round. ❑

FISHING THE DEEP WATERS

The clear blue waters around Madeira are a treasure trove

for commercial fishermen – and yield a few surprises, too

Whenever there is a short lull in the fishing calendar, Madeira's fishermen use the opportunity to service their boats. The beachside shipyards of Machico, Caniçal and Câmara de Lobos are fascinating places, with partially built boats lying amongst the debris of bent and distorted wooden planks. Amongst this hopeless mess you might think there was nothing but rubbish – or at least nothing suitable for building a boat.

Yet it is just such twisted bits of wood that are the boat-builders prize. The different-shaped planks, guaranteed not to warp, are fitted together like a puzzle and they offer the hull, beams and stern the greatest resistance to the waves.

Tunny on the line

On the whole, Madeiran fishermen are easy-going characters who do nothing in a hurry. But occasionally you'll see them rushing to their boats in the middle of the afternoon. This can only mean one thing: a school of tuna has been spotted, either with the naked eye or by using electronic sounding instruments.

In addition to a lot of spare time – and a constant thirst for the island's red wine – Madeira's fishermen appear to have a sixth sense which tells them where to find a tuna school. During the summer months it's the *bonito,* or *gaido,* as it is called here that can be found offshore, while in the autumn the red tuna, *Thunnus thynnus*, makes its annual appearance.

These fish are among the ocean's most adept predators. The torpedo-shape of their body gives a clear indication of their lifestyle: they are exceptionally fast swimmers and use a great deal of oxygen, as the dark colour of their flesh indicates. They can survive in tropical as well as sub-tropical waters, and swim in great schools on the lookout for food.

Tuna fishing in Madeira is still seen as a job for the tough guys, although stark necessity, rather than a love of sport fishing, forces these men out to sea. Their equipment consists of two things: a simple rod and line, plus the stamina to endure a tiring fight. Live mackerel are used as bait – they're thrown overboard in bucketfuls

and a whole school of tuna will appear to attack them. The surface, smooth only seconds beforehand, will churn madly as the fish bite.

Doing battle

A successful catch depends on how fast the fishermen can react. Once more live bait has been forced mercilessly on to large metal fishing hooks, the line is cast and within seconds pulled in again. There is no pause, just a continual in-and-out action; the tuna bite immediately, and so to pull the rod in successfully, mastering the correct swing is all-important.

Sometimes it is impossible to heave the tuna aboard – a big fish fights far too well for that.

PRECEDING PAGES: the grim-looking *espada* fish is caught in deep waters.

LEFT: fishing-boats at Câmara de Lobos.

RIGHT: mending the nets is a regular job.

When a particularly large one is hooked, the men attach the line to a wooden capstan and let the fish swim itself to death. If they did not, even the strongest man could be tugged overboard*.

Smaller fish fly rapidly on to the deck where they toss about energetically trying to escape. Their energy seems boundless, and the wriggling, colliding bodies make an extraordinary noise, like a furious drumroll. Yet as soon the boat sails home they are gutted, and their insides thrown overboard for the seagulls.

In other countries, the gutted tuna would be refrigerated immediately, but such techniques are still too advanced for many of Madeira's

will not find crustaceans – those for sale at great expense in the island's restaurants are imported. But you can't avoid the intriguing scabbard fish – the *espada* – whose very existence was unknown until 150 years ago.

A certain João Gomes, sailing far out at sea, earned a just reward for his spirit of adventure when he caught the first *espada* using a line that was at least 800 metres (2,500 ft) long. When he drew the line in, he came face to face with a strange-looking monster, weighing over two kilograms (5 lbs) and measuring more than a metre (3 ft) long. As black as coal, it had a huge mouth full of razor-sharp teeth and a pair

fishermen. When they get back home with the catch, the cleaned fish are usually laid out on the quay to attract a buyer. Meanwhile the deck is swabbed down, ready for another day.

Fish large and small

As well as tuna, fish including marlin, swordfish, mackerel, sardine and shark are all caught off Madeira, usually en route between their spawning and their feeding grounds. You may also see flying fish in Funchal's market: capable of swinging themselves on their pectoral fins, these are able to glide like birds when they wish to escape a persistent predator.

Because of the depth of Madeira's seas, you

of enormous eyes. Fortunately for Gomes, the terrifying creature was already dead: decompression kills these monsters of the deep before the reach the surface.

The *espada (Aphanopus carbo)* is unique to the waters around Madeira and to certain equally deep troughs around the islands of Japan. As the large eyes and the black coloration of this eel-shaped creature indicate, the *espada* lives at depths where sunlight does not penetrate – usually at 800 metres (2,500 ft) below sea level.

The fish is carnivorous, and it rises during the night to depths of 500–200 metres (1,600–600 ft) in order to feed, using its large eyes to spot potential prey. This is when Madeiran fishermen go out to hunt the creatures that they call the "pirates of the deep". They use a line measuring over 1.5 km (1 mile) in length, with upwards of 150 hooks – spaced at 2-metre (6-ft) intervals – baited with squid.

Apart from its nocturnal feeding habits, almost nothing is known of this mysterious creature. Even its breeding habits remain a puzzle. Marine scientists do not know at what depth the *espada* spends the first few months of its life, nor whether the fish is hatched as an egg or born already formed like a shark. What is not in doubt is the flavour and versatility of the succulent white meat, which Madeiran restaurants serve in a variety of ways – fried in butter with banana, for example, or marinated in wine and vinegar and then fried in olive oil.

Hard times

Câmara de Lobos is the centre of the *espada* fishing industry, and if you rise early enough in the day you can visit the informal harbour side market, where most of the island's annual catch of 1,500 tonnes is sold.

In theory, the fishermen who make this catch should be relatively prosperous. Instead, you will see scenes of great poverty around the market. Despite the picturesque appearance of the harbour, with its brightly painted boats lined up on the beach, and its rows of pastel-painted houses, many fishing families live in slum-like conditions. Along with nearby Cabo Girão, this is one of only two places on Madeira where ragged children will approach tourists to beg (sometimes with aggressive persistence).

One cause of the problem is not hard to pin down: much of the cash earned from the sale of fish is immediately spent in the harbourside bars. Seen through the eyes of a welfare worker, there is much here that needs reform. But fishermen have ever been thus – hard drinking is a part of the culture, as is religious devotion tempered with superstition. Before they go out to sea and as soon as they return, fishermen pop into the tiny whitewashed harbourside chapel to cross themselves and say a prayer of thanks for safe deliverance.

Câmara de Lobos has one of the largest and most splendidly decorated modern churches on Madeira – it stands on the hillside to the west of the harbour. But the fishermen remain faithful to their own ancient chapel, which their predecessors built using pebbles from the beach.

Scarcely big enough to hold a congregation, it is dedicated to St Nicholas, patron saint of seafarers as well as the prototype for Santa Claus. Painted on the walls are scenes from the saint's life, including vivid depictions of shipwrecks and drownings – reason enough to understand why hard-working fishermen might want to celebrate their daily survival through wine-fuelled conviviality in the local bars. ❏

A THREAT TO THE FOOD CHAIN

Madeira's clear waters may look inviting, but beneath the beautiful veneer lies little more than a desert. Because the island is the crowning summit of a 6,000-metre (19,000-ft) drowned mountain range, it has only a very narrow shelf of shallow water surrounding it, not enough to support an abundant marine life. This relative dearth is exacerbated by some local fishermen's persistent (and illegal) misuse of dynamite, which grants them an easy catch but also destroys all life forms from the primary plankton to the larger fish. Naturally, various laws have been passed forbidding such practices, yet as long as dynamite is freely available, it's not difficult to obtain for less worthy causes.

LEFT: these exceptionally long lines baited with squid are used to catch *espada*.
RIGHT: tuna are usually gutted on board the boat.

THE LAST OF THE WHALERS

In an extraordinary turnaround, Madeira's former whalers

now advise conservationists fighting to save the whale from extinction

When the film of *Moby Dick*, the whaling classic written by Herman Melville, was released in 1956, the following, somewhat ponderous advertising slogan appeared on cinema hoardings all over the English-speaking world: "In all the world, in all the seas, in all adventure, there is no might like the might of Moby Dick."

Directed by John Huston and starring, among others, Gregory Peck and Orson Welles, the opening scenes – set in an open boat with giant waves, fierce winds and saturating spray – have an authenticity and an edge that is lacking from much of the rest of the film. They were shot on Madeira using real whaling boats, real whalers and real whales, although filming this gripping sequence made the crew and stars so seasick that they retired to the safety of the special effects studio for the rest of the shoot.

Though none of the Madeiran whalers who appeared in that film are still alive, there are men in Caniçal today who earned their living as whalers right up to 1981, when whaling finally ceased in Madeiran waters – the very last place in Europe to forego it.

The whalers were offered a new deal that amounted to a total reversal of their past experience: instead of pursuing Moby Dick with harpoon and spear, they were asked to pass on their intimate knowledge of these complex marine mammals to conservationists working to save the whale from extinction.

An ocean refuge

Since 1986, the 200,000 sq. km (77,000 sq. miles) of open sea that lie between Madeira and the Ilhas Selvagens *(see page 247)* have been protected as a marine reserve for ocean mammals. Within this ocean refuge, fishermen are forbidden to kill or injure such endangered species as the sperm, the finback and the humpback whale, as well as various varieties

of dolphin that the whalers used to hunt as a source of food. Monk seals, regularly culled by Madeiran fishermen because they were perceived as competing for commercial fish stocks, were also brought under the protectionist umbrella, and from being on the verge of extinction, these mammals now have a safe

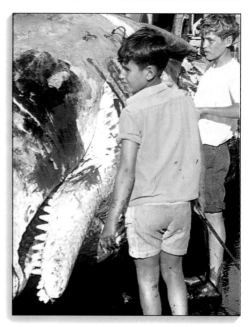

haven on the Ilhas Desertas *(see page 245)*. Thousands of other marine species will also benefit from the creation of this "national park" for ocean mammals.

As for the whalers themselves, they continue to make harpoons, albeit not for killing whales but to sell to tourists as souvenirs. For the same reason they carry on building whaling boats, in the form of small-scale models. And as in the old days, they continue to man their old posts on the Ilhas Desertas – not to scan the seas for schools of sperm whale, however, but to ensure that fishing boats keep well away from sites used by monk seals for rearing their pups.

Still others are employed as curators at the

LEFT: whales were harpooned off Madeira until only a few decades ago. **RIGHT:** these magnificent marine creatures were mainly slaughtered for their oil.

whaling museum in Caniçal village, which is also the headquarters of BIOS (Associacão para a Protecção da Natureza), the organisation set up in May 1990 to monitor the marine reserve. Tourists and scientists, schoolchildren, students and other interested visitors all come here to discover a wealth of fascinating information on the historical and practical aspects of whaling, on marine biology, and especially on whales and other ocean dwellers.

Pride of the museum is a 14-metre (45-ft) fibreglass model of a sperm whale mounted on the wall above an original whaling boat. Collections of scrimshaws (bones, carved and

their quarry and their habits – ironically, the whalers speak of the whales and their habits in terms that betray a strong affection for the very creatures whose destruction they sought.

Herd instincts

Swimming leisurely at a speed of up to 5 km (3 miles) an hour, small herds of sperm whales move around the deep, crystal-clear waters of the Atlantic – aimlessly, it would seem, at least to us. About once a day or at night, some gather for a rendezvous. Up to two dozen sperm whales have been observed at such meetings, which involve much physical contact. The

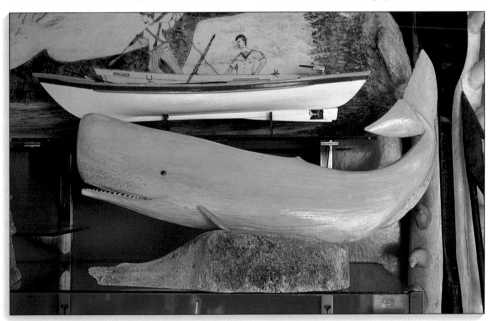

coloured by the whalers in their spare time), and other relics from Madeira's whaling past are also on display. None of these will delay the casual visitor for very long – to fully understand the transformation that has taken place in Caniçal, you have to watch the museum's rather slow-moving black-and-white video.

This 45-minute production tells the story of whaling on Madeira and includes much live footage of whaling in progress. As well as bringing home the barbarity of the practice, it gives you an insight into the lives of the whalers and their tough and dangerous industry. In order to hunt sperm whales successfully, the whalers developed an intimate knowledge of

whales rub themselves against each another, as if trying to compensate for being unable to embrace and caress each other with their short pectoral fins. With their heads close together they look as though they are exchanging some juicy item of gossip; endearingly, they also prop one another up in the water and give their offspring rides on their backs.

Schools are matriarchal, and bulls are only tolerated at mating time. This exclusion of the males plays an important biological role: the far bigger bulls are prevented from becoming food rivals for the cows and their calves.

The formation of schools is evidence of a high degree of solidarity and sociability, but it also serves a defensive purpose: by banding together, the females safeguard themselves more effectively against attacks by sharks.

Ironically, it was this same herd instinct that made the whales vulnerable to the whalers' harpoons. Whalers say that once one whale was injured and in distress, the others would stay alongside, wanting to help a fellow member of their herd now fighting for its life, and vainly hoping to find safety in numbers.

Even when the other members of the school realised that their comrade was doomed, the whale was not left to die alone. Its companions formed a circle, heads pointing inwards and their tails outwards, ready to be used as a powerful weapon. In this position, with only the lobe of their tail fanning the water, they neither attempted to attack nor to escape, but stayed motionless at their post until the bitter end. Faced with this group behaviour, the whalers didn't bother to use their harpoons on the rest of the school. They could easily slaughter them with their spears.

A complex social structure

Sperm whales are absolutely unpredictable, suddenly appearing and disappearing with no seasonal regularity whatsoever. Young cow whales and their calves tend to spend much of the year in the waters of the Madeiran archipelago. The "old ladies" – cows passed breeding age – travel further south, possibly to the Azores or the Canaries and back – although what route they take is still a mystery to the island's veteran whalers. Even marine biologists admit that they know very little about these creatures' migratory movements.

While the young female offspring of the mother whales appear to stay in these schools, the young males are driven away as soon as they have grown to the size of their mothers and aunts. Adolescent males join together to form their own schools and behave rather like teenage louts. Only once they reach the age of 25 are the males sexually and socially mature and ready to become fathers.

This complicated social structure – with a very slow rate of reproduction – has unfortunately had catastrophic consequences for the whales, particularly in the North Pacific. Here, the slaughtering of far too many sexually mature male whales continues to cause a serious decline in whale populations; even if no further sperm whales are killed, their populations are not likely to recover until the first decade of the third millennium, thanks to a lack of potential fathers.

Madeira's attempts to protect the whale and help restore their numbers is still at an early stage, but thanks to this initiative, it might not be long before more of us can enjoy the marvellous sight of a school of whales playing in the island's waters. ❏

LEVIATHANS OF THE DEEP

Although you have to be very lucky to catch a glimpse of a whale off Madeira these days, several species occasionally visit. Apart from the aforementioned sperm whale, there is the killer whale – actually not a killer at all, but a sort of sanitary policeman patrolling the seas (there is no evidence that these attack humans). Relatively little is known about the fairly prolific pilot whale, so called because of its unusually close social structure – schools are prone to outbreaks of mass hysteria, which frequently lead to strandings. There are rare sightings of humpback and finback whales, but not of the North Atlantic right whale – the last one was killed by Madeiran whalers 30 years ago.

LEFT: a model of a whale, carved from scrimshaw (whale bone), in Caniçal's Whale Museum.
RIGHT: the bad old days: handling a dead whale.

A STITCH IN TIME

Begun over a century ago, during a slump in the wine trade,
Madeira's embroidery industry is now famous all over the world

Madeira is the home of wineries,
And extremely expensive embroidered fineries.
I seem to sense a relation tender
Between vintner and embroidery vendor.
Free sample sippings of the grape
Inflate the tourist to a shape
In which, by the time he's embroiled in
*   the embroidery imbroglio*
He will pay for a dozen doilies the price
*   of an authentic First Folio.*
*   —Ogden Nash*

Nash may well have been a little fanciful in his conclusions about the relationship between Madeira's vintners and needle-women, but he correctly identified their importance on the island: wine is the most famous of Madeira's export commodities, but manufacturing industries based on traditional handicrafts, especially embroidery, come a close second. Since its large-scale introduction to the island in the middle of the last century, embroidery has become pre-eminent among the high-quality products made in Madeira.

It is doubtful whether crowned heads reposing on the tenderly embroidered flowers of their Madeiran cushions appreciate the hard work that goes into their production, but the embroiderers know. And one doesn't have to look far to see the importance the Madeirans attach to this art. The *bordadeira* – embroiderer – is one of the island's most popular motifs. Embroidery features on murals, on postcards, even on stamps.

A cottage industry

For many Madeiran women outworkers and their families, the products of this mainly home-based industry are a vital part of household income. But, despite the high prices the needlework fetches on the international market, the share that trickles down to the women

PRECEDING PAGES: hand-made embroidery from Funchal's Patricio & Gouveia workshop. **LEFT:** designs come in all shapes and sizes. **RIGHT:** samples on display in Funchal's embroidery institute (IBTAM).

who actually do the work isn't great: "My father is a fisherman and my mother is an embroiderer," says Lília, who is sent by her parents to beg on the streets.

Originally it was women from the traditional fishing villages or the villages deserted by emigration who spent their time embroidering.

They used to do it while waiting for their men to return, and it is still a craft passed on from mother to daughter, although these days few daughters are around quite as much. School is compulsory now, and it is illegal for girls under the age of 14 to be registered as embroiderers.

Leandro, an embroidery designer and employee of the Instituto de Bordados, Tapeçãrias e Artesanato da Madeira (IBTAM – Madeiran Institute of Embroidery, Tapestry and Handicrafts) which supervises the local handicrafts industry, believes that the often-quoted figure of 30,000 island embroiderers is more than a little exaggerated. "We have perhaps 10,000 true mistresses of their art," he says.

Yet wherever you go on Madeira the industry is hard to ignore, with vendors spreading out tablecloths, collars, napkins, table runners, scarves and handkerchiefs with an incessant stream of sales talk. And while the elaborate flower and leaf patterns are certainly eye-catching, the price of these works of art often dampens the enthusiasm.

Nonetheless, resistance along the lines of: "What happens if I knock over a coffee cup?" will be met with a stream of reassurances. Nothing to worry about: Madeira's fine embroidery is both washable and long-lasting – provided that it is the real thing– check

But perhaps it is due in part to British influence on the island over the years, and to the colonial spirit they instilled, that Miss Elizabeth ("Bella") Phelps, daughter of the wine merchant Joseph Phelps, is so often presented as the mother of Madeiran embroidery.

Miss Phelps, an unmarried English lady with a delicate constitution, came into contact with an orphanage in Santana in which she spent a certain amount of time herself in 1844, since the climate on the north coast was better for her health. While she was there she taught the orphans how to embroider cotton, and on her regular trips back to England, took some of

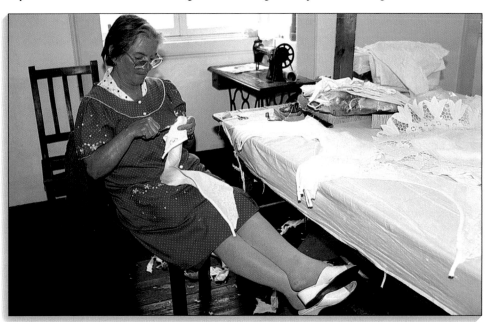

before you buy that products bear IBTAM's special metal seal (currently being replaced by a hologram), a guarantee of authenticity.

Before and after Phelps

Leandro, who also trains embroidery designers, is keen to emphasise that embroidery was not introduced by the English, as is commonly claimed. He points to Gaspar Frutuoso who, in his historical work of the 16th century – interestingly enough in a chapter concerning the psychology of the Madeiran women – wrote about the skilled work that they produced on cloth. Then there are the island's nuns, who have embroidered since time immemorial.

PAINTING WITH THE NEEDLE

With its intricate patterns of flowery baskets stitched by hand on to white cotton backgrounds and fringed with filigree lace, handmade Madeiran embroidery is world-famous – and much copied. Yet is there anything about the style that makes it authentically Madeiran? After all, nowadays it isn't just white cotton that forms the background to the embroidered motifs; coloured linen, organdie, batiste and silks are all sewn using a variety of techniques. Nor is white thread compulsory – sewing with blue and brown is common, too. Perhaps it is simply the high standards set by the best embroiderers, for the finest pieces still take thousands of hours of careful work.

their work with her in the hope that she would be able to make some money for the convent.

In England the Phelps family was well-known for its missionary work, and it is probable that it was Miss Phelps herself who was successful in bringing Madeiran embroidery to the attention of the ladies of the royal court. However, she could not in her wildest dreams have suspected the effect her act of charity would have on Madeira economically.

Not only did the embroidery win great favour at court (and at innumerable fashionable tea parties), but in 1851 Bella was invited to display her wares at the Great Exhibition in London. The English entrepreneurs Frank and Robert Wilkinson became her agents and established themselves on Madeira in 1862, thus laying the foundation for industrialisation and export on a large scale.

Essentially, not much has changed since then. It is still the agents, working on a commission basis, who provide the embroiderers with new material and collect the finished articles, although some of the women manage to cut out the middleman and take their work to the factories themselves. ("Factory", by the way, is slightly misleading: what happens here is that the designs are stencilled on to the outworkers' material with a specially adapted machine, while the finished work is washed, stamped with its seal of approval and finally packed up for sale.)

The industry expands

From 1891 onwards, German traders took over the market, rationalising and reorganising it, and concentrating production on Germany and the United States. By 1906, six of the eight existing embroidery firms were under German control. It was a time of prosperity: more and more wealthy people were embarking on cruises to Madeira and the beautiful embroidered goods were packed into small boats and transported to the cruise liners where they were sold to the passengers.

During World War I, however, all German possessions in Portugal – including the embroidery firms on Madeira – were confiscated. From 1916 the business was largely taken over by Americans of Syrian-Jewish origin. It was they who were responsible for developing the industry and giving it the status it had hitherto been lacking.

Although by 1923 about 70,000 people were involved directly or indirectly in the embroidery trade and the standard of living of many Madeiran families had improved, the quality of the embroidery itself slowly deteriorated. In the rush to make as much money as possible the true originality of the product was lost.

When the effects of the Depression hit in the 1930s, the American manufacturers pulled out, relinquishing the market to the Portuguese, who

in 1937 founded an umbrella organisation, the *Grêmio*. Soon the reputation of Madeiran embroidery was on the mend, for the *Grêmio* set about introducing strict standards of quality control as well as establishing embroidery schools, calculating prices, granting subsidies towards housing and making sure that the industry was well represented at international trade fairs. A percentage of the income earned by the industry as a whole was reserved to fund the organisation.

After the 1974 revolution, the *Grêmio* was dissolved and replaced by a commission. Production continues to flourish today, giving work to some 20,000 Madeirans. ❑

LEFT: the embroidery trade gives work to thousands of Madeirans, most of whom work from home.
RIGHT: island *bordadeira* immortalised on a stamp.

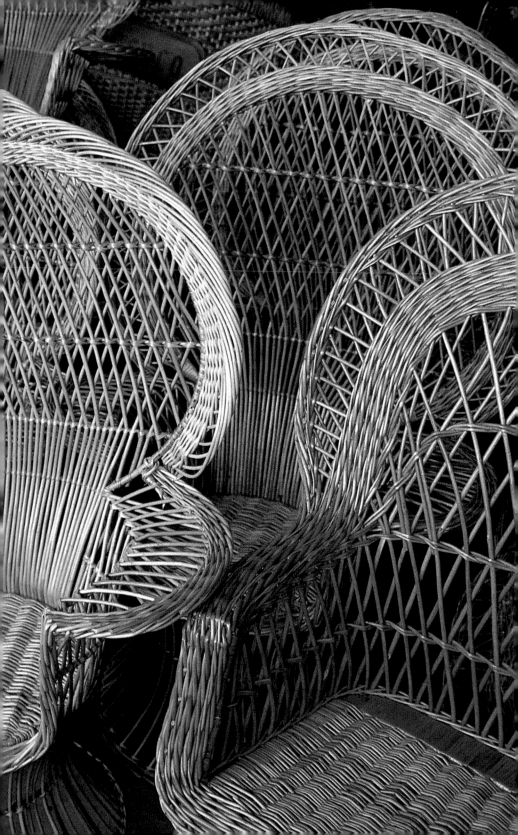

ISLAND WICKERWORKERS

Willow plantations in the humid valleys of the north supply raw materials

for Madeira's internationally renowned wicker industry

amacha, a small village on the east side of the island, is where Madeira's wicker industry began and where it is still concentrated today. There are people who will tell you that 90 percent of the island's population is directly involved in the industry, but in fact, it gives employment to some 2,500 people (wickerworkers, middlemen and export salesmen), most of whom are based in Camacha.

The focal point of the village is the Café Relógio ("Clock Café") in the main square. This large wickerwork emporium is on every tour operator's itinerary, and is usually packed with shoppers. Often, demonstrations of willow-weaving are held in the basement, and these definitely are worth seeing – the weavers work at amazing speed. In addition to baskets (available in every possible shape and size), there are over 1,200 other articles for sale, some real works of art. The middle floor is home to the celebrated "zoo", complete with wicker elephants, lions and monkeys, although most of the animals look somewhat out of place among all the practical products.

The souvenir market

Top of the sales chart has to be the clothes basket, which airlines usually allow to go through as a suitcase. The tea trays, potplant holders and picture-frames also make good souvenirs, along with more substantial purchases like furniture – the kind which you would otherwise normally only find in smart design stores back home.

Freight can be arranged, although a 40 to 50 percent surcharge on the actual sale price should be expected as well as a two- to three-month delay before the goods arrive. Small articles will usually be accepted by the airlines without any problems, but not larger items. However, exceptions are sometimes made if there is sufficient freight space available. It is certainly worth asking your airline.

Funchal itself also has a few wicker centres (in the Rua da Carreira, the Rua do Carmo and the Rua do Castanheiro), which you can browse through at your leisure, although there is not the same amount of choice as in Camacha.

LEFT: wickerwork makes a great souvenir – but try getting these in the plane's overhead locker.
RIGHT: harvesting the willow-canes at Boaventura.

AN INSECURE PROFESSION

Madeira's wickerwork industry has always been susceptible to slumps, as one can see looking at the ups and downs in the export figures over the years. Fashions change, weather can never be relied upon, and, since wicker goods take up so much space, transport costs are bound to be high. What's more, the wickerworkers do not have full-time contracts, either, and so are at the total mercy of their clients. There is no recognised quality control system as there is in the island's embroidery industry, although the wicker industry also falls under the umbrella organisation, IBTAM, which supervises the island's handicrafts.

The raw ingredients

Many farmers in the high, humid northern valleys around Boaventura and Ponta Delgada earn a living by planting willow bushes – a cross between *Salix alba* and *Salix fragilis* – and selling the osiers to weaving workshops.

After the harvest, which takes place between January and February, only the bald *cabeças* – heads – of the canes are left standing. Every plant delivers between 2–5 kg (4½–11 lbs) of cane, reaching their peak of production when they are four years old. Canes can stay productive for up to another 12 years, depending on the quality of the soil and the amount of water

approximately as long as it takes for them to sprout a second time. After peeling, it is soft and white enough to be made into exceptionally hard-wearing baskets. The processed cane is now bound according to strength and size and can be sold at various prices per kilo.

The wickerwork industry is organised on a similar basis to the trade in handmade embroidery. Through their agents, the weaving workshops deliver orders to the farmers, most of whom run family wickerworking businesses on the side. Later, the finished goods are collected, varnished, packed and sold locally, or exported worldwide.

they receive. Dry and windy seasons can severely reduce the harvest.

Before the canes are ready to be made into wickerwork they are cooked in enormous vats, sending thick clouds of steam billowing out over the village and filling the air with a distinctive aroma. This is the "warm" method, during which the canes adopt their familiar brown colouring. Then the bark is peeled off and they are left to dry, often on the roofs of the farmers' houses.

The long, drawn-out "cold" method is rapidly dying out and is only used when specifically requested by the wicker workshops. The cane is soaked in cold water for four to six weeks –

A long tradition

The Madeiran wicker industry has a long history. Even during the building of the first *levadas* at the time the island was settled, workers were lowered down the steep cliffs sitting in baskets. The oldest and most typical basket is the *barreleiro*, made of raw, untreated willow, which even today is still exported to wherever Madeirans are living and continuing this craft. This includes places as far away as Brazil and South Africa.

It is mainly at the market that the *barreleiro*, with its distinctive plate-shaped rim, can be seen. Nowadays it is only generally used for domestic purposes such as carrying fruit and vegetables, although it will still sometimes be used to transport stones on building sites if a crane isn't available.

When baskets were first produced as pieces of handicraft on Madeira, they were made not of willow but of broom, and the smaller, more delicate pieces continued to be made from this material right up until the 1950s. Unfortunately, this craft has now died out. The small baskets on display in Café Relógio are historic items. There are courses available to teach young people the ancient skills, but in general there is little interest in carrying on the art of broom wickerwork as a commercial enterprise.

How it all began

The origins of the island's wickerwork industry are shrouded in mystery. One story goes that a man from Camacha used the time he spent in Limoeiro Prison in Lisbon to acquire the trade from a fellow prisoner. Upon his return he shared this knowledge with his fellow villagers. Others claim the craft took root in Funchal's own prison in 1845. Still others maintain that the beginning of the industry dates back as far as 1827, when a delegation came over from Gonçalo, a village in Northern Portugal and the hub of the Portuguese wicker industry, and left only after having imparted their skills.

Other people point to William Hinton, a 19th-century sugar baron, as the man who brought wickerwork to Madeira, and it is certainly true that Hinton – whose descendants continue to operate businesses on Madeira to this day – was the main driving force behind the industrialisation of the craft.

The story goes that a local man named Anónio Caldeira was inspired to learn the secrets of the weavers' art after catching a glimpse of a particularly fine straw mat that had been imported from England to decorate Hinton's home. Camacha was where the Hintons and other well-to-do British families had their summer residences, and it was when they began to commission replicas of the elegant cane furniture – so fashionable back in England and Germany – that the local wickerwork industry really got off the ground. Soon, pieces were being produced for hotels in Funchal, becoming so popular that wickerwork developed into a booming export business. Baskets were even brought in from Italy to be used as models.

Yet despite this long history, it seems that Camacha's younger generation is no longer interested in joining the industry. They tend to opt for clean, nine-to-five jobs, and it is often only the older villagers today who know how to make particular products.

The growing competition from China and Poland is also regarded with trepidation by the locals – a fear they share with their fellow weavers in southern Portugal as well.   ❑

LEFT: wickerwork for sale at Camacha's Café Relogio.
RIGHT: one of Camacha's wickerwork *maestros*, Augustino Jesús Freitas.

A MADEIRAN FEAST

Based on a fine range of local produce, from fish to fruit, the simple yet tasty cuisine of Madeira appeals to most palates

Madeira does not really have a cuisine to call its own. What there is could probably best be described as Portuguese, with a dash of Arabian spice. Most dishes are solid and simple, with a heavy reliance on local produce. Fresh fish – headed by the stalwart tuna and the black eel-like *espada* – takes pride of place on island menus. Exotic tropical fruits in all shapes, colours and quantities come a close second. Meat and vegetables, however, are mostly imported, thanks to the island's small size and relatively low agricultural yield; consequently, they are more expensive.

The standard ways of cooking meat or fish are *frito ou grelhado*, roasted or grilled. However, that doesn't mean that the food is boring; it's the seasoning that counts. The aromatic smells of fennel, garlic, lemon and laurel which float around the Madeiran gardens and countryside in summer also waft from the cooking pots. Cumin is also used in abundance and no cook would dream of leaving out a dash of local wine. And it is, of course, also perfectly possible to order dishes which are *cozido*, boiled, or *assado*, braised.

Local produce

Fruit salad, prepared from a rich choice of fresh ingredients, is a popular dessert in many restaurants. Madeira owes its wide range of subtropical fruits to the fertile volcanic soil and mild climate on the island. Available in abundance are custard apple, papaya, passion fruit, guavas, mango, citrus fruits of all kinds, avocados, bananas, cherries and apricots. If you want to stock up on fruit, pay a visit to the *mercado* in Funchal, the largest market on the island, where there are always plenty of bargains to be found.

As for fish, although the waters around Madeira are crystal-clear, they are consistently

PRECEDING PAGES: Mercado dos Lavradores in Funchal. **LEFT:** fresh tuna sold fresh from the block at the fish market in Funchal. **RIGHT:** no guessing what's on the menu at this Old Town restaurant.

over-fished, and some species (grouper, for example) have already become expensive rarities in restaurants. Fortunately, the *atum*, as tuna is called in Madeira, is still widely available. It appears on every menu, and is typically fried and served with an accompanying spicy onion sauce.

Another traditional Madeiran dish is fried *espada (see pages 104–105)*, the black, eel-like scabbard fish with its delicious firm white flesh – not to be confused with *espadarte* – the more familiar swordfish.

Although this evil-looking creature with its rapier-like teeth occurs widely throughout the Atlantic in waters up to 800 metres (2,500 ft) deep, it is only fished off the coast of Madeira and in the Azores. No doubt this is due to the elaborate methods needed to catch it: fishermen head out to sea at night in small open boats and lower lines over 1.5 km (1 mile) long. Pulling in the line is usually done manually, and can often take several hours: a distinctly arduous task.

With a bit of luck, though, two fishermen and one line can catch up to one hundred fish in a single night. Bacalhau, dried salted cod which is also popular in regions as diverse as Italy and Norway, is imported from the North Atlantic; it is a staple of Portuguese cuisine. Madeiran cooks also dry and preserve dogfish *(gata)* and a small species of tuna called *gaido* in the same way.

Not frequently found in the frying pan or on the grill in Madeira are *pargo* (plaice) or *bodiaõ* (parrot fish). *Truta* (trout) is

> ### COD PIECE
>
> A tip for cooks keen to try *bacalhau* at home: it should be soaked in a large container of water for at least 12 hours before cooking, to wash away the salt.

fire. On its own it makes an excellent hors d'oeuvre; as a main course, it is most commonly served with salad and chips.

Also popular is *carne de vinho e alhos*, a dish of braised meat which has been marinaded in wine with garlic and laurel or fennel. You should certainly make an effort to try this during your visit.

In addition to rice, potatoes, bread and noodles, other typical Madeiran side-dishes served with meat and fish include maize croquettes *(milho cozido),* or fried polenta

produced in fish farms on the island. Seafood is almost always imported; only *lapas* (limpets) and squid are found locally.

A carnivore's delight

Compared to the wide range of fish dishes available on Madeira, meat has a much lower profile, mainly because it is more expensive. *Bife* (beef) is largely imported from the Azores or South America; *porco* (pork) and *frango* (chicken) are locally farmed. The traditional celebratory dish at Easter time is *cabrito* (kid).

One of the most delicious local specialities in Madeira is *espetada* – skewered beef spiced with laurel leaves and then grilled over an open

(milho frito), flavoured with herbs. *Bolo de caco*, bread made from flour mixed with sweet potato and served hot with a little garlic butter, is another tasty local speciality.

Unfortunately, only a limited choice of salad and vegetables is offered in most restaurants. Tomato salad is usually served with just a couple of green leaves, onions, or, in the best cases, a few olives. The abundance of fresh

LEFT: the abundance of colourful, fresh produce often presents an irresistible temptation.
ABOVE: making bread the traditional way at a country Folklore Festival.
RIGHT: *bolo de mel*, a tasty molasses-flavoured cake.

produce available in markets doesn't seem to make its way onto restaurant tables.

A wine for every course

Madeiran wine ripens in huge oak barrels called "mother barrels". This name refers to the fact that the residue left over in the barrels is topped up with new wine, the idea being that the old wine will pass on its taste to the youngster. The four principal wines are the pale dry *sercial*, the medium-dry amber-coloured *verdelho*, the medium sweet red *boal* and the sweet, full-bodied *malvasia* (Malmsey). The first two are drunk before a meal, the last two afterwards.

On the whole Portuguese wines are served, and these can be very good. The delicate Matéus Rosé is at its best well-chilled, and accompanies meat as well as fish. Another good table wine is the light and sparkling *vinho verde*, "green wine" – so-called because it is drunk when young, or green. The *vinho de la casa*, a light, dry table wine, is available in open carafes at a very reasonable price.

Anybody wishing to sample the local beer should ask for Coral. Imported bottled beer (mainly brands from Germany and Denmark) is normally only available in the island's larger hotels or in Funchal's better bars. ❏

A GLOSSARY TO HELP YOU ORDER

acorda – bread soup with egg and garlic
almondegas – meatballs
bacalhau dourado – dried cod with potatoes
bolo de mel – cake flavoured with molasses and spices
cabrito – kid
caldo verde – cabbage and potato soup
caldeirada de peixe – fish stew
carne de vinho e alhos – meat prepared in a wine and garlic sauce
con camarão – with shrimps
con cebola – with onions
con cogomelos – with mushrooms

costeletas porco – pork chop
frango assado – roast chicken
manteiga – butter
milho frito – polenta croquettes
omeleta de peixe – fish omelette
ovos e bacon – egg and bacon
ovos mexidos – scrambled eggs
pão – bread
prego no prato – beefsteak sandwich with egg and chips
queijo e fiambre – cheese and ham
sopa de peixe – fish soup
sopa de tomate – tomato soup

MADEIRAN WINE

Every drop of the island's first-class fortified wine confirms
how perfectly the grapes have soaked up the sun

For most people, the name Madeira is more likely to evoke thoughts of a mellow, sweet wine than a beautiful island in the Atlantic. Even wine buffs may have no idea where to look on the map for this small archipelago whose sunshine is responsible for its wine's famous flavour.

William Shakespeare must have tasted the Madeiran wine at one time or another. In *Henry IV*, Falstaff's comment on poor Bardolph's nose, which has a rather distinctive hue, reveals a familiarity with the wine: "Thou hast saved me a thousand marks in links and torches, walking with thee in the night betwixt tavern and tavern: but the sack that thou hast drunk me would have bought me lights as good cheap at the dearest chandler's in Europe." And a couple of scenes further on, Falstaff himself does not escape ridicule when he is accused of having sold his soul for the sake of Madeiran wine.

The first vines

Shakespeare probably knew little else about the island of Madeira. In fact, its inclusion in the play is one of Shakespeare's famous anachronisms. *Henry IV* is set during a period when the island had not even been discovered, let alone planted with the noble vine. It was only after the colonisation of Madeira by the Portuguese at the beginning of the 15th century that young vines were planted on the island – offshoots of the equally well-known Malvasia (hence "Malmsey") grape from Greece.

Within less than 50 years after its introduction, Madeira wine had become a legend in its own right. When, shortly before his execution in 1478, George, Duke of Clarence was asked, in accordance with the court etiquette of the day, how he would like to meet his maker, he famously asked to be drowned in a barrel of Madeiran wine. Whether this was just a last desperate bid for attention or a sincere expression of his love for the island tipple is unclear.

LEFT: detail of the mural of the grape harvest that decorates the São Francisco wine lodge in Funchal. **RIGHT:** heading off to harvest.

A lucky accident

It was not without reason that the English soon began to "top up" their proverbial dry humour with the sweet product of the island. The enthusiasm the English ruling classes had shown for Madeiran sugar was soon to be matched by an equal enthusiasm for the island's wine.

In 1650 three factors led to the opening of totally new markets for this export winner: Madeira's production of sugar cane was drastically reduced owing to the stronger competition from the South American colonies, which meant that there was more land available for planting vines. Then love (or more probably politics) resulted in England's Charles II marrying the Portuguese aristocrat, Catherine of Braganza, a particularly lucrative match for English traders since part of her dowry included trade privileges on Madeira.

Finally, in 1651, the Navigation Act was passed by the normally strictly sober Oliver Cromwell. It gives a good indication of the place this wine already held in the English heart. The Navigation Act forbade the importation of all non-English wares to Britain from the colonies – with the sole exception of Madeiran wine.

From then on there was no looking back. Drinking a glass of Madeiran wine during dinner was considered the right thing to do, irrespective of whether you were an officer sitting in your mess in India or the Caribbean or a toff sitting around the dining table of your English stately home. The "Madeira-Shippers" made certain that no matter where you were in the world, further supplies were always available.

As far back as the 15th century, Madeira

away. His face lit up as the first taste touched his lips and trickled over his palate. Over the course of the voyage the grape had been tipped in a completely new, but positive direction.

At the time, the general consensus of opinion was that the secret behind this special wine had to be somewhere along the journey over the equator. Was it the rocking motion of the ship that had done the trick or the great difference between the temperatures recorded during the day and those at night? Or had seawater, either when transporting the wine on to the ship or else just splashing around in the stern, managed to penetrate the barrels containing the Madeira?

wine was carried by ocean-going ships as a cure for scurvy, because of its high mineral and vitamin content. At some stage, lost in the mists of time, it was discovered that the wine changed its character during long sea voyages. Legend has it that an ordinary sailor was responsible for the find. The boat on which he was sailing was carrying crates from Funchal which, for some unknown reason, were refused in Hong Kong. Shortly before returning to Madeira, the captain ordered that the barrels of "spoilt" wine to be thrown overboard.

The sailor – and who could blame him – thinking this a tragic waste, opened a cask and tried some of the wine destined to be tipped

Perhaps it was a combination of factors that contributed towards the new taste. Certainly the softer, mellower caramel taste of the wine was an improvement on its original flavour. Soon, Madeiran wine merchants were paying ships' captains to take wine on board as ballast for their long voyages to Brazil or the Far East. The resulting wine improved in value as well as flavour and was known to 18th- and 19th-century tipplers as "ameliorated" Madeira, or "round-trip" wine.

New luck, new disaster

Naturally, people endeavoured to get round the cost of transporting the wine over the equator by trying out all sorts of alternatives. One story tells of a tradesman who hung a barrel over the entrance to his office so that every customer that came to visit him had to move it before entering. But this simple technique proved – perhaps fortunately for the customers – not to work. Thus barrels were shipped back and forth over the equator right up until the mid-19th century, when scientific experiments finally determined that it was heat that transformed the wine, rather than the ship's motion, and so the modern practice of slowing baking the wine using the warmth of the sun in summer, and hot water pipes in winter, was born.

wine's shelf life by blending it with brandy. It was a method that subsequent sampling proved to be extremely successful. Further variations of this "fortification" process improved the quality of Madeiran wine even more.

This new luck lasted another 50 years and then a new disaster struck with a vengeance. The mildew epidemic that occurred in 1852 destroyed 90 percent of all Madeira's grapes. This time, the wine merchants were devastated. Almost all of the established British shippers subsequently departed for Spain and, of the 70 British establishments on the island in 1850, only 15 were left five years later.

Luck was again to play a major part in the growth of the island's wine industry. In 1800, Napoleon's brother Joseph occupied the entire Iberian Peninsula, hoping that, by blocking the sea route to Madeira, the French would be able to strike a devastating blow against England's prospering trade. The wine stocks in Funchal increased daily, as did the fear among producers that all this precious liquid would go to waste. In desperation, tradesmen started to experiment with the stockpile, endeavouring to prolong the

LEFT: the coopers' art is alive and well on Madeira. **ABOVE:** these barrels – crafted from Polish oak – are fine examples of the craft.

WHEN THE TIME IS RIPE

Madeira's wine harvest begins punctually on 15 August, and lasts well into November – the longest vintage in the world. Grapes planted down at sea level ripen first; last to ripen is the high-growing *Sercial*. Lorries collect the harvested grapes (left in giant wicker baskets along the roadsides) and take them to wine centres, where they are crushed in mechanical presses. In the old days, of course, the grapes were put into large containers and trodden by barefooted grape-pickers. This was more than a bit of rustic fun, for it ensured that the seeds were not damaged and that no tannin was released to mingle with the grape-juice – an advantage which can elude modern mechanical methods.

Only staying power – or British pigheadedness – helped the remaining tradesmen survive this crisis. They used the opportunity to stock up on old wine, a worthwhile investment because it was needed to blend with grapes picked from the young vines. In 1872, however, fate dealt another blow. The vine pest *(Phylloxera vastatrix)*, imported from America by accident with new vine stocks, completely destroyed the most of the remaining plants.

Wine growers on Madeira finally rescued the industry by planting hybrid vines (produced by crossing American wild vines with each other or with European vines). These hybrids were resistant to the virus but some say they yield an inferior-quality wine.

A fresh start

In 1979, a new state Wine Institute, the Instituto do Vinho da Madeira, was founded to observe and control the entire process of Madeira's wine production. This means that there is supervision right from the planting of the vine itself, through the fermentation and maturing process and until the cork is pushed into the newly filled bottle.

It is the Institute's responsibility to ensure that Madeira's wine is authentic, controlling every step of the production process. Only then is the wine granted its official stamp *(selo de garantia)* and individual number. In addition, it is responsible for the education of the island's wine specialists.

What to look out for

So when and on what occasion should one drink Madeiran wine? As a general rule, serve the *sercial* as an aperitif, a *verdelho* to accompany the main course, followed by a *boal* for the dessert, and the *malvasia* served as a finale to the meal.

These classic Madeiran wines are named according to the type of grape. The *sercial* is dry to extra dry and has an extremely powerful bouquet. The *verdelho* is a rich golden wine pleasing to the eye and with a dry finish. The *boal* is a medium-coloured wine with a rich flavour and well-rounded character. It is *malvasia* though, full-bodied, sweet and heavy, similar in many respects to a liqueur, that is responsible for Madeira's fame in the wine industry.

As most tourists quickly discover, the vintners frequently open up their cellars for wine-tasting and whoever wishes to learn more about the island's wine can, for a small fee, try a few small glasses of different wines and come to their own conclusions. Using this method aspiring connoisseurs can "work" happily at their preferences, and purchase a few bottles or cases of any that they particularly enjoy.

Naturally, it is not possible to have a quick sip from the real vintage bottles of Madeiran wine. After all, who is likely to open a 30, 80 or 120-year-old bottle for sampling? Some of the top-class wines of such vintages sell for a whopping £100 (US$160) a glass. And unfortunately, Madeiran wine that has made the jour-

THE ALCHEMY OF WINE MAKING

Madeiran wine is a masterpiece of alchemy. Once the fermentation process is complete, the celebrated heating process begins, which caramelises the wine. Over the past century, different methods have been developed, although even the quickest lasts two months and involves heating the wine in enormous tanks, then keeping it in constant motion. The maturing process – after a short cooling period – takes place in barrels made of Polish or American oak, which are officially closed by the Wine Institute (a banana leaf is wound around the bung and sealed in wax). The finest wines will now be left for 20 years before being bottled; the minimum time allowed is 18 months.

ney over the equator is no longer offered for sale. Whether bottles of this legendary wine are still available is very doubtful, since the owners of such a treasure are hardly likely to want to part with it, although – if the experts are to be believed – it would still be an enjoyable wine.

Packing a case

If you wish, many wine merchants are willing to ship wine abroad. They are extremely reliable and there is never any worry about receiving an incorrect delivery or your cases not turning up at all. It is worth considering

American and European vines. Wines of this type have an undefinable aftertaste vaguely resembling fruit wines. Since the quantities produced are insufficient to meet even local demands, a *mixtura* (blend) of hybrid wine and imported wines from the mainland is frequently served. Some people maintain that hybrid wines can be damaging to your health, so it may be best to err on the side of caution and enjoy them in moderation.

The name of the most popular table wine in Madeira is *vinho verde* (green wine), which was originally brought over from the Portuguese mainland. This light, slightly sparkling wine

since, even with the customs duties, it still works out a great deal cheaper than buying the wine at home.

According to EU regulations, the hybrid wine that is produced in rural areas may neither be exported nor bottled. You will, however, come across it on excursions into the island's interior and in local restaurants, where it is described as *vinho da casa* (house wine) or *americano*. Another popular wine, *jaquet*, is a product of hybrid grapes resulting from the crossing of

LEFT: testing the wine before it leaves the cellars.
ABOVE: the tasting-rooms in the Wine Lodge (Adegas) of São Francisco, Funchal.

with a green tinge is served chilled. It is exceptionally refreshing and its lower alcoholic content makes it especially suitable for drinking on hot summer days.

Should you decide to splash out on a case of 30-, 50-, or even 150-year-old Madeiran wine, however, bear in mind that the true connoisseur does something to his store that would make the hair of any other self-respecting wine buff stand on end. Every five to ten years he empties the wine out of the bottle, washes the bottle, dries it thoroughly and then puts the wine back in. This is supposed to give the wine that extra breath of fresh air necessary for its further "growth". *Saúde!* (Cheers!) ❏

MIXING PIETY WITH PLEASURE

Madeiran festivals celebrate both saints' days and secular events in the calendar with devotion and singularly high spirits

Madeiran island life is punctuated throughout the year by official parades put on mainly for the tourists, and by major religious festivals and local village celebrations. As there is a patron saint – sometimes even two or three – for every village, there is an excuse for a party most days of the year.

CHURCH FESTIVALS

Weeks before a major saint's day the streets will be decked with coloured bunting and fairy lights, and adorned with garlands of fresh-cut laurel brought down from the mountains. On the big day itself, it's not unusual for celebrations to last right through the night, ably assisted by a band in the church forecourt, lots of fireworks, and food stalls serving up vast quantities of the skewered meat dish known as *espetada*.

Next morning, after Mass has taken place in the flower-crammed church (to the sound of yet more fireworks being exploded outside), the local clergy carry the saint's statue through the streets in a solemn procession. They will be accompanied by black-clad villagers and a brass band, and often they will be treading on a carpet of flowers laid out by the women of the parish. As the rest of the day is traditionally devoted to the family, parents and children stroll the streets, dressed in their Sunday best.

▷ **FOLK COSTUME**
A colourful member of Camacha's Grupa Folclorico.

▷ **TAKING STEPS**
Each year on 15 August, pilgrims climb the 74 stone steps of the Nossa Senhora do Monte (Monte's 18th-century parish church) on their knees in a striking gesture of penitence.

△ **MOTHER LOVE**
A devotee kisses the hem of a sacred effigy of the Virgin at Monte's Festival of the Assumption (15 August), the island's biggest pilgrimage event.

▷ **FLOWERED UP**
Funchal's dazzling Festa da Flôr (Flower Festival) is traditionally held in the second or third weekend of April, just as the spring blossom gets underway.

▽ **PEOPLE'S CHOICE**
Madeira's best-known professional folk band, the Grupa Folclorico da Camacha, bring a touch of traditional music and song to island celebrations.

OTHER ISLAND FESTIVALS

January:
5th: *Santa Amaro* is celebrated at Santa Cruz.
20th: *São Sebastião* at Caniçal, Câmara de Lobos.

June:
Fins de Semana Musicais: classical music performances in Funchal; various weekends.
29th: *São Pedro*, patron saint of fishermen; boat procession at Ribeira Brava.

August:
Madeira Wine Rally (a moveable feast, but usually early August).

September:
8th–9th: *Festa do Senhor dos Milagres*. Nocturnal procession honouring the Lord of Miracles at Machico.
13th–15th: Madeira Wine Festival. Wine tasting and exhibitions in Funchal and Câmara de Lobos.

December
8th December–6th January: Christmas illuminations are switched on in Funchal.
31st: Grand New Year firework display in Funchal, one of the best-known and most spectacular in Europe.

◁ **BLOOMIN' GORGEOUS**
Not only are houses and shops decorated with flowers during Funchal's spring Flower Festival, but richly adorned floats take to the streets as well.

▽ **IT'S MY PARTY**
Carnival starts on the Saturday before Shrove Tuesday and includes a major Rio-style street parade in Funchal.

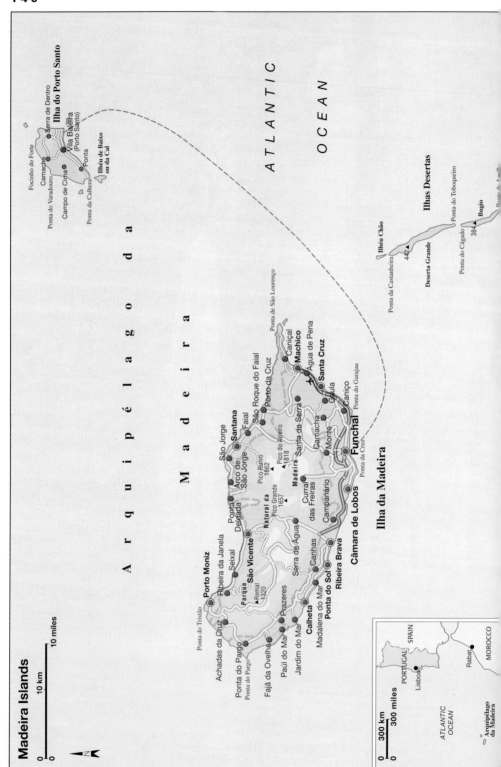

Madeira Islands

0 — 10 km
0 — 10 miles

N

Ilha do Porto Santo

Serra de Dentro
Camacha
Focinho do Forte
Ponta do Varadouro
Campo de Cima
Vila Baleira (Porto Santo)
Ponta
Ponta da Calheta
Ilhéu de Baixo ou da Cal

A T L A N T I C   O C E A N

Ilhas Desertas

Ilhéu Chão
Ponta da Castanheira
Deserta Grande
Ponta do Cágado
Ponta do Toboqueiro
442▲
384▲ **Bugio**

A r q u i p é l a g o   d a

M a d e i r a

Ilha da Madeira

Ponta de São Lourenço
Caniçal
Machico
Agua de Pena
Santa Cruz
Gaula
Caniço
Ponta do Garajau
Funchal
Ponta da Cruz
Porto da Cruz
São Roque do Faial
Faial
Santana
São Jorge
Arco de São Jorge
São Jorge
Pico do Arieiro 1818▲
Santa da Serra
Camacha
Monte
Pico Ruivo 1862▲
Madeira
Pico Grande 1657▲
Curral das Freiras
Campanário
Câmara de Lobos
Natural da
Ponta Delgada
Serra de Agua
Ribeira da Janela
Seixal
São Vicente
Paul da Serra ▲Remal 1320
Porto Moniz
Achadas da Cruz
Ponta do Pargo
Ponta do Pargo
Ponta do Tristão
Fajã da Ovelha
Prazeres
Paúl do Mar
Jardim do Mar
Madalena do Mar
Calheta
Canhas
Ponta do Sol
Ribeira Brava

ATLANTIC OCEAN

0 — 300 km
0 — 300 miles

PORTUGAL   SPAIN
Lisboa
Rabat
MOROCCO

Arquipélago da Madeira

PLACES

*A detailed guide to the entire island, with principal sites
clearly cross-referenced by number to the maps*

Much of the following section is devoted to routes that can be explored by car or bus, or on foot. Indeed, anyone who wants to appreciate the full beauty of Madeira must be prepared to do some walking, and what easier way than to explore the footpaths lining the old aqueducts, or *levadas*? Some paths (such as the path to Balcöes from Riberio Frio, or the walk to 25 Fontes from Rabacal), are now so popular with tour groups that they don't always offer a peaceful escape into rural tranquillity – but for the dedicated walker, the *levadas* still offer an unbeatable combination of stunning scenery and solitude, far from all noise except for birdsong and the sound of gently running water.

The old port city of Funchal, with its narrow streets and grand mansions, now has to contend with traffic congestion and pollution like any other modern city, but there are still plenty of reminders of the Age of Discovery, the sugar boom and the wine trade's heyday. Meanwhile, the parks and gardens of the dignified old *quintas* (grand villas, built for the well-bred and the well-to-do) are a plant-lover's delight, crammed with exotic species indigenous to the island and others imported from all over the world. They're a convenient retreat from city hustle and bustle.

Be prepared to embrace modern Madeira, too, as it is shocked and shaken into the 21st century, propelled by generous EU funding. Local engineers have risen to the challenge of constructing a modern road network by blasting a series of tunnels through the island's volcanic heart and building some of the highest bridges in Europe. An increasing numbers of cars and trucks are an inevitable by-product.

In 2001, another engineering feat – a new runway, constructed on stilts over the steep terrain – increased the capacity of the airport, bringing more tourists as a result. Tourism is, of course, the islanders' biggest hope for the future – hence the host of modern hotels which now crowd Funchal's western outskirts, new ones sprouting every year. Outside the capital, untrammelled development continues, too.

Fortunately, though, the absence of sandy beaches mean Madeira will probably be spared the kind of mass tourism that has had such an unsightly impact on its Canary Island neighbours. What's more, if you hire a car and drive just a few miles outside Funchal into the mountains, you are soon well away from the crowds. All you need is to know where to go – and that is the job of this section. ❑

PRECEDING PAGES: south coast palm tree; every scrap of fertile land is terraced on this small island; Funchal's Jardim de São Francisco, a tiny jewel right in the heart of the city centre.

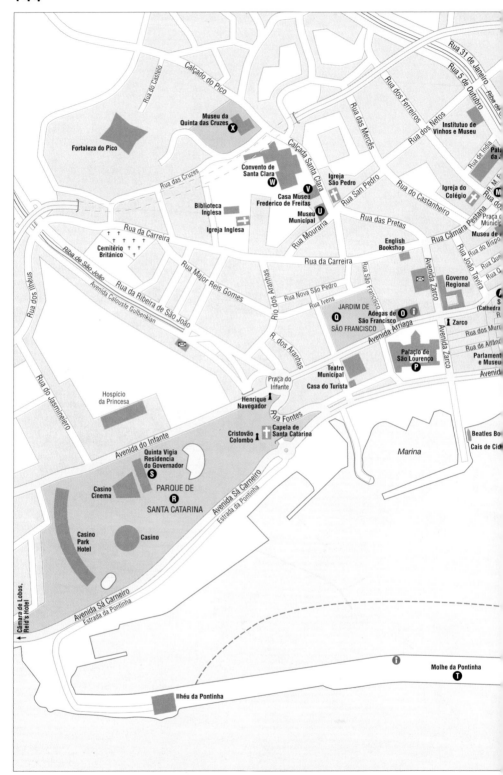

Rua 31 de Janeiro

Rua 5 de Outubro · Riba de ...

Calçado do Pico

Rua do Castelo

Rua dos Ferreiros

Rua dos Netos

Rua das Mercês

Museu da
Quinta das Cruzes X

Instituto de
Vinhos e Museu

Fortaleza do Pico

Rua de India

Pala
da J.

Calçada Santa Clara

R. M. F.

Rua das Cruzes

Convento de
Santa Clara W

Igreja
São Pedro

Rua do Castanheiro

Igreja do
Colégio

Rua M

Casa Museu
Frederico de Freitas V

Rua San Pedro

Praça d
Municip

Biblioteca
Inglesa

Museu
Municipal U

Rua das Pretas

Rua Câmara Pestana

Museu de

Rua da Carreira

Igreja Inglesa

Rua Mouraria

English
Bookshop

Rua do Bispo

Cemitério † † †
Británico †

Rua Major Reis Gomes

Rua da Carreira

Rua João Tavira

Rua Que

Rio dos Aranhas

Rua Nova São Pedro

Rua São Francisco

Avenida Zarco

Rua Q

Riba de São João

Rua da Ribeira de São João

Avenida Calouste Gulbenkian

Rua Ivens

Governo
Regional

Rua dos Ilhéus

R. dos Aranhas

JARDIM DE

Adegas de O
São Francisco

Zarco

S
(Cathedra
R

SÃO FRANCISCO Q

Avenida Arriaga

Avenida Zarco

Rua dos Muro

Rua de Alfand

Hospício
da Princesa

Teatro
Municipal

Palácio de
São Lourenço P

Parlament
e Museu

Rua do Jasmineiro

Praça do
Infante

Casa do Turista

Avenid

Henrique
Navegador

Rua Fontes

Cristovão
Colombo

Capela de
Santa Catarina

Marina

Beatles Bo

Cais de Cid

Avenida do Infante

Quinta Vigia
Residencia
do Governador S

Casino
Cinema

PARQUE DE

R

SANTA CATARINA

Avenida Sá Carneiro

Estrada da Pontinha

Casino
Park
Hotel

Casino

Câmara de Lobos,
Reid's Hotel

Avenida Sá Carneiro

Estrada da Pontinha

Molhe da Pontinha
T

Ilhéu da Pontinha

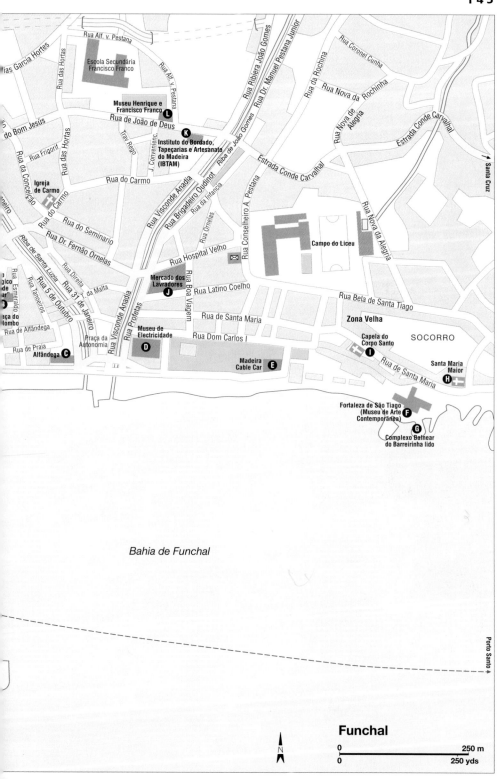

Rua Alf. v. Pestana

Rua das Hortes

ias Garcia Hortes

Escola Secundária
Francisco Franco

Rua Alf. v. Pestana

Museu Henrique e
Francisco Franco **L**

Rua de João de Deus

K Instituto do Bordado,
Tapeçarias e Artesanato
do Madeira
(IBTAM)

Rua Ribiera João Gomes

Rua Dr. Manuel Pestana Junior

Rua Coronel Cunha

Rua da Rochina

Rua Nova da Rochinha

Rua Nova de Alegria

Estrada Conde Carvalhal

Santa Cruz

do Bom Jesús

Rua Frigori

Rua da Conceição

Rua das Hortas

Igreja
de Carmo

Rua do Carmo

Trav Rego

J. Conveniento

Rua do Carmo

Rua Visconde Anadia

Rua Brigadeiro Oudinot

Ribca de João Gomes

Rua da Infancia

Rua Ornelas

Estrada Conde Carvalhal

Rua Conselheiro A. Pestana

Rua Nova da Alegria

Rua do Seminario

Rua Dr. Fernão Ornelas

Ribca de Santa Luzia

Rua Direita

. da Malta

Rua Hospital Velho

Campo do Liceu

Esmeraldo

Rua 5 de Outubro

Rua Tanoeiros

Rua 31 de Janeiro

Mercado dos
Lavradores **J**

Rua Boa Viagem

Rua Latino Coelho

Rua Bela de Santa Tiago

aça do
lombo

Rua de Alfândega

Rua de Santa Maria

Zona Velha

Museu de
Electricidade **D**

Rua Proletas

Rua Visconde Anadia

Praça da
Autonomia

Rua Dom Carlos I

Capela do
Corpo Santo **I**

SOCORRO

Rua de Praia

Alfândega **C**

E Madeira
Cable Car

Rua de Santa Maria

Santa Maria
Maior **H**

Fortaleza de São Tiago
(Museu de Arte
Contemporânea) **F**

G
Complexo Balnear
do Barreirinha lido

Bahia de Funchal

Porto Santo

Funchal

N

| 0 | | 250 m |
| 0 | | 250 yds |

A WALK THROUGH FUNCHAL

*You can turn the clock back centuries in Madeira's capital,
where a grand sea-and-mountain setting, lush gardens and
a wealth of historic sights make it a delight to explore*

Map
on pages
144–45

Funchal

Funchal is graced with an unusually dramatic setting. At its back, jagged mountains, 1,200 metres (3,600 ft) high, encircle the city like a giant amphitheatre, while its feet are lapped by the sea. The name supposedly comes from the Portuguese word for fennel *(funcho)*, which Madeira's founding father, Zarco and his explorers found in abundance on the river-banks when they arrived in 1419. Machico, on the east coast, may have been the island's first main settlement, but it was Funchal's magnificent wide, sheltered bay that drew most of the early settlers here instead. Today it is Madeira's largest town (pop. 120,000), and where nine out of ten tourists to the island spend their holidays.

Between the built-up areas, the original sub-tropical vegetation still thrives, although Zarco would hardly recognise the three city rivers. The Ribeiras de São João, de Santa Luzia and de João Gomes have each been bedded in concrete as part of a flood protection scheme; magnificent hedges of purple bougainvillaea, trained on wires above the dried-out canals, hide their most unappealing aspects.

The birth of a capital

In 1440, the Portuguese Crown officially presented Zarco with one half of Madeira – including Funchal – as his personal fiefdom. The island was united in 1497, and Funchal's stature as the main focus of Madeiran life began to grow. By the turn of the century, sugar exports had turned the place into a flourishing metropolis, attracting merchants from across Europe. The island's nobility also settled here, leaving the management of their country estates to tenant farmers.

In 1508, *Piccola Lisbonna* ("Little Lisbon", as Funchal was dubbed by the Italian sailors who docked here), was given city status by King Manuel I. Six years later, the king himself paid for the building of a Sé, or cathedral – the place where our tour begins.

Funchal's **Sé (Cathedral)** Ⓐ is, in fact, one of the city's few surviving Manueline-style buildings. The façade is simple and unpretentious, broken up only by the sturdy Gothic portal and the surprisingly small rose window above. The apse (at the eastern end) is much less austere with its embellished parapet and jaunty barley-sugar-twist towers, while the main tower's pointed cap sparkles with tiny coloured *azulejos* tiles.

Inside, the gloom makes it hard to see the beautiful, Moorish ceiling, carved from indigenous cedar and inlaid with ivory. Easier to admire are the elaborate 16th-century choir stalls, carved in Flanders and paid for with profits from the booming sugar industry.

If you want to find out more about the trade in sweet "white gold" that brought the city wealth, head east beyond the cathedral along the Rua da Sé to **Praça do Colombo**. The **Núcleo Museológico "A Cidade do**

PRECEDING PAGES:
the Fortaleza do Pico broods high on an upper-city rock.
LEFT: Funchal's harbour. **BELOW:** the 16th-century Sé, or cathedral.

Açucar" (Tues–Fri 9am–12.30pm, 2–5.30pm; closed Sat, Sun, Mon and public holidays) is set in the excavated remains of the house of 16th-century Flemish sugar merchant, Jennin Esmerandt ("João Esmeraldo" in Portuguese), a friend of Christopher Columbus *(see page 30)*. Documents and works of art trace the history of sugar production on the island and its impact on Madeira's development.

Head south to the seafront and the **Avenida do Mar**. A left turn brings you to the Old Customs House, or **Alfândega** ⓒ, now the seat of Madeira's parliament. Although it dates back to the 15th century, it is much altered (the southern façade has suffered a particularly dismal modern facelift); look out for the portal in Rua da Alfândega surmounted by the Portuguese coat of arms, which is one of the few surviving fragments of the original Manueline structure.

Into the Old Town

Despite the traffic, the Avenido do Mar's broad promenade and yacht-filled marina make it a nice place for a stroll. A short detour west brings you to the **Beatles Boat**, a luxury yacht once owned by the Fab Four but subsequently bought by a Madeiran and turned into a "floating" restaurant (ironically, it's firmly moored in concrete). This is a pricy tourist trap, but fun, nonetheless.

To the east, Avenida do Mar leads all the way to the **Zona Velha**, or Old Town, so called because this was the first part of Madeira to be settled. This rectilinear grid of narrow alleys is now crammed with tiny restaurants, whose tables spill out onto the cobbles of the traffic free streets in summer. On the left as you enter the Zona Velha is the new **Museu de Electricidade "Casa da Luz"** ⓓ (Rua Casa da Luz 2, Tues–Sat 10am–12.30pm, 2–6pm; closed Sun, Mon and public holidays). At one level, this is a museum about electricity-

TIP

Funchal is best explored on foot – not least because of traffic congestion. It can take longer to drive than walk back to your hotel during the evening rush-hour.

BELOW: the 17th-century Fortaleza de São Tiago, which is now a modern art museum.

generating, of interest only to specialists; on another level, it tells the fascinating story of the spread of electricity from Funchal to the island's remote communities – a formidable task, given the mountainous nature of the island's terrain.

Another engineering triumph is represented by the **Madeira Cable Car Station** ❺ (daily 9am–6.30pm in winter, to 8.30pm in summer, tel: 780 280, www.madeiracablecar.com). With its stylish glass-and-steel base station, the cable cars harness Swiss technology to carry passengers high above the city's rooftops up to the hill village of Monte.

Map on pages 144–45

Right at the end of Avenida do Mar, beyond the Porto Santa Maria hotel, is the **Fortaleza do São Tiago (Museu de Arte Contemporânea)** ❻ (Mon–Sat, 10am–12.30pm, 2–5.30pm; closed Sun and public holidays). Built at the eastern end of the Old Town in 1614–37, when English and French pirates were threatening the island *(see page 38)*, the fortress commands a superb view over the bay of Funchal and is used to display a small collection of contemporary art.

Immediately east of the fortress, the **Complexo Balnear da Barreirinha lido** ❼ (daily 8.30am–7pm in summer, till 5pm in winter) provides access to the sea for bathing. High above it is the elegant baroque façade of the church of **Santa Maria Maior** ❽, dating from 1803 and replacing an earlier chapel built by local people in thanksgiving for their salvation from plague.

Handmade boots on sale in the Mercado dos Lavradores.

To the market

Returning along the cobbled lane called Rua de Santa Maria, you will encounter spruced-up fishermen's houses, now used as craft centres by sandal makers and lace makers, as well as the little **Capella do Corpo Santo** ❾ (10am–noon and 3–5pm, except public holidays), a chapel built in 1559 by local people who

LEFT: relaxing at the Barreirinha lido.
BELOW: a trader outside the Mercado dos Lavradores.

formed a guild to provide help for destitute sailors and fishermen. One of the altars is dedicated to St Lawrence, in memory of the name of the ship in which Zarco and his crew sailed to Madeira.

Numerous bars and restaurants line Rua de Santa Maior, which is the oldest street in Funchal, and the Rua Dom Carlos I, which runs parallel. Many of the simple buildings lining both streets were slums until very recently, when their occupants were rehoused as part of a scheme to improve the area. You will still see plenty of examples of real poverty in and around the market that stands at the western end of the Zona Velha. Called the **Mercado dos Lavradores ❶** (or Farmers' Market), this is housed in a sleek liner-like Art Deco building, designed in the 1930s by Edmundo Tavares (daily except Sunday, 7am–8pm). The market itself is a major tourist attraction, full of the colours and scents of the island's tropical fruits and flowers, not to mention freshly caught fish in the basement. Around the market, farmers up from the countryside for the day set up informal stalls selling their home-grown produce among the sellers of lottery tickets, cobblers offering instant shoe and umbrella repairs or knife sharpening and stall-owners selling household goods at rock-bottom prices.

Island arts and crafts

The hustle and bustle of the market spills out onto the pavements in front of the market, from where you can look across one of the city's canalised rivers to the brand new Anadia shopping complex, with its basement supermarket, arcades of shops and cinema. Crossing to the supermarket and turning right (uphill) you will pass the Patricio & Gouveia Embroidery Factory, with its tempting sales rooms. A short way further up the hill, you will reach the **Instituto do Bor-**

TIP

Look out for the pretty *casas de prazeres* (boxy summer-houses) on the walls along Rua de João de Deus. In the 18th century, they were a favourite venue for society tea-parties.

BELOW: this pretty café abuts the English bookshop in Rua de Carreira.

dado, Tapeçarias e Artesanato da Madeira **K** (IBTAM, or the Institute of Embroidery, Tapestry and Handicrafts, Mon–Fri 10am–12.30pm, 2.30–5.30pm; entrance fee; *also see page 113*). If you have an interest in fine embroidery, take a peek at the beautiful pieces in the small museum upstairs.

A little further up, turn left into the **Rua do Bom Deus**, where at No. 13, on the right-hand side, you will find a curious temple-like structure with a pillared entrance. This is the **Museu Henrique e Francisco Franco O** (open Tues–Sun 10am–12.30pm, 2–5.30pm), dedicated to two brothers – one a landscape and portrait painter, one a sculptor. During the first half of the 20th century, they were among Portugal's most-celebrated artists. Follow the street all the way along as it crosses another dry river-bed and finally comes to a halt at the imposing **Praça do Município**, Funchal's main square. Dark volcanic basalt was used both for paving the square (the mosaic design is supposed to represent fish scales) and for decorating the surrounding buildings; the result is splendid.

At its eastern end is the grand 18th-century **Câmara Municipal (City Hall) M**, originally designed for one of Madeira's richest residents, the Conde de Carvalhal. An arch at the far end of the entrance hall leads to a pretty tiled courtyard, where a marble fountain offers a marble sculpture of Leda and her swan; upstairs, a small museum (currently closed for restructuring) traces Funchal's history.

Diagonally opposite looms the **Igreja do Colégio**, a Jesuit church that predates the City Hall by some 150 years. The façade – adorned with statues of Jesuit saints, including Ignatius of Loyola – is deceptively sober; don't miss the chance of a peek at the fabulous baroque interior, resplendent with rare coloured *azulejos*, gilt carvings and Mudejar-style wall paintings.

A Flemish feast

The best, however, is yet to come. Head across the square to its southwestern corner, and turn left, past the elaborate 17th-century stone portal of little **Capela do São Luiz,** down on to **Rua do Bispo**. The baroque bishop's palace at the end of the street houses the **Museu de Arte Sacra N** (Tues–Sat 10am–12.30pm, 2.30–6pm; Sun 10am–1pm; entrance fee), best known for its magnificent cache of 15th- and 16th-century Flemish paintings, bought by local merchants with the profits of the flourishing sugar trade.

Head for the top floor to see a fine *Annunciation* by Joos van Cleve and collaborators, a powerful red-robed *Santiago*, (St James), attributed to Dieric Bouts, and a gripping but faintly repellent *St Nicholas*, the snakeskin-like glitter of his robes offset by his icy-blue gloves. The small painting, *The Meeting of St Anna and St Joachim*, meanwhile, actually depicts a bearded King Wladislaw of Poland, who went into self-imposed exile on Madeira in 1414 *(see page 51)*.

Downstairs, admire the gorgeously embroidered liturgical vestments (the work of local nuns), statues and religious artefacts. An elaborate gilt processional cross, donated to the cathedral by King Manuel I in 1514, takes pride of place here.

Backtrack north to the main square now and find Rua Câmara Pestana heading west. This street turns into **Rua de Carreira**, lined with green-shuttered

Many paintings in the Museu de Arte Sacra were bought with sugar money.

BELOW: a statue of the explorer Zarco, near the Cathedral.

Map on pages 144–45

19th-century buildings. No. 43 has an English bookshop and a café in a patio shaded by banana trees and is a nice spot for a well-earned break.

A left turn from here into leafy **Avenida Zarco** takes you downhill past the baroque seat of the **Governo Regional** and – across the road – the stately **Bank of Portugal** building with its giant orange turret. Jacaranda-lined **Avenida Arriega**, the wide boulevard bisecting Zarco, is one of Funchal's most elegant streets. Next to the tourist office at No. 28 is the **Adegas de São Francisco** ⦿ or wine lodge (also known as the Madeira Wine Company), in a romantic old building that was once a convent (guided tours Mon–Fri at 10.30am and 3.30pm; Sat 11am; fee). Tours are informative, taking you through the entire history and process of making Madeiran wine, and finishing off with a tasting session. If you don't know much about the famous local tipple, this is a good place to start.

Arms and *azulejos*

The bulky white **Palácio de São Lourenço** ⦿ dominates the other side of the street *(see also page 40)*. Begun in the 16th century, it's been much modified over the years, although the battlemented East Tower is a remnant of the original Manueline design (note the King of Portugal's coat of arms here: a shield with a crown and Crusader's cross, flanked by two armillary spheres used for navigation during sea voyages). You're not allowed into São Lourenço – it's now the headquarters of the Madeiran military – although if you make reservations in advance you may be admitted to one of the vaults in the North Tower where there is a display on the fortress's history. Enquire at the tourist office.

Next comes the 19th-century **Chamber of Commerce**, decorated with jaunty blue-and-white *azulejos* (tiles) showing traditional island scenes. The beautiful

BELOW: the outdoor café next to the Teatro Municipal is one of Funchal's most fashionable coffee houses.

iled main hall is now a car showroom. For more glimpses of graceful *fin-de-siè-le* detail, peek into the entrance-hall of the offices next door, and into the splendid tiered **Teatro Municipal** a little further along. To the left of the theatre, the narrow Rua do Conselheiro José Silvestre Ribeiro (a street almost shorter than its name) leads down to the **Casa do Turista** – probably the island's best-known souvenir shop, with top-quality goods housed in a grand old mansion.

Opposite the Chamber of Commerce and the theatre is the **Jardim de São Francisco Ⓠ**, a tiny jewel of a park crammed with lush sub-tropical plants and trees, some with edifying nameplates. The outdoor café at the northern end of the park is a great spot for people-watching over a coffee or an ice cream.

Avenida Arriaga finally gives way to the **Avenida do Infante** at a busy traffic roundabout, adorned with a monument to Henry the Navigator. This marks the end of the city centre and the start of a long, sloping bluff which was traditionally one of Funchal's grander residential districts, filled with lavish *quintas* commanding majestic views over the seashell-shaped bay.

Along the seafront

The green expanses of the **Parque de Santa Catarina Ⓡ** stretch along the first part of the rise, sprinkled with statues, flowerbeds, a children's playground and huge wrought-iron bird-cages. Its benches are a big hit, and no wonder – the views of the sea and mountains are superb. The park's most important monument is the small disused **Capela de Santa Catarina** at its eastern end, marking the spot where Zarco's wife, Constança Rodrigues, erected Funchal's first chapel in 1425. Most of this present building is baroque, although the belltower and holy-water font under the canopy of the church date from the Manueline period.

A fine seated statue commemorates Columbus in the Parque de Santa Catarina.

BELOW: Parque de Santa Caterina.

THE STORY OF THE QUINTA VIGIA

Originally built for a wealthy Madeiran landowner, this romantic old villa has a poignant history. In 1853 the Empress of Brazil came to stay here with her daughter, Princess Maria Amélia, who had tuberculosis. Sadly, the rest cure was a failure; after only a few months the princess died aged just 22, and the house was shut up for years.

As far as the popular imagination went, though, this combination of blue blood and suffering was a heady one. Quinta Vigia is often associated with another empress, the glamourous Elisabeth (Sissi) of Austria, who spent the winter of 1860 on the island recuperating from a marriage crisis with her husband, Franz Joseph. But although legend has her sadly sipping tea in the estate's splendid summer-house overlooking the harbour and wandering the grounds in an angst-ridden daze, Sissi actually never spent any time here at all, preferring instead the comforts of Reid's.

In the 1890s the estate was bought by the Comte de Lambert, an envoy from the Russian court. True to form, he was a lugubrious sort who closeted himself away behind his lovely home's formidable iron gates. The local rumour-mill, of course, had an explanation: the count was haunted by guilt after the suicide of a rival in a love affair gone wrong. Quinta Vigia's melancholy spirit lived on.

To the west, a magenta building stands out among tropical trees: the splendid **Quinta Vigia** . This 18th-century villa now serves as the official residence of the Governor of Madeira and a guest house for state visits, but members of the public may stroll round the lovely garden as long as it isn't being used for an official reception. Although it is called the Quinta Vigia, this is not the original mansion of that name. It was rechristened in 1982 after the controversial demolition of the historic Quinta Vigia (where crowned heads used to stay – *see page 153*). The original building was bulldozed in the early 1970s to make way for the ugly modern casino and adjoining **Carlton Park Hotel**.

From the southern end of the park, there are good views down to the ships in Funchal's harbour where ships once had to anchor behind a small mole while their passengers were rowed ashore. Today, ships berth within the **Molhe da Pontinha** ⬤, the massive harbour wall visible below the park. The harbour is mainly a container port, and the arrival of a cruise ship is always a big event.

Several huge dragon-trees dot the luxuriant grounds of the **Hospício da Princesa** just across the avenue from the park. Founded in 1859 by the Empress of Brazil, in memory of her daughter (Princess Maria Amélia – *see page 153*), who died of tuberculosis, the hospice building isn't open to the public, but you can walk in the grounds and you could ask one of the nuns if you can have a quick look inside the chapel. It houses an exquisite marble Madonna donated by a grieving Emperor Maximilian of Mexico, who had been engaged to the young princess.

The hotel zone

West of the casino complex is where most of Funchal's big tourist hotels are situated, dotted on either side of the big, busy **Estrada Monumental**. Not much of Old Madeira has survived round here, although there is one celebrated exception: **Reid's Palace Hotel**, set in rolling clifftop gardens with fine views down to the sea. Afternoon tea on the terrace here is a highly recommended experience *(see pages 160–61)*.

Another grand old estate to have escaped the developers' clutches is the **Quinta Magnólia,** just north of Reid's Hotel along Rua do Dr Pita and behind the Quinta do Sol hotel. Formerly the British Country Club, it is now a delightful public park with a children's playground, swimming pool, squash and tennis courts and a keep-fit track (summer: 7.30am–9pm, winter: 8.30–5pm; entrance to the garden is free but there is a small charge to use the facilities).

The house itself was built by the former American consul, T.H. March, a passionate botanist. Later, it belonged to a certain Herbert Watney, an English medical doctor, who also took a particular interest in the estate garden; it is thanks to them that the grounds contain their valuable collection of palm trees and other exotic plants.

City streets

The last leg of our tour starts back in the city centre, just north of the Jardim de São Francisco. Head north up Rua São Francisco, turn right into Rua da Carreira, and left into the **Rua das Pretas**. The word *pretas* means "negresses" and dates back to the time of slavery

Brazilian architect Oscar Niemeyer (who designed much of his nation's capital, Brasilia) was also responsible for Funchal's casino, built in the shape of a giant crown of thorns.

BELOW: Niemeyer's casino, next to the Casino Park Hotel.

on Madeira, when blacks were confined to ghettos and bound by a strict evening curfew. Today, incongruously, this is one of Funchal's smarter shopping areas, dotted with trendy boutiques and antique shops.

Squeezed between two houses at the junction with Rua San Pedro is the little 16th-century **Igreja de São Pedro**, notable for its fine 17th-century tiling. A left turn leads to the **Rua Mouraria** ("Street of the Moorish Quarter") and the **Museu Municipal ⓊU** (Tues–Fri 10am–6pm, Sat–Sun and public holidays noon–6pm; entrance fee), housed in the gloomy 18th-century Palace of São Pedro. There's an aquarium on the ground floor and a rather lacklustre collection of stuffed animals on the upper ones; the building itself – with its elegant inner courtyard, double staircase and dark wooden fittings – is the main attraction here.

The Upper Town

The dauntingly steep Calçada de Santa Clara leads up past the church of São Pedro, but it's worth the climb, not least for the deep-pink **Casa Museu Frederico de Freitas ⓋV** (Tues–Sat 10am–12.30pm, 2–6pm; entrance fee) about halfway up. This fine late-17th-century villa is crammed with antique furnishings, carvings, religious paintings and china, amassed by a local lawyer who bequeathed the lot to the nation upon his death in 1978. A separate, newly designed building, called the House of Tiles, displays historic *azulejos* tiles from demolished buildings all over Madeira, dating from the earliest examples of 1514 up to splendid Art Nouveau examples from the late 19th century.

A little further up the hill is the historic **Convento de Santa Clara ⓌW** (open daily 10am–noon and 3pm–5pm except during services), founded in 1496 and still a convent today. The first abbess was Zarco's granddaughter, Dona Isabel,

Map on pages 144–45

BELOW: Reid's Palace Hotel, one of Funchal's most famous landmarks.

Map
on pages
144–45

Many of the graves in Funchal's British Cemetery belong to youthful victims of TB who had been brought to Madeira in the vain hope that the climate would spur on a cure.

BELOW: the pace of life in Funchal is pleasantly relaxed for a capital city.

and the nuns were high-born young ladies, many despatched there by impecunious parents unable to stump up a suitable dowry. Ring the bell at the entrance if you'd like to be shown around; there's no charge, but a small donation will be requested at the end of the tour.

The tour takes in several of the splendid baroque rooms leading off the tranquil cloister. To the north is the convent church with its richly painted ceiling and walls covered in blue-and-yellow 17th-century *azulejos*. Zarco himself is buried beneath the high altar, with the tombs of two of his daughters. An iron grill at the back of the church separates off the public part of the church from the area reserved for the nuns and is a reminder of the secluded lives the nuns embraced; they sat behind it during church services and whenever visitors were received, thus avoiding any direct contact with the outside world.

More tombs can be found in the 19th-century **Cemitério Británico** (daily, dawn to dusk; ring the bell at the gate for entry), southwest of the convent off Rua da Carreira, and filled with memorials to the island's Protestant community. The domed Neo-classical **Igreja Inglesa** nearby is also worth a visit; its neat gardens house an English library (open to visitors) attached to the chaplaincy.

Immediately north of the convent is the lovely **Museu da Quinta das Cruzes** ✪ *(see page 157)*. If you have any energy left after viewing this, continue all the way up the punishingly steep Calçada do Pico until you find the level Rua do Castelo on your left after 300 metres (985 ft). This leads to the **Fortaleza do Pico** (Peak Fortress; daily 9am–6pm), built in 1632–49 for sea surveillance and stil occupied by the Portuguese armed forces. Members of the public are allowed to walk around the walls, from which there are stunning views across the red-tiled rooftops of Funchal. ❑

Quinta das Cruzes

One of Madeira's finest features is the wealth of aristocratic *quintas* (mansions) that grace its streets and countryside. The earliest date from the 15th century, built for the Portuguese nobility who settled on the island. Many were added in the 18th and 19th centuries when the booming trade in Madeiran wine attracted scores of British merchants, who settled down and joined the island's elite.

Architects were hired to follow the latest fashions from Europe, while teams of gardeners toiled to create lush landscaped oases brimming with exotic plants. At one time there were a few dozen such large estates and several hundred smaller "summer *quintas*" on the island.

The ordinary public, of course, was never allowed more than a glimpse of these lavish mansions, concealed as they were behind high stone walls. All that's changed today. While many have fallen victim to property speculation – some divided up, others demolished – a few survivors have been converted into museums or institutional headquarters. Funchal's share includes the Quinta Magnólia (now a park and sports club) as well as the grand Quinta do Palheiro Ferreiro with its celebrated public gardens *(see page 168)*.

Most impressive of all, however, is the **Quinta das Cruzes** ("Mansion of the Crosses"), lying in a beautiful park just above the Santa Clara convent in Calçada do Pico. This was where Captain Zarco – the island's founding father – took up residence in the 15th century, although all that remains of his original farmhouse today are just a few foundation walls. Like many buildings in Funchal, this quinta was rebuilt in baroque style after its predecessor was damaged by a major earthquake in 1748.

The *quinta* then became a museum in 1953 (Tues–Sat 10am–12.30pm and 2–5.30pm; Sun 10am–1pm; entrance fee). The grounds of the estate house an Archaeological Park, a fascinating collection of masonry and stonework (including two fine

Manueline window-frames) dotted amongst the trees. Look out for the fragment of Funchal's pillory (actually a copy), which once stood near what is now the covered market; the original was moved here in 1835 after three centuries of gruesome use. To the south is the memorial stone of the master builder of Funchal's cathedral, Pedro Anes.

Orchids are grown on shady terraces at the top end of the gardens, which have a tranquillity all their own; not many tourists find their way up here, and a short spell on one of the benches is very restful. Giant specimens of lady's slipper bloom in the park during winter and spring, and you can also admire huge tree ferns, ornamental bananas, Indian laurels, fuchsias and azaleas.

The grand old house contains some equally impressive exhibits. On the ground floor you will find some fine examples of sugar-box furniture *(see page 119)* along with silverware, engravings, *azulejos* and old pewter. Upstairs are valuable collections of Oriental and English furniture, Flemish paintings and French porcelain. ❑

RIGHT: the museum inside the Quinta das Cruzes contains some exquisite antiques.

THE BLUE ART OF MADEIRAN *AZULEJOS*

A classic feature of Portuguese architecture, these tile mosaics not only adorn buildings but also protect them from wind and rain

Portugal's decorative wall tiles belong to a venerable design tradition that stretches back to the 13th century. They're known as *azulejos*, after the Arabic term *al zulecha,* meaning "burnt clay". Lisbon's earliest tile-workers were, in fact, Mudejars, or Moors who had converted to Christianity and settled in Europe.

Few examples of their work can still be seen *in situ* on Madeira, although the 16th-century tiles decorating the turret of Funchal's cathedral are an honourable exception. Santa Clara Convent also has some fine Mudejar tile decoration on the floor surrounding the high altar.

Later during the 16th century, the majolica technique from Italy was developed, making *azulejos* much easier to produce; veritable "tile carpets" soon became fahionable (the transept of Funchal's Igreja do Colégio is a good example). During the 17th century, tile-making flowered on Madeira, and scores of outstanding examples are now displayed in the Casa Museu Frederico de Freitas *(see page 155),* including Dutch-influenced blue-and-white tiles, and tile pictures depicting religious and secular stones.

◁ **GARDEN DECOR**
This 18th-century tile picture is one of several dotted round the Monte Palace Tropical Gardens.

◁ **BAROQUE DRAMA**
This substantial tile panel stands out in gleaming contrast to the stark white façade of the 17th-century parish church of Nossa Senhora da Piedade in Vila Baleira, Porto Santo.

▽ **WATERING IT DOWN**
This fountain in the Machico valley dates from the 1800s, when mass production of tiles started on Madeira: the expert eye of the tile-maker was now replaced by the stencil.

THE ISLAND'S MODERN *AZULEJOS*

The 19th century was not a particularly good time for Madeiran *azulejo* art. This was a time when tile-production in Portugal was profoundly influenced by developments in Brazil, where it had been discovered that tiled walls provided ideal protection against the damp and heat. Soon, as people started to render entire walls with mass-produced plain tiles, ceramic factories on the mainland eagerly launched themselves into this new market.

In Madeira, however, such industrialisation was scorned. Instead, tile-decorators seemed to deliberately wallow in nostalgia, adorning walls and corridors with highly romanticised copies of earlier designs (such as the *azulejos* above, which are from Funchal's former Chamber of Commerce building, now a car showroom). In fact, it wasn't until the beginning of the 20th century that Madeira's tiling industry was revitalised. Good examples of quality modern work include the fountain in front of the Carlton Hotel, and the tiles on the terrace of Reid's Palace Hotel.

▷ **FRESH PRODUCE**
A frieze of modern *azulejos* by Portuguese artist Outeiro Agueda decorates the entrance to Santa Cruz's market-hall

◁ **TOURIST TRAP**
This 1930s panel shows a tourist in a sedan chair. It is found on an exterior wall of Funchal's former Chamber of Commerce on Avenida Arriaga.

Map
on page
166

Reid's
Hotel
Funchal

REID'S HOTEL

A byword for old-fashioned luxury and exclusivity,
and with the strictest regard for social convention,
this grand old dowager is still going strong

It was the winter of 1950 that Sir Winston Churchill, then 75, said he wanted somewhere "warm, paintable, bathable, comfortable and flowery" to convalsece after a stroke. A friend came up with a perfect fit – the island of Madeira and a suite at **Reid's Hotel ❶**.

Anyone with a yen to stay in a classic *fin-de-siècle* grand hotel, built exclusively to cater to the whims of the well-bred and well-to-do, will find what they are looking for at Reid's. The rates may be stratospheric, but then the standards of service are high; not for nothing is this still – after more than a century – one of the most famous hotels in the world.

Yet its founder's origins were modest, to say the least. Thanks to England's long-standing alliance with Portugal (going back to 1376), British entrepreneurs had by the 18th century established a virtual monopoly over the wine trade. A 14-year-old Scottish youth called William Reid – one of 12 children of an impoverished crofter – arrived in 1836 with £5 in his pocket, having run away to sea and worked his passage to Madeira. By the age of 25, Reid had become a prosperous wine merchant in Funchal, and was diversifying into renting and managing *quintas* for well-to-do invalids from northern Europe.

Some of these villas he converted into hotels, and, in due course, he acquired a fine site on a high promontory overlooking Funchal's harbour, on which he planned to erect the luxury hotel of his dreams. Alas, Reid did not live to see the longed-for opening: he died in 1887, and his two sons, Willy and Albert, were left to complete the project on his behalf. In the end, it was only in 1891 that the hotel first threw open its doors.

A dream inherited

In 1937, Reid's passed into the hands of the equally famous Blandy family, another great British-Madeiran dynasty, and then in 1996 was acquired by the British-owned Orient-Express Hotels company. They have restored the hotel's original name, "Reid's Palace" and given the grand old lady a minor nip-and-tuck, getting rid of a few gloomy bits but keeping the best – the enormous lounges, the four hectares (ten acres) of lovely gardens, the teak-panelled library with its leather-bound books, and the art deco bathrooms.

Although it has grown substantially over the years, spreading over its clifftop site in varied architectural style, the effect is still harmonious and Reid's remains what it has always been: the epitome of discreet, old-fashioned luxury. Upper-class and business-class Brits still make up 40 percent of the guests; most of the (elderly) regulars still spend the entire winter season here, arriving in September and leaving soon after New Year.

BELOW: one of the heated salt-water swimming-pools at Reid's Hotel.

As a result, the hotel enjoys a wonderful sense of quietude. The reading room is disturbed by nothing more irksome than the occasional rustle of London's *Times* or *Daily Telegraph*; the lounges enlivened by nothing louder than the tinkle of bone-china teacups and the muted murmur of polite small talk. In the chandeliered main dining-room, the dress code is strictly black tie or dark suits for the men, and, for the women, evening gowns.

There are other five-star hotels in Funchal that may offer better value for money, but it's highly unlikely that this extraordinary, time-warped atmosphere could ever be duplicated in a modern tower block. If you'd like a small sample, reserve a place for the traditional English afternoon tea, complete with crustless sandwiches, scones and clotted cream, which is served daily between 3pm and 6pm on the beautiful main terrace overlooking the sea.

If you check in for a stay, you can look forward to a lavish range of amenities, from the three heated salt-water swimming pools and the rock pool down at the foot of the cliff to the tennis courts and saunas (one each for ladies and gentlemen). There is also (of course) a billiard and snooker room as well as a bridge room, and – reassuringly for non-sporty types – a host of padded sun-loungers scattered invitingly around the tranquil gardens.

Organised activities include painting-classes and *levada* walks. Recently, the hotel has branched out with its own high-class version of murder-mystery weekends, with trips on the famous Orient Express as prizes.

Afternoon tea on the terrace is a ritual that should not be missed.

Celebrities' meeting place

As the guest book verifies, Reid's has played host to emperors, kings and queens, including some fallen on hard times: ex-King Umberto of Italy, for example, who visited in 1965. He was preceded in 1921 by Karl I, the last emperor of Austria, who spent the first part of his exile here after being deposed from the Austrian throne. Stricken with pneumonia within months of his arrival, he died in 1922 and is buried in Nossa Senhora church at Monte *(see page 165)*.

Various dictators, both ruling and deposed, have used the hotel as a bolt-hole – Cuba's General Batista, for example, forced to flee his homeland by Fidel Castro, arrived with a large entourage and took over an entire floor. Ian Smith, former Prime Minister of Rhodesia, has also visited, as has South Africa's former Foreign Minister, Afrikaner Pik Botha.

William Churchill became a regular after his 1950 visit. On that occasion, he hosted a formal dinner at Reid's for Madeira's British community, who presented him with an unusual gift – an unopened demijohn of Madeira wine previously given to Napoleon when he anchored here en route to St Helena. The old curmudgeon was so tickled that he tucked a napkin over his arm and assumed the duty of serving all his guests himself.

In its understated way, Reid's can even claim a place in literary history. George Bernard Shaw signed up for dancing lessons during his stay, despite his advanced years (he was 71), signing a photograph for his teacher, Max Rinder, with the dedication: "To the only man who ever taught me anything…" ❑

BELOW: during the 1950s, Winston Churchill and his wife were regulars.

AROUND FUNCHAL

Map on page 166

*Some of Madeira's loveliest public gardens
and most arresting mountain scenery make easy
excursions from the centre of Funchal*

E ven if you don't intend hiring a car and exploring Madeira from top to bottom during your stay, there are a handful of half-day excursions from the capital with sights and scenery good enough to tempt the most dedicated of sun-worshippers away from the hotel swimming pool.

The first trip is to the leafy hillside suburb of **Monte ❷**, some 6 km (4 miles) from Funchal. If you would prefer not to tackle the steep road on foot (Monte's a 600-metre – or 2,000-ft – climb above sea level) take a taxi or bus 20 or 21, a winding 30-minute journey from the city centre. At the turn of the 20th century visitors had another option: a little rack-and-pinion railway, shut down in 1939 after a disastrous accident with an exploding boiler. A new cable-car carries passengers high above the rooftops of Funchal from the Zona Velha *(see page 149)* all the way up to Monte, an exhilerating (or vertigo-inducing) trip lasting around 15 minutes.

If you come by bus or taxi, you will be deposited in **Largo da Fonte**, the main coach terminus – a shady, cobbled square with a large bandstand (Monte has always been a favourite venue for weekend outings from the capital). If you come by cable car, you will end up on Caminho das Babosas, at the opposite (eastern) end of the village. Wherever you arrive, all paths in Monte lead to the twin-towered **Nossa Senhora do Monte**, gazing down over Funchal. This pretty white church was built in the late 1700s on the site of a chapel 300 years older, the work of the first person born on Madeira (and christened Adam, appropriately enough).

On the high altar there is a wooden statue of the Virgin Mary, discovered in the 15th century at nearby **Terreiro da Luta**. The diminutive sculpture is believed to work miracles, and every year on the Feast of the Assumption (15 August) penitents climb the 74 steps up to the church on their knees to pray to her.

A side-chapel to the left of the entrance holds the tomb of the last Austrian emperor, Karl I, forced to abdicate his throne after World War I. He died of pneumonia in Madeira aged only 35, soon after going into exile here in 1921 *(see page 53).*

PRECEDING PAGES:
Monte's toboggan drivers wait for customers.
LEFT: musicians at Monte festival.
BELOW: keeping that camera steady can be a tricky job.

Checking in

The main reason for visiting Monte, however, lies just around the corner from the foot of the church stairs. In 1987 the old **Monte Palace Hotel** was acquired by one of Madeira's richest men, José Berardo, who made his fortune in South Africa with a method to sift Johannesburg's mine-dumps and extract the last residues of gold. Now he has restored the hotel as his home, and spared no expense in turning the vast gardens (open Mon–Sat 9am–6pm; entrance fee; tel: 782 339) into a splendidly over-the-top horticultural stage-

The novelist Ernest Hemingway – with, one would presume, his tongue firmly in his cheek – described Monte's toboggan run as "one of the most exhilarating experiences of my life".

set, filled with lakes, pools, statuary, urns and pagodas, as well as plants from all over the world. You'll see Scottish heathers, Japanese azaleas and rare cycads (a kind of giant tree-fern) from South Africa, along with oriental plants and a garden of species native to Madeira. Fountains alternate with secret grottoes, while blossom-filled terraces are adorned with fragments of *azulejos*.

Outside the gates, just south of Largo da Fonte, in a deep ravine surmounted by the old rack-and-pinion railway bridge, is the lush **Parque do Monte** (open daily; free). A winding path leads down through this lovely municipal garden – filled in summer with hydrangeas and agapanthus – to a stream. Back at the church steps, brave visitors can make their descent to Funchal on Madeira's famous toboggan run, where you hurtle down the steep, cobbled streets in a giant wicker basket. Energetically steered by guides, the toboggans don't reach dangerously high speeds – in fact, the *carreiros* usually have to push more often than they brake. You can choose to get off in **Livramento**, or continue for 3 km (2 miles) further to the end of Rua de Santa Luzia in Funchal city centre.

Indigenous flora

It's an even shorter bus ride (29, 30 or 31 from the city centre) to the **Jardim Botânico ❸** (open daily 9am–6pm; entrance fee, which also allows admission to the Jadim dos Loiros; tel: 211 200), just southeast of Monte. Originally the summer retreat of the Reid family, the old Quinta do Bom Sucesso still retains the charm of a private estate, although the house itself has been turned into a rather lacklustre **Natural History Museum** (open Mon–Sat 9am–12.30pm, 2–5.30pm).

With its gardens laid out in sections according to the plants' geographical origin or species, this is a good place to come if you want to start familiarising

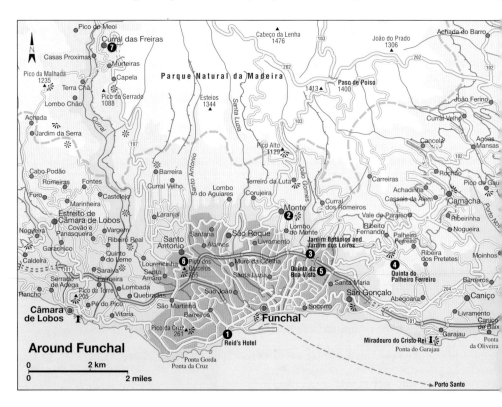

Around Funchal

0 — 2 km
0 — 2 miles

yourself with Madeira's exotic flora. Many of the plants are indigenous; there's a good selection of tropical trees and shrubs, a herbarium, a variety of ferns and creepers and some exceptional cactii. The gardens are beautifully laid out, spreading across terraces that climb from 200 to 350 metres (660–1,150 ft). Paths wind between dragon and coral trees, hibiscus bushes and bird-of-paradise flowers (strelitzias) to the original stock of trees in the upper part of the estate. *Miradouros* (viewpoints) offer magnificent views of the Ribeira de João Gomes gorge, and of Funchal.

Feathered blooms

You'll hear the **Jardim dos Loiros** (open daily 9am–6pm; entrance fee, which also allows admission to the Jardim Botânico) long before you reach it. The blooms in this garden – just a short walk downhill from the gates of the Botanical Gardens – are brilliantly coloured tropical birds, whooping and squawking for all they're worth. Ducks, geese and waterfowl roam the grounds, although the lories, macaws, parrots and parakeets are confined to their cages.

From here, follow the signs downhill and right to the **Jardim Orquídea** (open daily 9am–6pm; entrance fee; tel: 238 444), a working nursery about 15 minutes' walk away. Orchid varieties from around the world are cultivated here, then planted out in greenhouses and polythene tunnels, but time your visit carefully. Between the end of November and early April (orchid-flowering season) you can feast your eyes on an exploded rainbow of blooms, some fragile and delicate, others spiky and covered in spots and splashes like mad dragonflies. During the rest of the year, though, you'll have to use your imagination – or make do with the display panels.

Map on page 166

Two of the feathered "blooms" in the Jardim dos Loiros.

BELOW: a neatly kept patchwork quilt of beds in the Jardim Botânico.

Unquestionably the island's most magnificent garden is the **Quinta do Palheiro Ferreiro ❹** (open Mon–Fri 9.30am–12.30pm; entrance fee; tel: 793 044), just 8 km (5 miles) northeast of Funchal off the 102 Camacha road – and, incidentally, a delightful two-hour walk east from the city along the Levada dos Tornos. You can also reach it from the city centre on bus no. 37.

This was once the hunting lodge of one of Madeira's richest residents, the Conde de Carvalhal. He inaugurated the estate's splendid collection of camellia trees, which today number more than 10,000 – like the orchid garden, they're best seen between November and April. In 1885 the place was bought by the Blandys, one of the island's best-known British wine-exporter families, and it was they who laid out the 12-hectare (30-acre) garden.

A feast of rarities

With its holm oaks and chestnut trees, long borders, pergolas and lily pools, this could almost be an English country garden – until you look more closely at the foliage. In fact, there are enough rarities here to keep plant-lovers happy for hours; within the tranquil **Ladies' Garden** alone you'll find South African aloes and king proteas, South American agaves, and enormous ferns. Elsewhere, an Australian Flame Tree (Captain Cook brought the seed to Madeira) is now the size of the giant redwood that stands next to it.

Signs lead to a wilder corner of the grounds known as the **Ribeiro do Inferno** (The River of Hell), a somewhat misleading name for this patch of cool, shady woodland with its trailing creepers and lush ferns. Closer to the house, don't miss the elegant baroque chapel, supposedly positioned so that the dissolute Count could observe Mass without having to leave his shady verandah.

BELOW: orchid greenhouse, Quinta Boa Vista.
RIGHT: well-swept cobbled paths lead up to Monte's parish church.

Map on page 166

A climb up to Rua Luís Figueiroa de Albuquerque, northeast of the city centre (or a short taxi-ride) brings you to **Quinta da Boa Vista ❺** (open Mon–Sat 9am–5.30pm; entrance fee; tel: 220 468) and yet more horticultural treats. This is the home of Betty Garton, daughter of pioneer British orchid-breeder, Sir William Cooke, and she has filled these terraced gardens with greenhouses containing thousands of orchids – some destined for the cut-flower trade, others very rare and for use in hybridisation programmes. It's not all orchids, though; look out for the unusual hybrid passion-flowers, the bromeliads and the rare trees.

To the mountains

Apart from Monte, the other favourite local Sunday-afternoon drive is up **Pico dos Barcelos ❻**, one of the mountains that encircle Funchal. It's just a few kilometres west of the city on the 101 and then north on the 105, or take city bus no. 9 or 12. Once you've passed through the capital's western suburbs and **São Martinho** village, the road starts to climb. Look out for the viewpoint at 364 metres (1,200 ft); there is a restaurant and snack bar here, and a series of terraces offering marvellous views down over Funchal.

A longer excursion can be made from Funchal via Pico dos Barcelos to the **Curral das Freiras ❼**, or "Nun's Valley", an outstanding beauty spot. The valley's name dates back to 1566, when the nuns of the Santa Clara Convent fled here to escape a pirate attack *(see page 39)*. It's only 15 km (9 miles) northwest of the capital, yet it's a 45-minute drive – par for the course on Madeira's winding mountain roads. You can also take bus 81 from the city centre.

From Pico dos Barcelos, get on to the 107 (confusingly, some maps call this the 203). The bumpy road twists and turns up through forests of eucalyptus and pine, often smudged with patches of mist. Look out for the road-sign pointing the way to the **Eira do Serrado** *miradouro*, reached from the car park in front of the shop and café. A ten-minute walk along a path leads to the lookout-point, perched 800 metres (2,600 ft) above the valley below.

The view is amazing: a huge valley cupped in the crook of some venerable mountains, whose steep, amphitheatre-like cliffs give credence to the theory that the Curral is an extinct volcanic crater – although geologists now think this effect was caused simply by erosion. Familiar sounds (clanking buckets, barking dogs) float up from the tiny village far below, but it still feels as though you have stumbled upon a secret valley; it is easy to see why the nuns felt secure here.

If you have time to spare, walk down to the village on the old *verada* that until 1959 served as the villagers' only link with the outside world (the zig-zag footpath starts just beyond the shop at the sign that says "Eira do Serrado alt 1,094m". The path is steep, but the reward is more breathtaking scenery along the way.

As you descend, you'll see chestnut-trees growing on the valley slopes; this area is famous for its chestnut-flavoured soups and cakes and its chestnut liqueur. Chestnut bread is another speciality; ask for a slice with your coffee from one of the bars on the village's small main square. ❏

Chestnut liqueur is a speciality of Curral das Freiras.

BELOW: Pico dos Barcelos offers marvellous views of the Funchal area.

EASTERN MADEIRA

An introduction to the island's diverse range of landscapes, from bustling coastal resorts and cool green highlands to the stark, barren wastes of the dry easternmost tip

Map on page 174

Funchal

The shoreline stretching east from Funchal is changing fast. Until just a few decades ago this was a sleepy part of the island, where the locals went about their business as fishermen or farmers pretty much undisturbed – as their fathers and grandfathers had done before them. Today, tourism has gained a toe-hold, with hotels and holiday apartments (mainly frequented by Germans) springing up around Garajau and the villages nearby. Returned emigrants have escalated development, too – having made their fortunes abroad, many have come home to build brash modern villas in prime sites overlooking the sea. But that doesn't mean there's nothing to see. The following tour should take about half a day; more if you stop en route for a snack and a swim or two.

Ocean views

Two roads lead east from Funchal to Caniço: while the fast new motorway goes there directly, the winding coastal **Estrada Conde Carvalhal** is splendidly scenic. Having wound its leisurely way through the capital's suburbs – which now stretch almost as far as the village of **São Gonçalo ❶** – the road starts to hug the clifftops; a lookout point along the way offers dramatic coastal views.

The former fishing-village of **Garajau ❷** (named for the large number of *garajaus*, or terns, which once nested here) is now a rather nondescript modern resort, but the observation point signposted as the **Miradouro do Cristo Rei** is worth a detour; drive right through the village to find, on the cliff-edge, a giant statue of Christ, gazing out to sea above a 200-metre (650-ft) drop. The view from the terrace is quite magnificent, sweeping across from Funchal Bay in the west to the Desertas in the east, with miles of wrinkled blue ocean in between. Yet the cliff has a grim history: until quite late into the 18th century, this was where the bodies of dead Protestants were dumped in the sea, for non-Catholics were not allowed to rest in island soil.

A rough track leads down to a small, stony beach and a handful of ramshackle fishermen's huts. Follow the paved footpath round the base of the cliff and you'll find another rocky beach which is usually completely deserted – it's a good place to soak up the sun after a swim off the causeway.

From here, head back to the main road, where a short drive east leads to little **Caniço ❸**, some 3 km (2 miles) inland. Despite the clusters of new holiday apartments, the place doesn't seem to have lost its rural soul, and village life still centres on the jacaranda-shaded main square overlooking the sea. The handsome 18th-century parish church is worth a look, too: with its white-painted altars and just a sprinkling of gold leaf, the overall effect is refreshingly

PRECEDING PAGES: Ponta de São Lourenço, the easternmost tip. **LEFT:** on the rocks at Caniço de Baixo. **BELOW:** Garajau's imposing Miradouro do Cristo Rei .

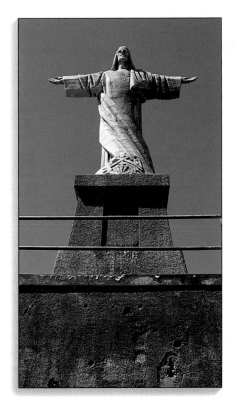

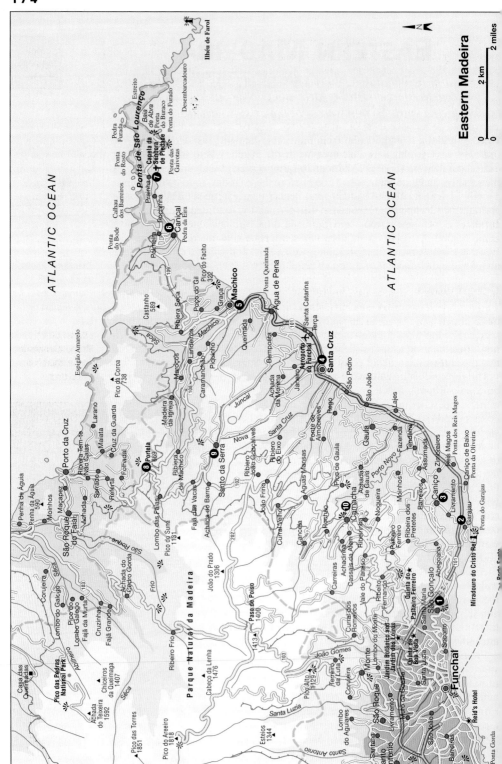

Eastern Madeira

low-key. Caniço also has a good reputation for fish restaurants *(see Travel Tips)*.

Santa Cruz ❹, the next town of any note, lies some 7 km (4 miles) further east along the main road. The town's proximity to the airport means many visitors overlook it as a holiday option: a shame, because this is a beguiling place for a short stay. The pebbly beach – dotted with bushy palm trees and the odd brightly-coloured fishing-boat – borders a small, neat park, with a pretty café at one end and the local fish market at the other. A little further on, past the **Praia das Palmeiras** lido (the swimming-pool here is guarded by a bizarre model of a sperm whale) and the open-air theatre, you'll reach a spacious open-air terrace with a fine view of a clump of prehistoric-looking dragon-trees – a good spot for a breather.

Like so many small Madeiran towns, Santa Cruz has some splendid historic architecture. Set back from the sea in the centre of town, the parish church – the **Igreja de Santa Maria de Santa Cruz** – was begun in 1479 but only completed in 1533. Both Gil Eanes and Pedro Anes, the master builders responsible for Funchal's Sé, were involved in its construction, which may be why this three-aisled building with its squat whitewashed tower is the largest church on the island outside Funchal. The main portal, the rose window and the small portal facing the parvis all have fine stone carvings dating from the Manueline era, while inside, the sacristy contains several excellent examples of 16th-century azulejo tile work from Seville.

Across the square, the **Town Hall** has fared less well – clumsy renovations mean that only sections of the early 16th-century façade remain. Close by is a magnificent park, its flowerbeds overhung by giant Indian laurels.

Just outside Santa Cruz, to the right of the road, lies the **airport**, built largely on reclaimed land.

Second city

Despite being the oldest settlement on Madeira and the island's second-largest town, **Machico ❺**, 5 km (3 miles) east of Santa Cruz, has for five centuries been little more than a sleepy provincial backwater. In the last few years, however, tourism has created something of an economic upswing; hotels and an untidy sprawl of holiday bungalows and apartments on the outskirts of town have been followed by restaurants, cafés and shops.

History has it that Machico was named after an Englishman, Robert Machin, shipwrecked here along with his mistress, Ana de Erfert, in 1344 *(see page 21)*. Not only did Machin's crew promptly mutiny and disappear with his ship, but Ana died of exposure only a few weeks later; Machin buried her under a cedar tree and built a small chapel nearby, before setting sail on a makeshift raft bound for the mainland. His story, with its intriguing details of the lonely grave on a mysterious island far out in the Atlantic, was to fuel many a legend.

After the archipelago was claimed by the Portuguese in 1419, Madeira was initially divided into two fiefdoms. Machico became capital of the eastern half of the island, a position it held until 1497, when Funchal became the first city of a united Madeira.

The colourful frieze of azulejos adorning Santa Cruz's market-hall is by the noted Portuguese artist, Outeiro Agueda.

BELOW: Santa Maria, the historic parish church at Santa Cruz.

Split down the middle by the reed-choked Machico River, the town's east bank is home to the little quay, or **Cais**, where Zarco and his band of explorers allegedly first set foot on Madeira. True or not, the view is excellent, taking in the whole of Machico Bay from the boatyard where wooden fishing-boats are still built to the unsightly Dom Pedro Baía Hotel – the town's tallest building – way over on the left. Nearby is the 18th-century **Forte de São João Batista**, one of three forts built in the bay as a (largely ineffectual) defence against pirates. It's now a private residence.

The famous crucifix kept in Machico's "Chapel of Miracles" is known as the Senhor dos Milagres, and is thought to have special powers to heal the sick.

Historic churches

The road running along the edge of the harbour leads away from the shore and into the town itself. If you're visiting during the afternoon, you may pass *espada* fishermen repairing their long rods here: the lines they use can run to 1.5 km (1 mile) in length, with upwards of 150 hooks *(see page 104)*.

Stay on the east bank and you'll soon reach the **Largo Senhor dos Milagres**, a small cobbled square shaded by tall Indian fig trees. The little 19th-century **Capela dos Milagres** (Chapel of Miracles) here – supposedly built on the site of Machin's original chapel – contains a much-venerated Gothic wooden crucifix, washed out to sea in a flood in 1803, yet miraculously retrieved and returned by a passing American ship. The islanders promptly renamed the chapel in honour of the event and still celebrate it every year in October with a large festival. Pilgrims arrive from all over Madeira for the climax, a procession where the cross is solemnly paraded through the town. Those seeking to be healed from disease often carry wax effigies of the various body parts they want restored to health.

BELOW:
boat-building
at Machico.

A small hump-backed bridge – with cows grazing peacefully beneath it – eads over the river to the oak tree-lined **Largo do Município** and one of Machico's oldest buildings, the 15th-century **Igreja da Nossa Senhora da Conceição**. The graceful side portal, with its three slim white marble pillars, was a gift from King Manuel I, as was the original organ. As with so many other churches on the island, the interior was radically altered during the baroque period; the altar with its gold-leaf decoration and the coffered ceiling both date from that time, but two of the side chapels (on the north side of the nave, opposite the entrance) are Manueline survivors. One of them – depicting a phoenix rising from the ashes – contains the blue coat of arms of the Vaz Teixeria family, the first rulers of the eastern half of the island.

A plague of pirates

Now head in the direction of the sea along Rua General António Teixeira de Aguiar, the narrow street opposite the church. **House No. 15** has a curious display window containing ancient wine bottles covered with cobwebs and dust – inside are priceless vintages dating back to 1842, before the *phylloxera* crisis.

On the right a few steps further on is Machico's **old market** (a tile next to the entrance still bears the inscription *Mercado Velho*), now converted into a pleasant café. The ochre-coloured, triangular building directly opposite is the **Fortress of Nossa Senhora do Amparo**, built in 1706. It owes its existence to an island governor who decided to put a stop to Machico's problem with marauding pirates once and for all: the town was duly given three fortresses (only two of which survive) so that the buccaneer's ships could be attacked from all angles if they entered the bay. What's more, Fort Amparo's triangular

Map on page 174

Ornate pillar in Machico's Capela dos Milagres.

BELOW: Machico fishermen.

TORCH MOUNTAIN

Head north-east from Machico in the direction of Caniçal and after 5 km (3 miles) or so you'll notice a turnoff to the right marked *Pico do Facho*, or "Torch Mountain". The winding cliff road leads to an intriguing landmark, dating back to the days when pirate raids posed a real threat to the archipelago. Realising that they had little real hope of defending themselves and their property once the buccaneers – skilled in handling their ships' cannons and usually armed to the teeth – had actually landed, the local farmers and fishermen decided that their best bet was to devise an efficient early warning system.

Accordingly, sentinels were posted on round-the-clock watches on high points along the coast – above Machico, at Garajau, and on a mountain near Serra de Fora on Porto Santo. The first to spot vessels on the horizon with the dreaded Jolly Rogers flying from their masts would light a huge bonfire – and the alarm would pass along a chain of torches. Thus notified, the Madeirans would make for their hiding-places in the hills as fast as they could.

Today, Pico do Facho is a popular picnic-spot, kitted out with benches and barbecue-sites. Climb up the stone steps to the paved observation-point for a glimpse of the old sentinels' magnificent view.

The fishing industry is still a key one in the east coast towns.

shape allowed its cannon to be pointed seawards on two sides. It now houses Machico's tourist office.

Back down on the seafront are the three bustling open halls of the **Lota**, where freshly-caught fish – mainly tuna – is auctioned. Follow the harbour promenade right to the end; the small chapel here, the **Capela de São Roque** contains several valuable baroque *azulejos* showing scenes from the life of St Roche, but unfortunately the building is seldom open to the public.

Arid landscape

Immediately beyond the turnoff to Pico do Facho (*see box, page 177*, the motorway heads into a tunnel and emerges into a different world entirely. Suddenly the landscape is dry and brown, the terraced fields have disappeared and the road is lined with palms.

The highlight of a visit to **Caniçal ❻**, the next stop on our route, is the **Museu da Baleia** or Whaling Museum (open Tues–Sun 10am–noon and 1–6pm; entrance fee), near the harbour. Whaling off the coast of Madeira has been banned since 1982, and the sperm whale is now a strictly protected species (*see page 107*), but Caniçal was once the centre of the local industry; display cases are filled with harpoons and scrimshaw (whalebone) carvings, while a 35-minute video – in English, French and German – gives background detail.

Away from the museum, the town has a rather desolate air: a few of the old whalers have found a new lease of life advising conservationists fighting to save sperm whales from extinction, but the ban dealt a death-blow to the local economy. A **Free Trade Zone** (Zona Franca) has been set up just east of the village but it has not attracted much foreign investment or created many jobs.

BELOW:
young sunbathers,
Caniçal.

Map on page 174

From Caniçal the road continues east, past a rugged landscape where volcanic boulders striped with coloured lava poke through dry, scrubby grass. Soon the land narrows to a jagged line of cliffs – the **Ponta de São Lourenço**, Madeira's easternmost point. While the road ends at a car park at **Baia d'Abra**, it's possible to continue on foot from here along a narrow path to the very tip of the island *(see page 223)*; the walk there and back takes about three hours. You won't be able to reach the lighthouse visible from the car park, though – it stands on a rocky islet just offshore.

Once, this peninsula was covered in thick indigenous forest, but that was all chopped down centuries ago so that the area could be used as pastureland for goats; the trees never grew back. Now, however, it is a nature reserve, and although it looks starkly barren for most of the year, visit in early spring and you will find this harsh, bare region covered in a fine mist of flowers. At any time of year, a clear day brings wonderful views of the three Desertas Islands.

The Ponta de São Lourenço was named by the pioneering Portuguese explorer, Zarco, for the boat that first brought him ashore on Madeira.

Pick of the picnic-spots

As you drive back from Baia d'Abra to rejoin the main road, look out for a track leading to the left. A short walk down it brings you to a windswept lookout point and picnic-spot, with good views of the pretty **Capela da Senhora de Piedade** on the top of a round, bare hill. The chapel is the focus of another popular island festival: every year in September, a procession of villagers carry a sacred statue of the Virgin from the parish church at Caniçal down to the beach, where a fleet of decorated boats awaits; these deliver the statue to this chapel.

At the bottom of the hill – a long-extinct volcano – is the **Prainha** ❼, Madeira's only natural sandy beach, It's not very large, and the sand is a gritty

BELOW: Caniçal, set against a backdrop of rugged hills.

volcanic black, but it is immensely popular and gets very crowded in summer. There's a seasonal café and several more picnic sites here, too.

A change of scene

The last leg of our journey heads inland. Retrace your route west along the main road as far as the Machico crossroads and take the second turning right on to Highway 101, following signs for **Portela** ❽ and being careful not to take the new road signposted to Porto da Cruz, as this by-passes Portela and takes you through a very long tunnel straight to the north of the island. At first the eucalyptus-lined road winds gently up through the Machico Valley with its neat patchwork of emerald terraced fields, but it soon grows steeper as you start to climb the Santo da Serra plateau, some 700 metres (2,300 ft) above sea level.

Traditionally, the tiny hamlet of Portela has been a place for travellers to break their journey, standing as it does at a junction of roads leading to the south and north coasts. You'll notice a drop in temperature as soon as you step out of the car: the weather up here can get decidedly damp and cold in the winter, and it's easy to understand why the rather comical-looking traditional woollen hat with earmuffs (the *Barrete de Lã*) is still so popular with the locals.

At the head of the Portela Pass is a rather rough-and-ready log-cabin style restaurant *(see Travel Tips)*, which locals swear makes the best grilled *espetadas* (beef kebabs) on the island. Outside, there's a fabulous view down to the north coast and the villages of Porto da Cruz and Faial, sandwiched in between the giant loaf-shaped **Penha de Águia** (Eagle Rock).

It's some 5 km (3 miles) south across the plateau from Portela to the "hill station" of **Santo da Serra** ❾, the traditional summer retreat of the island's well-

TIP

The grilled *espetadas* at the **Casa de Portela** are served the traditional way: that is, strung on a giant metal skewer which is then hung from a hook above your table.

BELOW: bringing home the fuel.

eeled British residents. The gracious old **Quinta do Santa da Serra** (grounds open daily until sunset; free) here used to belong to the Blandy family, one of the island's foremost wine-trading dynasties, and is definitely worth a visit: head for the village square and look for the modest wooden gates at its southern end. The pink mansion half-hidden behind enormous lichen-splotched trees is now state-owned, but the gardens – complete with small zoo, playground and tennis courts – are a public park. Visit in spring and you'll catch the camellias in full bloom; in summer, look out for the splendid white and blue agapanthus and hydrangeas.

A cobbled path leads to the less-manicured rear section of the garden and a belvedere known as the **Miradouro dos Ingleses**, which has excellent views down over the east coast. A look-out used to stand here and report to the head of the family whenever trading vessels came into view on the horizon, whereupon Mr Blandy would set off for Funchal to negotiate his business.

Just outside the village is Madeira's oldest golf course, the **Campo de Golfe da Madeira** (see Travel Tips).

Wickerwork centre

The road now twists and turns south down towards the coast again, in and out of aromatic stands of eucalyptus and pine and past lush terraces thickly planted with fruit and vegetables. Above the road is thick forest: this is where the cloud layer starts.

As you near **Camacha** ❿, some 11 km (7 miles) away, you'll notice small white willow bushes growing alongside the road: Camacha is the centre of the island's wicker trade (see page 117), and many farmers in this region earn their living planting these trees and selling the resulting osiers to wicker-weaving workshops. In the town itself you may also see sheaves of canes stacked against the walls of the houses.

Drive down through the town, past the 18th-century parish church, until you reach the circular main square. A plaque in the centre of the square states that the first-ever football match on Portuguese soil was played here, in 1875. A student named Harry Hinton came out from England for the summer with a football packed into his suitcase, and organised a proper game.

At the southern end of the square, an observation point affords splendid views down to the sea, over forests and terraced fields. Next door is Camacha's most famous building, the **Café Relógio**, with its eye-catching clock-tower like a miniature white-painted Big Ben. Its first owners were a wealthy 19th-century British family who used it as a summer residence. Today it's the headquarters of Madeira's largest wicker goods export company, with a sales room packed with wicker products of all shapes and sizes including a curious collection of animals.

From here, it's 10 km (6 miles) back to Funchal via **Vale do Paraiso**, a delightful drive through spreading orchards; in spring, the apple blossom contrasts magnificently with the azaleas and camellias growing wild by the roadside, while in summer, the bright blue agapanthus comes into its own. ❑

Map on page 174

You won't only find wicker baskets on display at Camacha's Café Relógio.

BELOW: wicker craftsman at work in Camacha.

CENTRAL MADEIRA

*A spectacular route zigzagging north over the island's
main mountain range with its jagged peaks, then west
along an equally dramatic coastal corniche road*

Map
on page
186

Funchal

his is one of Madeira's classic drives, taking in the very best the island
has to offer, from jagged mist-capped mountains to lush subtropical coast.
You'll need to 0set aside the best part of a day for it, though – the route covers some pretty rugged and hilly terrain, and involves a good many twists and
turns. Indeed, wherever you drive on Madeira, it's worth remembering that dis-
ances as they appear on the map can prove highly deceptive. Places which
ook like a stone's throw away from each other usually take a lot longer to reach
han you might think.

The other thing to bear in mind is that this tour passes through several micro-
climates: light clothing like a T-shirt and shorts won't be sufficient on their
own, even on the loveliest summer's day. It can get distinctly chilly up at the
higher altitudes and it is often the case that while Funchal on the south coast is
bathed in glorious sunshine, the northern half of the island huddles under a
thick carpet of rain clouds. The Madeirans' fanciful claim that the five continents
converge on their island is not as extravagant as it may sound.

PRECEDING PAGES:
hiking the central
mountain range.
LEFT: the traditional
Barrete de Lã hat
is still worn today.
BELOW: Virgin
monument at
Terreiro da Luta.

Into the mountains

Take Road 103 heading north out of Funchal. Some 6 km (4 miles) from the
centre of town is the leafy suburb of **Monte ❶**, filled
with grand old *quintas* gazing down on the city from
their cool and lofty heights *(see page 165)*. As soon
after the twin towers of the parish church disappear
from view behind you, the road delves into a dense
plantation of eucalyptus trees and mimosa, the latter
covered in spring in bright yellow blossom. You may
encounter patches of thick mist: you're above the
cloud line here.

The road winds up to the turnoff for **Terreiro da
Luta ❷**, approximately 300 metres (1,000 ft) above
Monte. At the junction lies an old train station, the
last stop on the funicular railway that until 1939
hauled passengers up and down from Funchal. It has
now been converted into a restaurant. The statue of
Zarco here is by the local artist Francisco Franco, and
was erected in 1919 to mark the fifth centenary of
Madeira's discovery.

Just beyond the restaurant is a huge **Monument to
the Virgin**, with a statue of the Madonna perched on
a mighty basalt pedestal. Although Madeira saw little
action during World War I, she did not escape entirely
unscathed: in 1916, soon after Portugal entered the
war on the Allied side, a German submarine surfaced
off Funchal harbour and sank three ships anchored
there before shelling the city itself. The terrified locals
marched up to Monte in a long procession to pray for
peace; the local priest, meanwhile, vowed to build a

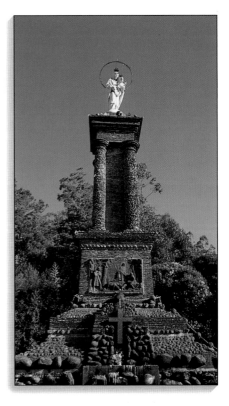

Funchal cathedral's magnificent carved roof is made from the wood of the indigenous cedar tree: look out for specimens as you ascend from Terreiro da Luta.

monument to the Virgin if only the bombardment would end. Miraculously (or so it seemed), his wish was granted, and so – albeit some 10 years later – this statue was erected in fulfilment of his vow *(see page 56)*.

A steep ascent

Now the road climbs still higher into the mountains, leaving the eucalyptus forest behind. Pines enshroud the way here, interspersed with stands of majestic Madeiran cedar trees. A turnoff to the left brings you to **Pico Alto ③** mountain (1,129 metres/3,704 ft); where there's a picnic-site and an *azulejo*-tiled *miradouro* offering more splendid views down to Funchal. Back on the main road, you'll soon reach the **Paso de Poiso ④** crossroads; a left turn here leads to **Pico do Arieiro ⑤**, Madeira's third-highest mountain at 1,818 metres (5,965 ft).

It's only a short drive to the summit, but the landscape alters quickly and dramatically, the thick forest giving way to bleakly rolling moorland and the occasional windswept pine. You can see enormous swathes of the island from

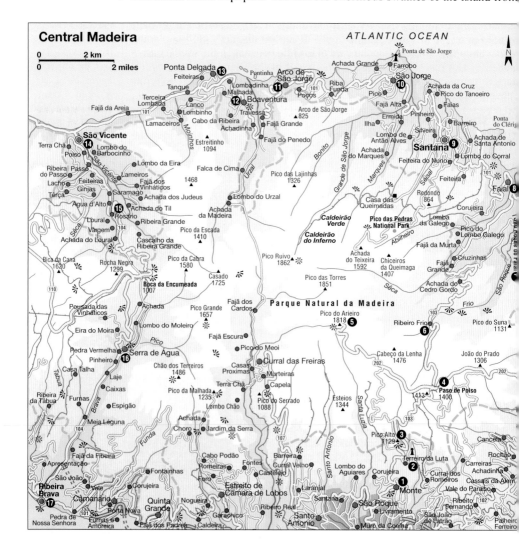

Map on page 186

TIP

You'll need to wear a jacket or a sweater on the summit of Pico do Arieiro – even on a hot summer's day, it's chilly up here, and the weather can change in minutes.

up here, but the views of its volcanic heart immediately below are much the most impressive. Mist boils up out of deep, lava-caked ravines, streaked at odd angles by green heathers and tough grasses. A ridge of barren mountains – forced up out of the bowels of the earth by volcanic explosions, and then carved into odd serrated shapes by wind and rain – stretch away into the distance. It's a desolate scene, but starkly beautiful at the same time.

One of the finest hiking-trails on the island winds north from Arieiro's summit to Madeira's highest mountain, **Pico Ruivo** *(see page 230)*, a tough but exhilarating morning's climb. Arieiro's café-restaurant is a good place to stock up on supplies; there's also a state-owned *pousada,* which makes a handy base for longer hiking trips through the mountains. If you check in here, make sure you try a glass of *poncha,* the house speciality: this fiery concoction of sugar-cane spirit, honey and lemon juice is practically guaranteed to lend new strength to the limbs, whatever the weather.

Rural glimpses

Retrace your steps back to Poiso and turn left back on to the 103; it's 5 km (3 miles) north to the farming hamlet of **Ribeiro Frio** ❻ ("Cold River"). The road rolls down through the lush indigenous forest which is a trademark of northern Madeira: dripping wet lichen hangs from the mahoganies and laurel-trees, while the shaded floor is thick with wild geraniums, foxgloves and ferns. Observant explorers may be rewarded with a glimpse of a purple Madeira orchid peeping out between the tree-trunks in early summer. Along the roadside, mean-while, other flowers – agapanthus and hydrangeas in summer, pink belladonna lilies in autumn – add splashes of colour along the way.

If you'd like to know more about the island's indigenous flora, the forestry commission has estab-lished a **Botanical Garden** (free admission) in the centre of the village, with a small collection of neatly labelled plants. Across the road is a state-owned **Trout Hatchery** (free admission), where fish of all sizes mill about in troughs. Plenty of trout find their way on to the menu at Victor's Bar down the road – this cosy log-cabin-style restaurant has a welcoming open log fire and is usually full of hikers sipping hot drinks and recovering from their exertions.

Their presence is not surprising: there are some really good walks in the Ribeiro Frio region. One par-ticularly easy detour (it takes roughly 30 minutes there and 30 minutes back) is signposted off the road which leads below Victor's Bar. Follow the **Levada do Furado** to the left through forests and spreading orchards of apple and pear to the observation-point known as **Balcões** – a series of wooden balconies built high on a ledge – you'll be rewarded with huge views of Madeira's central mountain range, including all its tallest peaks.

If you'd prefer something slightly more taxing, head along the *levada* in the opposite direction. After a two-and-a-half-hour walk through pristine indige-nous forest you will reach the **Lamaceiros** water-house; immediately after this a path descends to a smaller *levada,* where you can pick up a track leading

BELOW: handmade woolly hats for sale on Pico Arieiro.

The lush landscape around Ribeiro Frio is a walker's delight.

down to **Portela** – about another 30 minutes' walk. This route doesn't have any really taxing ups and downs, but good shoes and a head for heights are essential, all the same.

Ribeiro Frio provides a glimpse of rural Madeira at its most picturesque. A stream rushes noisily beneath a wooden bridge, and the air is clean and cold. You'll see small thatched cowsheds half-hidden by apple-trees dotted across the hillsides, and farmers heading down the road balancing vast bundles of hay – cow fodder – unsteadily on their heads; such is the shortage of flat, safe grazing-ground on this mountainous island that the animals are kept tucked away in these steep-roofed huts instead.

Tropical crops

Back on the 103, the temperature warms a degree or two as the road descends towards sea level, leaving the forest behind. Innumerable small terraces in luscious shades of green now line the road; the crops round here are much more diverse than those grown in the south, and you may spot sugar-cane, medlars, papayas, mangoes, passion-fruit and even kiwi-fruit.

Some 5 km (3 miles) from Ribeiro Frio, a right turn at the fork in the road leads to **São Roque do Faial** ❼, a pretty rural village which – like its namesake **Faial** ❽, just a few miles away – is utterly dominated by the massive flat-topped hill known as the **Penha de Águia** ("Eagle Rock") looming in between. Faial is the plainer of the two villages, but scores points for its stunning location high above the sea.

Now the road follows the coastline in the direction of **Santana** ❾, 12 km (7½ miles) away. Don't miss the observation-point, or *miradouro*, on a bend

BELOW: Ribeiro Frio means "cold river" – and so it is.

just above Faial: it offers marvellous views down over the Eagle Rock area with the spiky dragon's tail of the São Lourenço peninsula – Madeira's easternmost tip – far beyond.

Cottages and cascades

Although it's set in some of the most beautiful and unspoilt countryside in all Madeira, there's not much to see in Santana. It's become an obligatory stop on all the coach-party itineraries, however, thanks to its one architectural quirk: a collection of quaint *palheiros* (cottages) in a style unique to the area. With their pointed gables and thatched roofs reaching nearly to the ground, these are perfect for the Madeiran climate, staying pleasingly cool in summer and warm in winter. Nonetheless, only a few are still inhabited; many have been converted into storehouses or even stables for cows.

Head down the main road until you see the parish hall on the right; next door is a particularly photogenic cluster of neatly renovated huts, two of which are open to the public. The tourist coaches all pull up here for this very reason, but, if you're after something slightly less artificial looking and more authentic, there are a few more, inhabited houses down in the village that can be inspected on foot.

The other reason people come to Santana is to walk. The town is the starting-point for some of the most spectacular hikes on the island, through the **Pico das Pedras National Park** and on to Pico Ruivo *(see page 225)*. The turnoff is signposted left off the main road as you drive in from Faial.

As you leave town, you'll pass a turnoff leading right for the **Quinta do Furão**, a package-tour hotel owned by the Madeira Wine Company. It's a good

Map on page 186

All sorts of tropical crops, including bananas, are grown around Faial.

BELOW: road worker near Santana.
RIGHT: Faial is stunningly located.

TIP

Santana's nearest
beach is small and
rocky, but peaceful.
Look out for the *Praia*
("beach") sign just
after the Ilha turnoff,
about 6 km (4 miles)
north of Santana on
the main road.

place to stop for a snack – the food is decent, if unremarkable and there are fine sea views from the restaurant. However, even better ones can be had from the vineyard behind the *quinta*, where you can see the waterfalls that cascade down the cliffs straight into the waves.

The north coast

Santana and its neighbouring village of **São Jorge ⑩**, 7 km (4 miles) further north, are divided by a deep ravine carved out by the São Jorge river, which the road crosses with some difficulty and many hairpin bends. São Jorge is worth the time it takes to get to, though, for not only is it remarkably pretty, but it's home to an unexpectedly grand baroque **parish church** as well. Only Funchal's cathedral can compete with the sheer mass of detail here: highlights include a chancel ornately decorated in gold leaf, and a trumpeting angel perched on top of a pulpit similarly gilded and carved in rich designs. At the main altar there's a small statue of St George, along with reliefs and frescoes depicting scenes from the saintly one's life. Unfortunately, the gold leaf is flaking quite badly; this sumptuous interior is seriously in need of restoration.

If you want to explore the village further, there are also a couple of pleasant parks in the village centre, filled with strelitzias and azaleas, and a charming chapel shaded by three towering palm-trees.

Now the route hugs the north coast clifftops, passing still more orchards, terraces dense with vines, and banks of ferns and flowers. Just beyond the Cabanas hotel complex is a little *miradouro* with breathtaking views down to the sea and the red-roofed houses of the next village, **Arco de São Jorge ⑪** at the bottom of the cliffs. Several more hairpins must be negotiated to reach it, though,

BELOW: a pair of
traditional thatched
cottages, Santana.

winding down through foliage so lush it seems almost like tropical rain forest. A dank, narrow tunnel connects Arco de São Jorge with its neighbouring valley, densely wooded and ringed by hills with jagged peaks, as if drawn by a child. The government plans to upgrade the rough track (the "107") running south across the island from here to **Curral das Freiras**; for the moment, though, the area still seems wonderfully remote and unspoiled, and full of opportunities for intrepid hikers *(see page 224)*.

A short drive further west leads you to the agricultural community of **Boaventura** ⑫, which despite its lovely clifftop setting overlooking the sea is fairly nondescript. Vineyards dominate here, along with willow-tree plantations down in the fertile valleys – the village is the source of most of the raw material for the island's celebrated wickerworkers *(see page 117)*.

A place of pilgrimage

Just 2 km (1¼ miles) along the coast is the small town of **Ponta Delgada** ⑬, filled with spruce modern houses well-spaced between patches of trellised vines. Head down towards the shore and you'll find a large **sea-water swimming pool** built into the rocks. It's replenished by hissing Atlantic breakers at every high tide – much to the excitement of any children who happen to be swimming in it at the time.

Once a year, on the first Sunday in September, Ponta Delgada becomes the focal point for pilgrims from all over Madeira, who pour in to worship at the **parish church** to the right of the pool. Legend has it that during the 15th century, a wooden statue of Christ – known as the *Bom Jesus* – was mysteriously washed ashore here, prompting locals to put up a church on the site. Today's

Map on page 186

The parish church in Ponta Delgada has a splendidly ornate interior.

BELOW: the north coast offers some stunning vistas.

building is modern, for the original burnt down in a fire in 1908 – but miraculously the crucifix survived. The charred figure is on display inside the church behind a glass panel, and worshipped just as fervently as before.

Along the corniche

Outside Ponta Delgada the 101 narrows to a slender coastal ledge in the steep, waterfall-splashed cliff, which makes the the 6-km (3¾-mile) drive to **São Vicente** quite a ride. On the outskirts of town, just off the main road, the World Wide Fund for Nature has set up a **park** (unlimited access) containing a good selection of coastal plants endemic to Madeira, from the Madeira geranium to the blueweed and the oxeye daisy. Visit in spring to see the blossom at its best.

Well-preserved São Vicente is one of Madeira's most attractive towns. To find the centre of the village, turn left off the main road away from the sea; you'll pass the small 17th-century **Capela de São Roque** – carved out of a hunk of solid rock – en route.

Standing right at the foot of the steep-sided São Vicente Valley is the **parish church**, adorned with blue-and-yellow *azulejos* and surrounded by tall palm trees. The black-and-white mosaic above the church door was put up in 1943 – the year in which extensive restoration works were carried out – although the original building dates back to the 17th century and is one of the most ornate on the island. Take a look at the chancel and side altars, decorated in typical Portuguese *talha dourada* style – richly carved and not sparing the gold leaf.

BELOW: driving the Encumeada Pass.

Opposite the church, a delightful cobbled side-street lined with green-shuttered houses winds uphill; inner courtyards, full of flowers, can sometimes be glimpsed here through open doors.

On the opposite side of the valley from the village you will find the **Grutas de São Vicente**, a cave complex with a difference (Sítio do Pé do Passo, São Vicente; tel: 842 404; Apr–Sept, daily 9am–9pm; Oct–March 9am–7pm; entrance fee). These caves were created by white-hot magma melting through weak joints in the rock of Madeira's central mountain range. Little by little, the intruding lava created a series of worm-holes, called lava tubes. A tour of the tubes only lasts 15 minutes, but takes in various different types of lava, including formations that look like smooth pools of molten chocolate; these turn out to be very solid if you try to dip your fingers in. Rainwater percolating through from the Paúl de Serra into the lava tubes creates numerous underground streams and a series of magical waterfalls. Dramatically spot-lit, these form the climax of the tour.

Map on page 186

Through the cloud layer

Now the route leaves the north coast behind and heads inland along the 104, winding gently up through the São Vicente valley. If you're travelling after heavy rain, keep an eye out for waterfalls glinting through the trees on the slopes on your right. Soon, on the left-hand side of the road, a distinctive chapel in the form of a single belltower comes into view; this marks the sleepy hamlet of **Rosario** ⑮, a few houses spread out amongst cowshed-studded terraces.

Beyond Rosario, there is a choice of routes, as a new road tunnel now bores straight through the mountains, carrying traffic to the south coast. You need to stay on the old road, which is sign-posted to Boca da Encumeada. The road south now twists more steeply upwards through thick forest, back on to Madeira's central plateau. After all this luscious, mist-smudged mountain scenery, it's quite a shock to suddenly break through the cloud layer and emerge on to the barren heights of the **Boca da Encumeada**, or the Encumeada Pass. It may be the island's lowest pass at 1,007 metres (3,300 ft), but, if the weather's good, you still get an amazing view right across the island from the Serra de Água valley in the south back to São Vicente. The north coast, however, is usually obscured by cloud, and you may even see clouds swirling by below you – what the experts call a meteorological divide.

BELOW: policemen stroll the streets of picturesque São Vicente village.

Towards Funchal

The drive down the other side of the pass has some good mountain scenery. If you want to stop and absorb the views, look out for the chalet-style **Pousada dos Vinháticos** hotel on the right-hand of the road. The road unfolds south towards the sea through the steep Ribeira Brava valley, with its conical peaks like witches' hats. First, though, you pass **Serra de Agua** ⑯ village: the name means "Water Saw" and recalls a sawmill which once stood here. Today it's the site of the island's oldest hydro-electric power station.

Down at the bottom of the valley the road is lined with poplar trees and giant reeds; the Ribeira Brava ("Wild River") itself is usually all but dry. Once you've passed through the bustling little resort town of **Ribeira Brava** ⑰, turn left on to the motorway. From here, it's a mere 20-minute drive back to Funchal through a series of tunnels. ❑

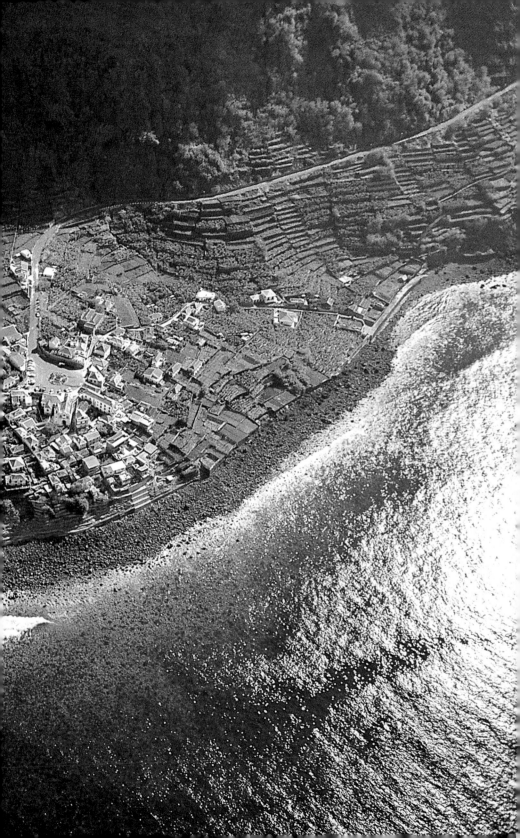

WESTERN MADEIRA

The pace gradually slows and the tour buses diminish
as you swap the built-up south coast with its popular sights
for the charming villages and scenery of the underrated west

Map on pages 198–99

Funchal

Sign up for a guided coach tour of western Madeira and you'll probably head up the coast as far as Ribeira Brava, stopping at the pretty fishing village of Câmara de Lobos and the high sea-cliff of Cabo Girão along the way, before striking inland along the Encumeada Pass or retracing your steps back to Funchal. Yet this underrated region has a lot more to offer than that – from coastal towns barely touched by tourism to some remarkable village chapels and churches.

The less-travelled route described below does, however, take a full day by car or taxi, which means an overnight stay in Porto Moniz or Prazeres may be worth considering. The towns and villages along the coast can be reached by bus, but not the Paúl da Serra plateau.

PRECEDING PAGES: Jardim do Mar, jewel of the south coast. **LEFT:** view towards Cabo Girão. **BELOW:** promenade café, Ribeira Brava.

Exploring the "Place of Wolves"

These days, thanks to the fast new motorway, you can race into Ribeira Brava from Funchal in around 20 minutes. This tour relies instead on the picturesque old coastal road, which meanders out through the capital's western suburbs past volcanic cliffs streaked with yellow lava, terraces lush with banana-trees and houses half-hidden behind giant hibiscus bushes.

It's 9 km (5 miles) along the coast to **Câmara de Lobos ❶**, named "Place of Wolves" by the 15th-century explorers, after the seals – "sea-wolves" in Portuguese – which they found frolicking in the ocean here. Today, the bay is full of open wooden fishing-boats; this is one of the island's most important harbours as far as the local fishing industry's concerned.

Don't miss the chance of a quick peek inside the **fishermen's chapel** of Nossa Senhora da Conceicão on the bay's western shore, just beyond the fish market. Built in 1420, it was the second chapel to be erected on Madeira, after the original **Capela dos Milagres** in Machico *(see page 176)*. Despite an extensive 18th-century overhaul (the altar dates from this period), the building still has charm; the nave is lined with paintings depicting scenes from the life of St Pedro Gonçalves Telmo, patron saint of Portuguese sailors, including one where an apostle fishes for *espada* on the shores of Galilee.

On the pebbly beach you'll see fishermen methodically mending the long lines they use to catch *espada* *(see page 104)*, or playing cards. The men only head out to sea three times a week, on average – the Atlantic is usually far too stormy for small craft.

It's a picturesque scene, but this is, in fact, one of the poorest villages in Madeira. In the narrow streets of the town you'll see women embroidering, trying to eke out the meagre family income, and children

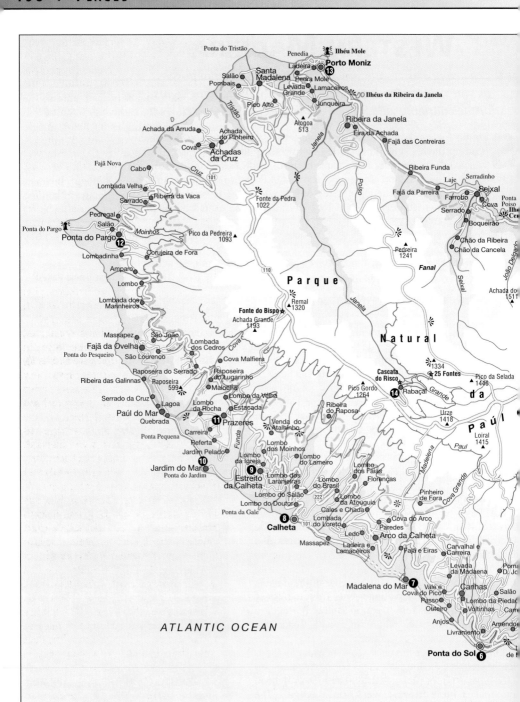

Ponta do Tristão

Penedia

Ilhéu Mole

Ladeira

Porto Moniz ⑬

Salão
Santa
Madalena
Pombais
Pedra Mole
Levada
Grande
Lamaceiros
Pico Alto
Junqueira
Ilhéus da Ribeira da Janela

Ribeira da Janela
Atogoa
513
Eira da Achada
Fajã das Contreiras

Achada da Arruda
Achada
do Pinheiro

Cova
Achadas
da Cruz

Ribeira Funda

Fajã Nova

Cabo

Laje
Serradinho

Cruz
101
Fajã da Parreira
Farrobo
Seixal

Lombada Velha

Ribeira da Vaca

Ponta
Poiso

Serrado
Serrado
Cova

Pedregal
Fonte da Pedra
1022

Boqueirão

Salão
Moinhos
Pico da Pedreira
1093

Chão da Ribeira

Ponta do Pargo ⑫

Chão da Cancela

Lombadinha
Corujeira de Fora

Pedreira
1241

Fanal

Amparo

110

Lombo

Parque

Achada do
1511

Lombada dos
Marinheiros

Remal
1320

Fonte do Bispo ★

Achada Grande
1193

Natural

Massapez
São João
Lombada
dos Cedros

1334
25 Fontes
Pico da Selada
1446

Fajã da Ovelha
São Lourenço

Cova

Ponta do Pesqueiro
Cova Malfieira

Raposeira do Serrado
Raposeira
do Lugarinho

Cascata
do Risco

Ribeira das Galinnas
Raposeira
599

Pico Gordo
1264

Rabaçal ⑭

d

Serrado da Cruz
Malcelra
Lombo da Velha

Ribeira
do Raposo

Urze
1418

Paúl do Mar
Lagoa
Lombo
da Rocha
Estacada

Quebrada

Prazeres ⑪

Venda do
Atalhinho

Paúl

Loiral
1415

Carreira

Ponta Pequena
Referta
Lombo
dos Moinhos

Jardim Pelado
Lombo
da Igreja
Lombo
do Lameiro

Paul

Jardim do Mar
Estreito
da Calheta ⑨
Lombo dos
Laranjeiras

Lombo
dos Faias
Florenças

Pinheiro
de Fora

Ponta do Jardim
Lombo do Salão
Lombo
do Brasil

Lombo do Doutor
222
Lombo
da Atouguia

Ponta da Gale
Lombada
do Loreto
Cales e Chada

Calheta ⑧
101
Ledo
Cova do Arco

Massapez
Paredes

Arco da Calheta

Carvalhal e
Carreira

Ladeira e
Lamaceiros
Fajã e Eiras

Levada
da Madaena

Madalena do Mar ⑦
Vale e
Cova do Pico
Passo
Canhas
Salão
Lombo da Piedad

Outeiro
Voltinhas

Anjos
Amêndo

Livramento

ATLANTIC OCEAN

Ponta do Sol ⑥

Western Madeira

0   2 km
0   2 miles

N

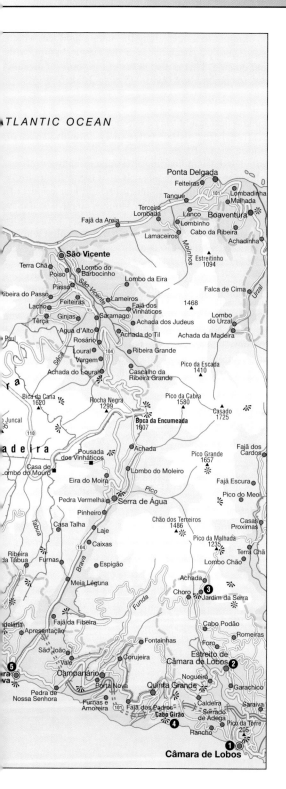

dressed in rags. Some houses here must rely on one tap per street, along with outside toilets and a communal bath-house.

Just off the **Largo Republica** – the small main square in the centre of the village – is the **parish church** of São Sebastião, worth a look inside for its blue-and-yellow *azulejos*. While the building dates back to 1430, it, too, was extensively altered in the 18th century.

Now the road winds inland; just outside town a right turn leads to the **Pico da Torre** *miradouro* (observation point) which has fine views down over Câmara de Lobos' lovely crescent-shaped bay and east back to Funchal.

Fertile fields

Back on the main road, bananas give way to vines as you climb through increasingly built-up countryside, bristling with modern villas built by returned emigrants. There's not much to see in little **Estreito de Câmara de Lobos** ❷ unless your visit coincides with the busy weekend market, when farmers arrive from all over the region to buy and sell livestock, vegetables and fruit.

Another high point in the village calendar is the September **wine harvest**. Harvested grapes in giant wicker baskets line the roadsides, waiting to be taken to wine centres to be crushed *(see page 127)*.

For a glimpse of what rural Madeira looked like before all the garish modern housing went up, you can take a short detour further up the mountain-slopes to the hamlet of **Jardim da Serra** ❸, set in delightfully pretty countryside and surrounded by cherry orchards. About a kilometre after you pass Estreito de Câmara de Lobos' big 19th-century church, you'll see a left turn signposted for the village; follow this until the road forks, then take the right-hand branch.

Retrace your steps to the main road; it's 5 km (3 miles) west via the 214 from here to **Cabo Girão** ❹, the second-highest sea-cliff in the world. The sign at the viewing platform says 580 metres (1,900 ft) – the distance downwards to the dark, pebbly beach and the seagulls wheeling far below. Amazingly, there are

Azulejo *tiles on the belfry offset the stern baroque façade of Ribeira Brava's São Bento church.*

BELOW: boats are still made the traditional way in Câmara de Lobos.

even a few *poios* (terraces) clinging to ledges along the steep cliff-face, which can only be reached by boat. There's a snack bar near the viewing-point, with toilets and room for parking outside. This is also the starting-point for an easy two-hour ramble back down to Câmara de Lobos *(see page 215)*.

A resort built on sugar

Double back from the cape and turn left at the crossroads on to the main road again. It's 12 km (7½ miles) from here to **Ribeira Brava** ❺ through a series of broad valleys densely scattered with villages.

The resort of Ribeira Brava itself is a bustling little place, with a seafront market and a promenade lined with modern cafés. It also has a surprisingly grand **parish church**, São Bento, built in the 15th century and located just off the main street, the **Rua do Visconde**. Like so many churches on the island, São Bento was given an extensive facelift during the 18th century, but some original Manueline features have survived – notably the carved stone pulpit and the prodigious baptismal font, adorned with mythological figures and set in its own chapel just to the right of the entrance.

Two more recent attractions lie further inland. One is the quirky **Colecção João Carlos Abreu**, a new museum devoted entirely to paintings and sculptures of horses (Estrada Reginal 104; tel: 952 548 ext 328; Tues–Sun 10am–12.30pm, 2–6pm; entrance fee). The other is the excellent **Museu Etnográfico da Madeira** (Madeira Ethnographic Museum; Rua de São Francisco 24; tel: 952 598; Tues–Sun 10am–12.30pm, 2–6pm; entrance fee). This is housed in a former convent that was later turned into a sugar-cane-crushing mill and rum distillery. The museum's exhibits cover every facet of island life, from fishing and

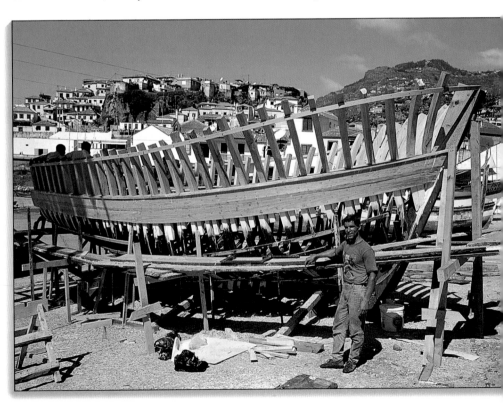

transport to agriculture, weaving, house building and the wine industry. There are frequent craft demonstrations, such as embroidery and weaving, and the museum has a small craft shop and café.

Along the new coast road

The 213 – a new road, and remarkably straight by Madeiran standards – runs between Ribeira Brava and Calheta, tunnelling through the lava-streaked coastal cliffs where it cannot arrow past their feet. Some 4 km (2½ miles) west along this route is **Ponta do Sol ❻**, another seaside village with an unusually splendid **parish church**, again built with sugar money. This one has a splendid green ceramic font which was a gift from King Manuel I, along with some rare yellow 17th-century *azulejos*, but the real highlight is the chancel's carved Mudejar-style wooden ceiling which dates back to the early 1500s.

A short drive further west leads to tiny **Madalena do Mar ❼**, a line of rather battered-looking houses bordered by frilly green banana plantations on the one side and the new coast road on the other. As there's not much to see here, press on to the town of **Calheta ❽**, southwestern Madeira's main settlement. Drive down towards the sea along a small ravine to find the massive grey **parish church**, begun in 1430 (the elegant stonework on the main portal here is Manueline) but subsequently renovated several times over. Ask next door if you want to have a look inside, as it's usually locked: treasures include a giant silver-and-ebony sacrarium, kept in the chapel in the side aisle, and the beautifully preserved wooden Mudejar-style ceiling in the choir.

Next door is one of the three Madeiran sugar mills that still produce rum and molasses. You'll see a disused mill – built more than 100 years ago – on the

Map on pages 198-99

The grandparents of the American novelist John dos Passos came from Ponta do Sol but emigrated to Chicago in the mid-19th century, as a plaque on the town hall testifies.

BELOW: tranquil Jardim do Mar.

This red-capped lighthouse marks the island's most westerly point.

BELOW: you don't need sand in order to soak up the sun.

beachfront here, a mute reminder of the time when sugar cane was still an important crop.

At Calheta, the 213 climbs up and inland to rejoin the 101, the winding old main road. The 16th-century **Capela dos Reis Magos**, the main sight at **Estreito da Calheta ❾** some 3 km (1¾ miles) further west, is reached down a narrow lane leading off to the right just before the turnoff to Jardim do Mar. With its whitewashed belfry and miniature windows, this tiny building is a refreshingly simple affair, despite the coat of arms of its wealthy landowner founder, Francisco de Gouveia, carved in stone above the entrance.

The chapel is always kept locked, but the key may be obtained from the house next door on request. It's worth the trouble: the altarpiece inside is some 460 years old, its wings marvellously decorated with Flemish panel paintings and with a splendid carving at its centre depicting the *Adoration of the Magi*.

Sea and forest

It is 4 km (2½ miles) to **Jardim do Mar ❿**, along a side-road that winds steeply down past banana-tree-clad cliffs. This unspoilt village of old stone houses, cobbled streets and lush gardens overflowing with flowering trees and vines has an almost Mediterranean atmosphere; it is certainly one of the most beautiful spots on the island. If you fancy a dip, there's good bathing off the rocks here. As you ease your car gingerly down the narrow road to the sea you'll pass a crumbling pink *quinta* on the left which once belonged to the Couto Cardosos, one of the oldest and most aristocratic families on the island.

Now retrace your steps to Estreito da Calheta and continue the route west. This road winds high above the sea, through tranquil forests of aromatic pine and

eucalyptus, mimosa and sweet chestnut. There is a sense of increasing isolation, for the only signs of human habitation are scattered along the mountain ridges; deep ravines separate the villages here. The clifftop hamlet of **Prazeres** ⓫, some 10 km (6 miles) farther on, is typical: unplastered one-room houses built from dark basalt in the old style, clustering round an oversized church with looming towers.

To the westernmost tip

More peaceful rural scenery is in store as you drive on to the most westerly point on the island at **Ponta do Pargo** ⓬. Apple and pear orchards line the road; small brown cows graze in the fields; women farmhands in bright head-scarves and wellies stride by, hoes slung purposefully over their shoulders. Modern life scarcely seems to have intruded here for decades.

At the village, follow the yellow signs for the *Farol* ("lighthouse"), a 3-km (1¾-mile) detour. Perched on a rocky headland tufted with thistles and heather, this sturdy red-tipped building overlooks a vast sweep of sea: next stop, America. This is also the starting-point for an excellent *levada* walk down to Prazeres *(see page 217)*.

You'll be lucky to pass more than two or three other cars as you head north to the seaside resort of **Porto Moniz** ⓭, 18 km (11 miles) away. The quiet clifftop road meanders through a few isolated villages, but the scenery here is mainly broom and eucalyptus forest, banked with flowers and bracken. The local farmers protect their gardens from the wind and salt with hedges of heather: the little *miradouro*, or viewpoint, just before you reach the turnoff for the town, has good views of some chequered countryside down at sea level.

Map on pages 198-99

A keeper still lives in the lighthouse at Ponta do Pargo, even though the light has been operating automatically for over a decade now.

BELOW: codfish drying in the sun.

THE NORTH COAST ROAD

If you're a nervous driver, then it may be best to avoid the high coastal road between Porto Moniz and Seixal, which was originally cut into the steep coastal cliffs with pickaxes. Despite various attempts to widen and improve it, it is still basically more of a ledge than a road, with extremely narrow passing-places, dank, dripping tunnels and more hairpins than the most teetering beehive hairdo. And let's not forget what the Madeirans call "the free car-washes" – the waterfalls that pour down on to the road unhindered after heavy rains.

It may demand skilful driving to negotiate it (with frequent bouts of reversing to let oncoming drivers past), but this is undoubtedly one of the most beautiful coastal drives in the world. Wherever the road allows it, park and soak up the view, from the silhouettes of Madeira's north coast stretching away into the distance to the Atlantic breakers crashing against the cliffs down below.

Beyond Seixal, the rest of the route to São Vicente is now enclosed in wide modern tunnels, but the original coast road (signposted "Antiga 101") can still be driven in one direction only, from east to west (ie from São Vicente to Seixal). Allow 45 minutes for the 16-km (10-mile) drive by the old route and 25 minutes for the new.

Map on pages 198-99

TIP

If the clouds part as you cross the Paúl da Serra moor you'll be rewarded with glimpses of all the south-coast villages that you drove through earlier on this route.

BELOW: sheep cope well with the wild and windy Paúl da Serra moor.

Porto Moniz is where many Madeirans come on holiday, and its handful of boarding-houses and hotels get extremely busy during the peak summer season, when various seasonal seafood restaurants also do a roaring trade. The resort's main drawcard is the **volcanic rock swimming-pools** down on the beachfront, gouged by waves and weather out of a single tongue of lava that poured into the sea thousands of years ago. Away from the crowded pool area, back up on the mountain-slopes, you'll find a peaceful main square and a little 17th-century church – pretty much all that remains of old Porto Moniz.

Over Paúl da Serra

The last leg of the journey heads inland, returning to Funchal over a vast stretch of windswept moorland known as **Paúl da Serra**. To find the turnoff, retrace your steps through Porto Moniz and backtrack for 7 km (4 miles) along the way you came. The moor is signposted off to the left: it's 77 km (48 miles) back to Funchal from here, about an hour-and-a-half's drive, with stops to admire the views. The road that climbs up to the plateau is a dramatic one, winding through thick cedar- and laurel-forest and passing broad valleys which drop away abruptly to the sea. The moor itself is remarkably flat, and cloaked in scrubby, goat-nibbled heathers; mist sweeps by like smoke from a vast bonfire.

After some 15 km (9 miles), you'll see a turnoff for **Rabaçal** ⓮ on your left, the start of one of the best walks on the island *(see page 218)*. A little further on, the road forks; the left option leads to the **Casa do Lombo do Mouro** and the start of another excellent hike *(see page 227)*, a right turn gets you back down to the coast via Canhas, some 12 km (7½ miles) away. Now head east to Ribeira Brava, where you can pick up the motorway back to Funchal. ❑

The Architecture of the Discoverers

Visitors to Madeira will encounter plenty of examples of the Manueline style – Portugal's celebrated "architecture of the Discoverers" – in the island's oldest buildings. The style is named after Manuel I, who became King of Portugal in 1495. Historians tagged him *O Venturoso* – "The Fortunate" – because it was during his rule that the country began to reap huge fortunes from its overseas territories.

The foundation stones for his success had been laid three-quarters of a century earlier by Henry the Navigator, who founded a nautical academy at Sagres on Portugal's southwestern tip. Here, with great military precision, he drew up a strategy to conquer the world.

To help him, he recruited the services of geographers, astronomers, shipbuilding engineers and naval captains who hailed from every European seafaring nation. Certain in the knowledge that the earth was round (many years before Columbus), and equipped with the Arab astrolabe and other navigation aids, the treasure-hungry adventurers set sail in their twin-masted caravels.

In 1419, they reached Madeira; in 1430 the Azores; in 1470 the equator. In 1488, Bartolomeu Dias rounded the southern tip of Africa and named it the "Cape of Storms". In 1489, Vasco da Gama pioneered the sea route to India's Malabar Coast. In 1500, Pedro Cabral set foot on Brazilian soil, and, in 1521, Fernão Magalhães – albeit under the Spanish flag – made the first attempt to sail round the world.

These successful voyages, and the discovery of far-away countries, were reflected in the art of the period. The basic architectural style did not alter: on Madeira it remained late Gothic while in the mother country, a transition to Renaissance forms could be observed. Yet when the stonemasons went to work on the buildings, they gave them an elaborate new decorative twist. Portals and façades were enhanced with nautical motifs, from anchors and fishing nets to astronomical instruments and exotic marine animals, all a reflection of the triumphs of the discoverers of the "New World".

On Madeira, these embellishments were far less prolific than on the mainland. For one thing, the island remained a fairly conservative and parochial place despite its economic prosperity, and secondly, the artists – including the Sé's master builder, Pedro Anes – came from the Alentejo, the region of flatlands and hills beyond Lisbon. Instead of importing European trends, the Alentejans looked to Moorish influences for their inspiration, and were particularly fond of *azulejos* in classic abstract designs.

This subtle blending of the Manueline and Moorish styles is at its best in the superb ceiling of the capital's cathedral. Other notable examples include the ornaments on Funchal's Alfândega, the interior of the parish church at Santa Cruz, the ceiling of the parish church at Calheta and the interior of São Bento church in Ribeira Brava. ❑

RIGHT: Ribeira Brava's parish church interior is a good example of the local Manueline style.

TRADITIONAL MADEIRAN PARKS AND GARDENS

Rooted in the island's rich volcanic soil and nurtured by a balmy climate, the grandest island gardens owe much to British influences

Madeira's parks and gardens brim over with exotic blossom, much of it first brought to the island in the 18th century by British merchants who settled here to work in the wine trade. Members of the small ex-pat community vied with each other to create the lushest and loveliest gardens and held regular competitions to see who possessed the latest botanical rarity.

A DAZZLING DISPLAY

Today, not only are several of those gardens open to the public, but they are all within easy striking distance of Funchal. The Quinta Palheiro, just 8km (5 miles) northeast of Funchal, looks at first glance like a Victorian garden in the depths of Surrey in England, all manicured lawns, long borders, pergolas and lily ponds. Yet proteas, aloes, agaves and other exotics proliferate.

Then there's the splendid Jardim Botânico, originally the summer *quinta* of the Reid family, who launched the celebrated Reid's Hotel. It has a huge collection of rare plants, along with splendid views over Funchal. And don't miss the Quinta Boa Vista, whose greenhouses nurse a dazzling range of orchids in rainbow colours.

△ **BLANDY'S BLOOMS**
Owned by the Blandys, one of Madeira's foremost old wine-exporter families, the Quinta do Palheiro is the island's most magnificent garden.

▽ **TROPICAL BLEND**
The Monte Palace Tropical Gardens are an eccentric mix of rare plants, *azulejos* and statuary, and there is an Oriental Garden, too.

△ **THE LADY'S GARDEN**
This corner of Quinta Palheiro near Funchal has been laid out French-style with hedges cut into unusual shapes.

◁ **RARE BLOSSOM**
The terraced gardens of the Quinta da Boa Vista are filled with thousands of orchids, most destined for the cut-flower trade.

HIGH DESIGNS ON FERTILE MADEIRA

Gardeners certainly have an easy time on Madeira. Thanks to the island's lack of a summer dry season, blossom grows in profusion all year round. Not only that, but plants which visitors may well be accustomed to seeing only in pots elsewhere here grow to enormous sizes in the carefully-tended parks and gardens. Look out, for example, for the towering Swiss cheese-plants in the grounds of Funchal's Quinta Vigia, which reach at least 25 metres (80 ft) high and are covered in long green fruits (the locals call these, simply, "the delicious fruit").

The Jardim Botânico (*see above*), meanwhile, has some extraordinary black-and-white bird-of-paradise flowers (*Strelitzia nicolai*), which grow 3 metres (10 ft) high, along with some equally imposing cacti. The Quinta do Palheiro Ferreiro, however, scores on its giant camellias, some of which are also over 3 metres (10 ft) high. The camellia garden was first planted at the end of the 18th century by the Conde de Carvalhal, and is best seen between November and April, when the flowers are in bloom.

ARCHAEOLOGICAL PARK
Heraldic emblems carved in stone, gravestones and crosses dot the grounds of the Quinta das Cruzes.

△ **SOWING THE SEED**
This statue is one of several to adorn Funchal's lovely Santa Catarina Park, with its terraced paths overlooking the bay.

◁ **ZARCO'S GARDEN**
Funchal's historic Quinta das Cruzes is surrounded by a tranquil park, hidden behind high walls and filled with flowering trees and shrubs.

ISLAND WALKS

In this chapter are described 10 walking routes, which traverse a wide range of landscapes and give walkers of all abilities a glimpse of Madeira's finest scenery

Map on pages 212–13

or its size, Madeira is one of the most scenically diverse islands anywhere in the world. Thanks to a labyrinthine network of old paths (*veradas*) and watercourses (*levadas*) which web the island's lush peaks and valleys, one of the most pleasant and easiest ways to savour the sights and scents is front-foot forward with your boots on. You can explore almost the whole of the island along these paths, from the stunning coastline to the top of the highest mountain at over 1,800 metres (6,000 ft). However, you need to be well-organised to do so, and walkers would underestimate changing weather and conditions underfoot at their peril.

If you're only moderately fit, you'll be pleased to know that many of Madeira's walkways – from the strips of well-trodden earth alongside irrigation channels to the neat stone paths engineered into valley cuttings – are not that difficult to manage. Indeed, the thrill of walking here is not so much the steepness of the ascent, but the extent of the view and the suddenness of the drop. Many routes demand a head for heights; vertigo sufferers will not enjoy the narrow ledges skirting some of the higher channels, where you need steadiness to make progress. That said, this walker (and vertigo sufferer) has found that by fixing his eyes firmly on his feet during the occasional difficult passage, most of the island is negotiable.

A sense of direction is important, too; path signposts in Madeira are still very few and far between. For the most part you have to do some homework, examine inexact maps and rely on word of mouth and common sense. Sometimes a painted direction on a lump of rock points the way – usually at a fork in the road by the side of a house whose occupant has, presumably, come to anticipate ramblers' enquiries.

Transport required

As any Madeiran will tell you, the *levadas* were originally designed for irrigation and later, hydro power. Similarly, the *veradas* – many of which are hundreds of years old – were built by isolated communities who knew where they were going. The point is that they were not constructed with tourists in mind, and some of the most spectacular pathways are also the most difficult to reach.

While the road network is capable, taxis can be expensive and buses infrequent to places far from Funchal. Often, it's only possible to drive to the start of a route, which means walkers must organise a pickup at the other end or retrace their steps. Taking an organised walking tour (*see Travel Tips for details*) is, therefore, an attractive option if you want to explore Madeira's more isolated reaches. Prices are reasonable, too, especially if you're part of a group.

PRECEDING PAGES: Penha de Águia ("Eagle Rock"). **LEFT:** this steep island is good for walkers, but cows have little pasture. **BELOW:** following the *levada*.

A LUSH TERRAIN THAT'S MADE FOR WALKERS

One of the best ways to savour Madeira's scenic diversity is by exploring the canal-paths which criss cross the island's mountains and valleys

HEADING NORTH ▷
The Boaventura area offers great variety for hikers, with everything from *levadas* through forests to outstanding coastal views.

AROUND RABAÇAL ▷
The mossy *Levada do Risco* leads through thick forest and past cliffs bright with waterfalls.

△ **TO THE LIGHTHOUSE**
The *Levada da Calheta* leads from Ponta do Pargo's lighthouse past the fishing village of Paúl do Mar (*above*).

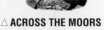

△ **ACROSS THE MOORS**
It's a steep climb up to the Paúl da Serra plateau from Lombo do Mouro, but the views are worth it.

△ **ON TOP OF THE WORLD**
The drive from Funchal up to the top of the Encumeada Pass, where several walks begin, offers spectacular scenery before you even put your boots on.

1. Monte to Vale do Paraiso
2. Cabo Girão to Câmara de Lobos
3. Along the Levada da Calheta
4. Rabaçal and around
5. Exploring Fanal
6. Ponta de São Lourenço
7. Around Boaventura: Fajã das Falcas to Fajã do Penedo
8. Pico das Pedras National Park
9. Lombo do Mouro to Bica da Cana
10. Pico do Arieiro to Pico Ruivo and Archada do Teixeira

◁ **HOME ALONE**
Santana with its quaint cottages is the starting-point for walks in the Pico das Pedras National Park.

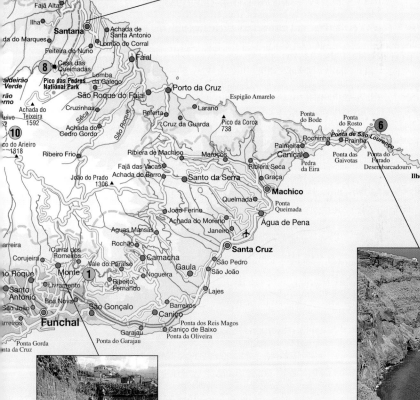

◁ **TO VALE DO PARAISO**
This walk from Monte is one of the easiest and most popular on the island.

△ **PONTA DE SÃO LOURENÇO**
The island's starkly beautiful easternmost point offers hikers dramatic sea views around every corner.

Walkers must resist the temptation to be whisked back to base in a Monte toboggan.

BELOW: black swan in the Monte Palace Tropical Gardens.

The top 10 routes

The 10 walks described below – graded from the easiest to the more difficult – cover the full range of Madeiran scenery, from rocky shores to forests full of ancient trees and hillside terraces bursting with fruit and vegetables. Two routes are near the capital, the rest are wider spread, but all involve the historic *levada* and *verada* systems. In some cases walkers will need to plan their transport arrangements with care, but it will definitely be worth the effort.

❶ Monte to Vale do Paraiso

One of the easiest and most popular Madeiran walks – close to the capital, with a fine range of scenery, and a good choice of refreshments at the end.

It's a half-hour bus ride (or 15 minutes by cable-car) up to Funchal's leafy suburb of **Monte**, where this walk kicks off. In the cobbled main square (Largo da Fonte), you will find cafés, toilets, souvenir-stands and, on the right, the lovely Parque do Monte *(see Around Funchal, page 165)*. A cobbled path to the right of the square leads up to the 18th-century church of **Nossa Senhora do Monte**, from whose forecourt you can gaze down upon the beginning of the famous Monte toboggan run. Resist the temptation to be whisked back to Funchal on a wicker sledge, and instead continue through the town, past the cable-car station and into a broad square with a chapel on the left and a viewpoint on the right. Straight ahead is the start of a wide *verada* – the real start of this walk.

The path zig-zags downhill at first, past a sign pointing left to **Camacha** save that demanding 8-km (5-mile) hike for a day when you're feeling especially fit. Soon you'll find yourself winding down a pretty bridge, then up through a valley cloaked in scented eucalyptus forests; at the top of the ridge is **Curral do**

Romeiros village, with fine views over Funchal. From here, ten minutes along a twisty path lead to a left turn up to the apple-tree-lined Levada dos Tornos. Turn right along the *levada*. The first stretch is agreeably level, offering ample opportunity to look at goats and listen to chaffinch and robin song echoing across the valley. After 20 minutes, you skirt the grounds of the new Choupara Hills Resort Hotel, before crossing a main road and rejoining the path at the *levada*-sign. The path borders the **Quinta do Pomar** gardens here, with wire-netting to stop you clambering into private property.

Time for tea

After the path crosses another road, some 30 minutes on, you will pass the entrance to an excellent tea-house set in lushly planted grounds. Called the **Hortensia Gardens** (entrance free; tel: 795 219), this is a spot to linger over salads, soup or cakes with views over Funchal. Alternatively, continue along the path for another 10 minutes to the famed Jasmine Tea House, which serves 50 varieties of tea and delicious homemade scones. Whichever of the two you choose, you will find that the No.47 bus passes the front door, taking you back to Funchal.

Stepping out

Length of walk: 8 km (5 miles), two-and-a-half-hours (with tea stop).
Conditions: Easy, after a steady climb up to Curral dos Romeiros.
How to get there: Easy. By city bus 20 or 21, half-an-hour from Funchal, or by cable car from the Zona Vehla.
Refreshment: There is plenty available at Monte where the walk begins, and at the two tea houses where you finish. Take water for the walk, nonetheless.

❷ Cabo Girão to Câmara de Lobos

An easy downhill ramble from the world's second-highest sea cliff (the highest is in Norway) to a pretty fishing village which Churchill loved to paint.

Start at **Cabo Girão**, a 45-minute bus ride from Funchal. The bus deposits you outside a café with a small photographic display of famous visitors to Madeira; you can smile at pictures of George Bernard Shaw learning how to waltz before crossing the road to admire the sea-views over the 580-metre (1,900-ft) cliff itself.

The walk proper begins just off the main car park by a new road, where you will find a *verada* initially shaded by pine trees. **Câmara de Lobos**, your destination, lies way down below, past steep terraces webbed by small *levadas* irrigating an astonishing variety of crops – from sweet potatoes and vines to pumpkins and hydrangeas. Ten minutes later, superb views of the south coast distract attention from the tiny, scurrying lizards at your feet.

Passing houses lined by orange, fig and avocado groves, you come to a main road; cross this to rejoin the path where it leads to a lookout point, with more marvellous views down to Funchal. On clear days, you can see the Desertas Islands, too.

The way now continues down past yet more terraces, these ones lush with mangoes, banana trees, strawberries and beans. Bear left past a slope thickly

Map on pages 212–13

A funicular railway once took passengers between Monte and Funchal but, after a serious accident on the line in 1939, journeys were suspended for good.

BELOW: stepping out near Monte.

covered in vines, cleverly angled along the hillside to catch the air underneath (this district is where some of the very best grapes for making Madeiran wine are grown). As if you needed any more reminders that you are in the heart of an agricultural region, you may also brush up against the odd goat, tethered to a stone shed alongside the path and kept to fertilise the soil.

Down to the coast

Scattered higgledy-piggledy about the hillside, the houses round here boast decorative carved figures (pigeons and bulldogs are especially popular) on their tiled gable-ends. There is nothing very decorative about the bank of 23 post-boxes fixed to a corner-fence on the road you join to complete your walk into Câmara de Lobos. Yet they are a poignant reminder of the island's remarkable geography – because so few homes round here sit on roads, most householders have to clamber up and down these steep terrace-paths just to fetch the post, as well as the shopping and everything else they need. Visitors use the pathways for their walking pleasure, but to the locals they are lifelines.

Soon the new pink-and-white fishermen's apartments of Câmara de Lobos come into view; you have reached the coast. The pebbly beach down here is as busy as the small main square with its cafés and early 20th-century bandstand, as fishermen pass the time of day and prepare for their night trips out to sea.

Our route now leads east from the main square, past the little fishermen's chapel of **Nossa Senhora da Conceição** and through a small boatyard where, in time-honoured fashion, workmen build the *canoas* used for fishing off the coast, and the larger *embarcações* for deep-sea fishing. Steps lead up to a look-out point by the main road with excellent views down over the town. A plaque

TIP

Look out for Madeira's dazzling national flower, the "bird of paradise" or strelitzia, as you descend to Câmara de Lobos – it adorns many pathside gardens here.

BELOW: fishermen taking it easy at Câmara de Lobos.

says it all: this is where Churchill came to paint in 1950, including, it may be presumed, scenes of the very cliff where you have walked.

Stepping out

Length of walk: Achievable in a gentle two hours – and it's downhill all the way. The whole trip makes an easy half-day excursion from Funchal.
Conditions: Easy, but the descent is steep, something to bear in mind if you have knee-trouble.
How to get there: Easy by bus (45 minutes from Funchal). Good connections at both ends.
Refreshments: There's a snack bar at Cabo Girão. The walk's not really long enough to merit any great need for sustenance, but bring water if it's a hot day.

❸ Along the Levada da Calheta

An easy linear walk exploring Madeira's isolated westernmost tip, flavoured with fresh, salty breezes and glimpses of traditional rural life.

Our starting point here is the lonely clifftop lighthouse at **Ponta do Pargo**. Some 3,600 km (2,200 miles) west across the vast, wrinkled *Oceano Atlantico* is Portugal's other island colony, the Azores, and far beyond them, Canada. You may spot flocks of wild canaries above the cliffs, perhaps homesick for their own namesake islands further south.

Backtrack up the main road for ten minutes to pick up the fern-lined Levada da Calheta, which leads east past cider apple orchards (be warned: the fruit's extremely tart) dotted with the odd horse-chestnut tree. The well-trodden path heads on past stone cowsheds, terraces planted with maize and the red roof-tiles of a lower building which almost grazes the lip of the *levada*.

Soon afterwards, the watercourse vanishes underground; to find it again, cross a main road, pausing at the nearby viewing platform for superb views over the west coast cliffs. Now the *levada* snakes past clumps of pine and bracken, offering wide views across serenely unspoilt open countryside. Soon you come to a fork in the way which gives you the option of leaving the path and descending to pretty little **Fajã da Ovelha**, and from there pushing west along the coast to **Paúl do Mar**, a quiet fishing-village which right up until the late 1960s could only be reached by boat. Otherwise, continue along the *levada* to the clifftop hamlet of **Prazeres**.

Stepping out

Length of walk: 6 km (4 miles), one-and-a-half hours, or 9 km (6 miles), two hours, depending on where you finish.
Conditions: Easy, if you pick up the walk on the main road above Ponta do Pargo. Good paths, no steep drops, and superb views of the west coast.
How to get there: Because Ponta do Pargo is fairly isolated, a hire car is the best bet; or hire a taxi for the day, for 'drop-off-and-pick-up' at your designated end-point. An organised tour is another good option.
Refreshments: There are seasonal cafés at Ponta do

Map on pages 212–13

BELOW: the dramatic west coast cliffs near Ponta do Pargo.

Pargo, and Ponta do Sol is handily placed if you want to stop for a meal on the way back to Funchal (*see Travel Tips*)

❹ Rabaçal and around

This short, circular route through the highlands of the interior is a firm favourite with walkers, and no wonder: although relatively undemanding, it embraces wooded valleys, mountains and waterfalls, and is also well-signposted.

To reach the start of the walk, head for Ribeira Brava and take the 104 heading north, turning left onto the 204 at Boca de Encumeada. The most exacting part of the journey is the right turn down to the small government holiday village of **Rabaçal**. This extremely steep, narrow lane is a truly hair-raising drive, especially if you meet a car coming the other way.

Steps from the main car-park alongside the government rest-house lead to a broad path, where you'll see signs for the **Levado do Risco** and **Levada dos 25 Fontes** ("Springs"). You'll come across gushing cataracts all over the place here; these and the humid temperatures are responsible for the amazingly lush jungly vegetation.

An easy 15-minute walk along the leaf-littered, mossy Levada do Risco brings you to a lookout point over Risco Falls, two narrow and seemingly endless cataracts plunging over a gorge. It's a dramatic spectacle, but don't get carried away: a danger sign warns against trying to cross the gorge by clambering through the tunnel on your right. Instead, retrace your steps to take the Levada dos 25 Fontes path, turning right once you reach the *levada*.

Some 20 minutes later, after a rather more testing journey along the *levada*'s lip (fenced in the steepest places), through a stretch of enchanted forest full of

BELOW: the mossy, waterfall-lined *Levada do Risco.*

huge, lichen-draped trees, you reach a lagoon fed by tumbling waterfalls. Most are slender threads emerging from cracks in the cliffs; come in winter, though, and you'll be greeted by a tumultuous cascade cutting a broad swathe down a cliff to the rear of the pool.

Map on pages 212–13

One step beyond

Most people walk to the waterfalls and straight back to the government rest-house, missing out on the following less well-known but highly rewarding appendix to their valley hike: retrace your steps from the 25 Waterfalls for ten minutes or so and turn right, passing by the **Levada do Rocha Vermelha** as you go. The wide path is not signposted, but zigzags steeply down through jungly ferns and flowers right into the crook of the mountains. You won't find people here, only birds, bees and butterflies, and – after a 15-minute walk – a shelter for *levadeiros (levada* maintenance-men), shaded by a walnut tree.

The gardens of the Rabaçal rest-house are filled with blossoming plants.

A ten-minute diversion following the **Levada do Norte** against the flow takes you past banks of wild strawberries and violets to a tunnel – the first of 27 between here and the Encumeada Pass. Ten hours, a torch and stamina is what you need to complete that hike; for now, keep going along the path back to Rabaçal. In some parts of Madeira, *levadas* are used to generate hydro-electric power; soon you'll be able to see where four separate channels meet, enabling water to surge down to **Calheta** on the coast for just this purpose.

Just after the confluence, a left turn takes you up on a steepish 20-minute climb back to the government rest-house along a lovely old *verada*, part of a centuries-old path that was once the main route for villagers and their donkeys to Funchal. Get your breath back at the picnic-table seats alongside the rest-house; it's tempting to forget when you're out walking in Madeira that, usually, the only way back is up.

BELOW: ancient laurels in Fanal's cloud forest.

Stepping out

Length of walk: 10 km (6 miles), three hours.
Conditions: Moderately easy. Good underfoot at the beginning; vertigo possible on short stretches along the *levadas*. Toughish long climb (about 20 minutes) back up to the Rabaçal rest-house from where the four *levadas* meet.
How to get there: By taxi, hired for the day. If you hire a car in Funchal, follow the 204 northwest to Porto Moniz over the Paúl da Serra plateau, but look out for the right turn to Rabaçal (the 204-1) en route. This walk is on every tour operator's list, but bear in mind that the groups will, most likely, not be small ones, which can make it difficult to appreciate the beauty of the landscape.
Refreshments: Take your own – the Madeirans always do. Picnicking's a flourishing tradition here; the tables beside Rabaçal's government rest-house are a big favourite with the locals, who arrive laden with all their own refreshments – and even cooking-pots.

❺ Exploring Fanal

A circular forest walk across a misty mountain ridge, offering some truly magical views down to the north-western coast.

The pathways around Fanal are lined with colourful flowers.

BELOW: the resort of Porto Moniz is where Madeirans come on holiday.

Our route begins on the coastal road outside **Porto Moniz** (the 101), where a signposted turnoff to the south takes you 1,000 metres (3,200 ft) up to Fanal mountain and **Forest House**, lying at the end of a rough, bumpy track. Only with care is this part of the road is negotiable without a 4-wheel drive vehicle; higher suspension is an advantage.

Just past the house, a path leads past the volcanic crater-lake of **Lagoa do Fanal**, full of water in winter and grazing cows in summer. Follow your nose past the heady scent of a lily-of-the-valley tree and take the first turning right into a wide, mossy roadway. Mountain swifts dart in attendance. You're walking through primeval woodland here, a landscape unchanged since the first Portuguese settlers arrived in the 15th century. Tall ferns flourish with indigenous black laurel trees, the jewel of Madeira's forests; some are 900 years old and still growing.

Sea glimpses

Now comes twenty minutes' gently-sloping walk up from the bottom of the ridge. The sandy path is lined with ferns on one side, but falls away to moss-covered stony outcrops on the other. Inevitably, you'll run into patches of mist (there are only sixty days of sunshine a year at the top of the Fanal), but through its ragged blanket you may hear the chatter of the chaffinch, blackbird and redstart, and glimpse the looping flight of the protected laurel pigeon. In summer a thick carpet of blue wild mint flowers pad out the path.

After about half-an-hour's climb, the ferns drop away to reveal, on the left your first view of the steep terraces – thick with vegetables and vines – which sweep down the hillside to the coast. After a further half-an-hour, you'll need

to take care not to lose the path as it starts to descend over steep rocky out-crops, overgrown in summer with tall, jungly ferns.

If you happen to lose your way, head back again to the top of the ridge and find an alternative route leading down through a small forest. Here, over the centuries, huge laurel trees have twisted themselves into amazing shapes, their vast, gnarled branches coiling on to the ground. With mist touching the tree-tops and a thick bed of leaves underfoot, this is a wonderfully peaceful spot in which to linger a while.

Cow sheds and cable-cars

An hour-and-a-half later, the path leaves the forest behind and starts following the coastline, visible far below. On the left is the fishing village of **Seixal**, with the emerald-green terraces and scattered houses of **Chão da Ribeira** just inland. After another half-an-hour's walk, the land suddenly flattens out to reveal a few wood-and-corrugated-iron cow-sheds, the first buildings seen since the start of the walk. Nearby, usually eerily half-veiled in mist, stands an old cliff-top pulley which once wound a cable-car loaded with loggers up and down the mountain to Chão da Ribeira – undoubtedly a nerve-wracking journey.

The Forest House is in sight, your car is parked nearby – and in three hours of walking, it's unlikely that you'll have met another soul. Drive (carefully) back down the track until you meet the main road leading to Porto Moniz.

From there, you can visit Seixal, head back into the mountains on another road to see the quaint old stone cow-sheds at Chão da Ribeira, or simply stare with amazement up at the old cable-car station where, just a little while ago, you stood in the mist at Fanal.

Map
on pages
212–13

It is easy to get lost on the Fanal ridge – the mist can lead you astray and the path-side ferns grow so thick and high in summer that you can quite easily become disorientated. This is not a place to walk on your own.

BELOW:
a well-preserved old stone cow-byre at Cháo da Ribeira.

Stepping out

Length of walk: 9 km (6 miles); two-and-a-half to three hours, depending how long you linger amongst the laurels.

Conditions: Unusual. Much cooler than on the coast, and often misty. Take a jumper and rainwear and wear boots because, although the surface is mainly peaty and even, it can be slippery when wet. There is some steady climbing up to the top of the ridge and a few rocky places, but nothing really difficult.

How to get there: This is a full day excursion, whatever your method of transport. It is more than a two-hour drive from Funchal through Ribeira Brava, north over the Encumeada Pass to São Vicente and west to Porto Moniz, turning left just before you reach town for the fairly rough and bumpy climb (the 209) that leads to the Fanal.

It is impossible to travel all the way by bus. Take a taxi (which would have to wait), or hire a car, which can be parked safely near the Forest House for the duration of your round-trip walk.

Refreshments: Take your own or stock up en route to Fanal; nothing is available for miles around once you're up there.

BELOW: cacti flourish in the dry landscape round Ponta de São Lourenço.
RIGHT: taking a break high up in the central mountain range.

❻ Ponta de São Lourenço

An occasionally challenging linear hike along Madeira's stark but beautiful easternmost tip, with dramatic sea-views round every corner.

Our walk begins where the tarmac road (the 101-3) heading east from **Caniçal** ends in a car park at **Baia d'Abra**, and immediately converts itself into a well-trodden footpath. Briefly head downhill (right) to catch a glimpse (to the left) of the uninhabited Desertas Islands, a haven for monk-seals and petrels.

Underneath your feet, however, the only signs of life will be the scurry and rustle of miniature lizards. Vegetation is sparse, although you will spot wild tomatoes and potato-vines. Time to climb for about twenty minutes, sliding your feet into whatever natural toe-holds you find, and enjoying the splendid long-distance views west along the headland. A left fork now leads about a hundred yards over to the north coast side where a striking reddish-purple triangle of rock juts out of the sea, surrounded by several smaller volcanic siblings also coloured rich shades of red. It's hard to imagine that three centuries ago, these were all thickly cloaked in vegetation, a hunting ground for Portuguese noblemen who came here to shoot wild pigs, deer and rabbits.

To the lighthouse

Back on the main path, don't be tempted to stray. The occasional white painted marker-post gives some reassurance, but the ground is very stony and undulating and after an hour you have to tackle a narrow, short steep descent with only the sea – far below – as a horizon. Happily, railings have now been fixed to give walkers some guidance, but the wind can blow with some ferocity across the gaps in the cliffs here.

The path now becomes crumblier, but offers enticing views of the sea round every corner. Finally, up ahead and to the left, you spot the oasis of the **Casa do Sardinha**, with its fringe of palm trees. It's the obvious place for a well-earned picnic – but only in 45 minutes' time, after you have climbed the hill behind the house. Oh yes, you must – **Pico das Gaivotas** gives an extra 300-metre (980-ft) high view of the whole of this extraordinary region – a national park – as well as a good glimpse of the lighthouse at the island's easternmost tip. Back at the

Map on pages 212–13

The lighthouse at Madeira's easternmost tip sits on its own islet, separated from the mainland by a 167-m (550-ft) channel and only reachable by boat.

BELOW: the island's rocky and dry easternmost tip.

Casa do Sardinha, the park ranger's house, accept his offer of a fill of your water bottle if it comes your way; his special supply comes from a spring at Porto Santo. You will need it – the only route back is the way you have come.

A short drive back along the coast towards Caniçal leads to **Prainha**, the only sandy beach on Madeira. A path winds down from the main road on to the tiny strip of dark volcanic sand, sheltered by high cliffs; be warned that it gets extremely crowded in high season.

Stepping out

Length of walk: 8 km (5 miles). A steady three-and-a-half hours.

Conditions: Quite challenging and vertiginous at times; very stony and uneven in parts (wear hiking boots). Exertion needed to climb and descend short stretches. Exposed, too, so sun hat and water bottle are necessities.

How to get there: By bus to Caniçal from Funchal, then taxi to the car park at Baia d'Abra, 5 km (3 miles) away. By hire car to the same spot. Organised walking tours are widely available from Funchal; most include a midday picnic.

Refreshments: The car park at Baia d'Abra usually sports a refreshment trailer, from about midday on. Take your own water, anyway, and sustenance just in case. Refills of spring water are often available at the park ranger's house.

❼ Around Boaventura: Fajã das Falcas to Fajã do Penedo

One of Madeira's most outstandingly scenic linear walks, along a high north coast *levada* where you feel as though you are teetering on the island's rim.

Bear in mind, though, that getting to the starting point by car is quite an achievement in itself: it's a 90-minute drive from Funchal to Ribeira Brava and

BELOW: *levadeiros* (maintenance men) near Boaventura.

São Vicente via the Encumeada Pass, then along the cliff road to Porto Delgado and finally the clifftop village of **Boaventura**, where the walk begins.

Map on pages 212–13

After the initial hard climb up from the village to find the *levada*, it's some consolation that the path starts out fairly level. Cross the river, pass by the neat vegetable-gardens of **Fajã das Falcas** hamlet and wind upwards for half an hour or so to look down on to pretty Boaventura with its red-tiled roofs.

Now the path narrows, winding steeply up to the left as the *levada* tunnels through the ancient forest cloaking the slopes of the surrounding mountains. Indigenous laurel-trees lord it over lily of the valley and wild geraniums; you'll also spot Madeiran mahogany trees, ironwoods and plenty of creepers and ferns. A further hour of solitary walking through these green, waterfall-cooled surroundings gives a deep sense of peace – and false security. So far, there have been only a couple of vertiginous sections of path to conquer, but now comes a stretch which leaves you feeling rather like a tightrope walker, with sheer drops away down the valleys to the north coast. Nonetheless, the huge views are thrilling; at one stage you can see not only the walk's finishing-point on the right, but the point over to the left where you began.

One of Boaventura's chief crops is willow-cane, supplying the raw materials for the wickerworkers at Camacha.

From forests to fields

Eventually (and, for vertigo sufferers, not a moment too soon), the path broadens out. You may hear the sound of a radio here, for there is a *levadeiros'* shelter just down the track. Now the path leads downhill to **Fajã do Penedo** village, past vines and fields that are ablaze in summer with vivid orange flowers. Look back up the valley for a good view of one of the most beautiful *levadas* on the entire island. As an alternative route home, you can drive east along the scenic north coast road via rural São Jorge, Santana and Faial and then head inland to Ribeiro Frio and Funchal.

BELOW: harvesting willow-canes near Boaventura.

Stepping out

Length of walk:13 km (9 miles), three-and-a-half hours.
Conditions: A steep hike to reach the *levada*, then a good level path most of the way above Boaventura – except for those extremely narrow ledges over sheer drops. Superb subtropical vegetation and views.
How to get there: You can reach Boaventura by bus from Funchal, but, as they don't run that frequently, it would be difficult to do the walk and return in a day. Instead, hire a taxi for the day for "drop off and pick up". Or arrange a hire car with someone to collect you at the finish. An organised tour would also be a good option for this longer, awkward destination.
Refreshments: Take pre-packed drinks and food.

❽ Pico das Pedras National Park

A choice of two circular walks – one relatively easy, one less so – through the beautiful **Pico das Pedras National Park** in northeast Madeira.

Both hikes start in the village of **Santana**, famous for its curious triangular thatched cottages (many now used as cow sheds) whose roofs almost touch the ground. Make for the southeastern outskirts of town where the walks begin with a 5-km (3-mile) climb up

a signposted stony track into the park, and then along an even narrower lane leading to the tiny government holiday resort of **Queimadas**. Alternatively, of course, you can drive to Queimadas and start from there.

Along the *levada*

From Queimadas' government rest-house, the Levada do Caldeirão Verde ("Green Cauldron") beckons. There are, however, two signposts: one marked Caldeirão Verde, the other for the hamlet of Pico das Pedras; we shall start with the latter, shorter route. Initially, the *levada*-path takes you through lush natural forest thick with ferns and lilies to a tranquil picnic-site, with stone tables set by a tumbling waterfall. Walk on for some 20 minutes to reach a small cave, which gives a modicum of shade if you want to stop for a snack.

From here the route heads downhill. The *levada,* meanwhile, keeps disappearing underground, forcing you to play hide-and-seek in order to keep to the path, until **Pico das Pedras** hamlet comes into view. There's not much to the place apart from a few Swiss-style bungalows built for walkers, a small riding school and a snack-bar; Santana is an easy downhill walk from here.

The alternative route to the **Caldeirão do Inferno** ("Hell's Cauldron") via Caldeirão Verde is longer and more strenuous, but spectacular. Follow the *levada* further west for 6.5 km (4 miles) across gorges and through one long and one shorter tunnel (torches advised) until you reach the "green cauldron" itself, a mossy pool fed by a 300-metre high (980-ft) waterfall.

Now keep to the path for another half-an-hour – past outstanding forest-and-mountain views – before climbing up some steps to join the Levada do Pico Ruivo. It's another half-hour hike (through several more tunnels) down to the

TIP

It is worth visiting Queimadas just for the idyllic park that surrounds the government rest-house: in spring, the azaleas and rhododendrons are particulary fine.

BELOW: free-range grazing is a rare sight on Madeira.

ottom of the Caldeirão do Inferno, a dramatic ravine which in olden times so pooked local shepherds that they refused to enter it, claiming it was the haunt f evil spirits. From here, retrace your steps back to Queimadas.

Map
on pages
212–13

tepping out

ength of walk: 5 km (3 miles), 2 hours up from Santana to Queimadas, then 8 km 5 miles) to Pico das Pedras village and downhill to Santana (2 hours). Queimadas o Caldeirão do Inferno and back takes 16 km (10 miles) and 4 to 6 hours.
onditions: The first walk is easy when the paths are dry and sun-baked; far nore difficult when wet. The longer alternative is altogether much more exact-ng, vertiginous and difficult to follow, especially in wet weather and particu-rly where the *levada* disappears underground.
low to get there: By bus or taxi to Santana; or by taxi as far as the government est-house at Queimadas
Refreshments: For the first walk, take drinks and nibbles; there are various ood spots to stop for a picnic. Santana has eateries while Pico das Pedras has ranch-style snack bar next to the riding school. For the alternative, pack drinks nd good rucksack sustenance. You will need it.

Thatched shelter built in the distinctive Santana style.

⯁ Lombo do Mouro to Bica da Cana

A challenging linear hike up to Madeira's central plateau, along *levadas* and *veradas* surrounded by dramatic peaks.
   The walk begins just off the main road which runs north from Ribeira Brava to ão Vicente. From the top of the **Encumeada Pass**, take the 204 leading south-vest to **Lombo do Mouro** and pick up the *levada* path just across the road from

BELOW: view from the top of the Encumeada Pass.

TIP

Watch out for falling rocks when you're out hiking in these mountains; they tend to tumble down the slopes after heavy rain.

BELOW:
grand views near Lombo do Mouro.

the parking area which overlooks the forest house here. At first the *levada* run along a high bank just above the main road, but that soon dips out of sight belov a tangled profusion of brambles and broom, wild roses and foxgloves, strawber ries, oregano and mint. A ten-minute climb is rewarded with heady mountain views east across to **Pico Grande** and Madeira's highest mountain, **Pico Ruivo**

Watch your feet and have your waterproofs handy – it gets wetter and more slippery as waterfalls spit and tumble down a cliff by the side of the path. Step take you up to an old *verada*, the original road bisecting the island from north to south, still used by local villagers to gather firewood for cooking and heating

A tricky climb

The locals must be blessed with a good head for heights, because the next bit i hairy – steep, with no protection, and a bottomless sheer drop on the left in front of high peaks rising out of the mist. Luckily, the path is wide enough to allow you to keep safely to the right.

A *levada* emerges from on high just before a clearing-cum-lookout point at th rock of **Pináculo**, with huge views over the north coast. Head along it; it i level for a while, but the climb up to **Paúl da Serra** plateau (following signs fo Bica da Cana) is more difficult. The rocky, vertiginous, slippery path (poorly repaired in parts) is negotiable with care – but a last push to the top is rewarded with a delightful change of scenery, the grassy tops of the surrounding volcano craters sprinkled with ferns and flowers, and the air filled with bird sounds Buzzards swoop, on the lookout for rabbits.

It is worth clambering up the extra 450 metres (1,500 ft) from here to the obser vation point at the top of **Bica da Cana** (1,620 metres, or 5,000 ft); your rewar

grand mountain views not only of Pico Ruivo and **Pico do Arieiro** a little urther south, but also right across the island to the north coast and **São Vicente**.

At weekends, the large picnic area next to the forest house at Bica da Cana is ll of Madeirans escaping Funchal's pollution, seemingly bringing most of eir cooking utensils with them. They will have driven up here by car along the ain 204 highway that crosses Paúl da Serra plateau. You are allowed to feel a it smug at having walked up instead – before remembering that your car is arked all the way down the road at Lombo do Mouro.

Map on pages 212–13

tepping out

ength of walk: 9 km (6 miles) to the plateau, three hours, 15 minutes.
onditions: Testing but glorious. Uphill most of the way, but the paths are uite good. A steep 15-minute clamber at the end up to the plateau. Precipitous n parts, with nothing to cling on to. Boots and wet wear recommended.
low to get there: Hire a taxi to drop you off and pick you up. If you don't mind etracing your steps, hire cars can be left on the verge overlooking the forest ouse at Lombo do Mouro. Plenty of organised tours also cover this route.
efreshments: Take water and a snack to enjoy at the lookout point at Pináculo. Aost organised tours include a meal at the Bico da Cana picnic spot. Or pack bit of skewered beef and a bay laurel leaf in your rucksack; you may well find friendly Madeiran willing to grill them for you on the family barbecue.

❿ Pico do Arieiro to Pico Ruivo and Archada do Teixeira

A tough but thrilling linear walk between Madeira's highest mountains and beyond, offering glorious views across the breadth of the island.

BELOW: on top of the world: observation-point, Pico Arieiro.

Map on pages 212–3

The journey begins with an hour-long drive which is spectacular in itself – up into the mountains along the 103 from Funchal, through the vast protected area of the **Parque Ecologico do Funchal**. A left turn along the 202 twists you up to the **Pico do Ariero**, where the walk begins. Both the vegetation and the air thin out considerably as you drive, offering dramatic glimpses of mist-shrouded peaks; there are superb views down to the north coast, too.

From Ariero, the line of the hiking trail (signposted 'Pico Ruivo') you can see winding through the mountains seems benign enough, but it masks some difficult ups and downs over stone steps and through ravines and tunnels, with many drops unprotected by railings. However, the first lookout is only 15 minutes' striding time away, offering good views of the jagged ridge of **Pico do Torres** Madeira's second-highest mountain at 1,851 metres (6,000 ft).

To the highest peak

Clear weather is essential if you want to pick put Funchal and **Pico Ruivo** (the island's highest peak at 1,862 metres, or 6,100 ft) from a second viewpoint reached after some 20 minutes including a steep 10-minute climb.

The needle-shaped **Pico do Gato** comes into view after another 50 minutes' climb, beyond the walk's first tunnel. Make sure you don't deviate from the most well-used path along here; landslides are common, and you should turn back if you come across wayside railings which have been badly damaged.

Three more tunnels now follow in quick succession, bringing you out amidst grass and broom for exceptional views west towards **Pico Grande** and the **Paúl de Serra** plateau beyond.

Another hour and twenty minutes' hiking brings you through the last tunnel to a rest-house, situated just below the mighty Ruivo. Time for a decision: will you head downhill along the fenced goat path to the taxi point at the **Achada do Teixeira** rest-house (25 minutes), where your transport home awaits – or will you continue up for 5 more minutes to conquer the summit of Madeira's highest mountain first?

Stepping out

Length of walk: 7 km (4 miles), and about three-and-a-half hours.

Conditions: Tough, with very serious risk of vertigo along much of the route. Steep climbs (over 450 metres, or 1,500 ft), and plunging descents. Boots are essential, plus sunhat and sunblock, a jumper (it can get pretty cold up here), rainwear and a torch. Check the weather conditions before you set out, and make sure you tell someone where you're going and what time you expect to return back to base. These are serious mountains, after all.

How to get there: By taxi or hire car to Pico do Aneiro. There's no road to Pico Ruivo, so you must arrange a pick-up at Achada do Teixeira,

Refreshments: Pack a rucksack with nourishing drinks and snacks, for comfort as much as sustenance. There is a small hotel, café and gift shop just below the summit at Arieiro, where you can stock up and a seasonal café at the base of Ruivo.

BELOW: you may spot the lovely king protea on the lower mountain-slopes.
RIGHT: exploring Madeira's highest mountains.

PORTO SANTO

*There's not much to see on Madeira's little neighbour,
the only other inhabited island in the entire archipelago,
but it does have one major asset – a long, golden, sandy beach*

Map on page 236

Funchal

Visitors who come to Porto Santo expecting a holiday full of action and high life will inevitably be disappointed. For most of the year, it is far too quiet. But that is precisely why many people do come here: for peace, tranquillity and a total escape from the pressures of the modern world. Throw in 8 km (5 miles) of golden sand, lapped by the turquoise waters of the Atlantic Ocean, and you have the perfect desert island.

Many of Porto Santo's summer visitors are Madeirans, come to enjoy the tropical paradise on their doorstep. They are joined in August – the Portuguese holiday month – by scores of Lisbonites, refugees from the hot capital hell-bent on escaping to Porto Santo's more equable climes. For one month, in high summer, Porto Santo is packed with visitors soaking up the sun by day, and dancing in the discos all night. Then September comes, and the tiny island goes back to its slumbers again.

Rather unfairly, the people of Madeira consider their near-neighbours to be slow and workshy. This supposed lethargy serves as a target for many Madeiran anecdotes and jokes. It is true that the inhabitants can often be seen sitting at street corners doing nothing for hours on end, languidly brushing away the flies and watching the world go by – but what else is there to do on a tiny island in the middle of the Atlantic, measuring just 10 km (6 miles) in length and 4 km (2½ miles) across?

Some people are driven to visions by the lack of other distractions. In the 16th century, a local farmer and his niece declared themselves to be *profetas* – prophets – able to work miracles and see into a person's soul. They also claimed the ability to itemise every sin you had ever committed, not foreseeing the official disapproval that inevitably followed: a magistrate was swiftly despatched to the island to arrest the fanatical *profetas,* and restore the island to the true path of orthodox Catholicism.

This small event earned locals the nickname "*profetas*", enterprisingly revived some years ago by a pop group that entertains in one of the seafront hotels.

A low profile

Precious little else has changed on the island in the past 600 years. Although Porto Santo was the first island in the Madeiran archipelago to be discovered, it was soon neglected in favour of its larger, more fertile and hospitable neighbour.

One early British traveller, a certain T. Edward Bowdich, who visited in the autumn of 1823, was astonished by its lack of development: "During the three days I resided there I could never discover that the governor had more than one king's servant under his command... he (distinguished by being clothed in

PRECEDING PAGES: dolphins play off Porto Santo. **LEFT:** the Ilhéu de Baixo from Ponta da Calheta. **BELOW:** the pace is relaxed in sleepy Vila Baleira.

tattered remnants of various uniforms) opened the gates, hoisted the flag, beat the drum at sunrise and sunset, swept the yard, helped in the kitchen, and waited at table when the governor had company."

Bowdich went on to describe the governor's humble home: "[It] looked like that of the lawyer in a small village in England; it was very neat, of one storey, and contained but two sitting-rooms... and a row of cannons, some of which had fallen from their carriages, whilst the others, from their monstrous touch-holes and rusty condition, were emblems of peace rather than war, and fit subjects for a society of antiquaries."

Not brown, but gilded

The climate here is dry and stable (a rain-shower in winter can turn the island a rich green colour overnight), but there is little summer rain, and the landscape is mostly a patchwork of yellows, ochres and browns. Older travel guides described Porto Santo as the "brown island", by contrast with Madeira's "green".

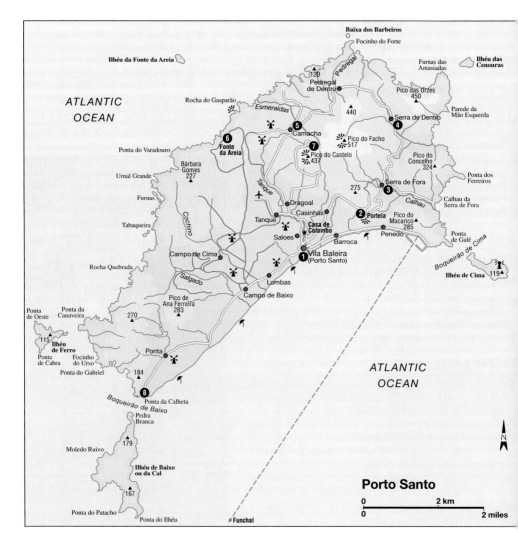

Porto Santo

0   2 km
0   2 miles

Nowadays, though, the local tourist office, with a keen ear for more saleable epithets, has dubbed it the Ilha Dourada – the gilded (or sunkissed) island.

Maps:
Area 236
City 238

Not much remains of the island's indigenous vegetation. Early settlers came here to exploit the sap of the legendary Dragon Tree, which was used to make dyestuffs. Juniper also thrived, along with tree heather – although now you will have to search hard for these plants. Agricultural production on the island is also limited. The soil is not very fertile and produces meagre crops of melons, figs and pumpkins in fields sheltered by dry-stone walls. In recent years, attempts have been made to re-introduce trees, especially cedars and Aleppo pines, which are able to withstand prolonged periods of drought.

More successful are the grapes that grow along the south coast. Most of these are cultivated for eating but a small part of the harvest is used to produce *Vinho do Porto Santo*, a heavy red wine with a distinctive reddish-brown colour. It has a pleasant taste and tempts many first-time samplers to drink a glass too many. The wine is available in small quantities of varying quality and can be sampled in local bars and restaurants.

Porto Santo's heavy red wine goes down surprisingly easily.

Tourist potential

Local politicians have made bold plans for the island's future development. A sewage works has already been completed, while alternative sources of energy, in the form of wind-powered generators, are beginning to compete with traditional windmills.

As for tourism, to date there are some 800 beds available to visitors, and many more are planned (several new hotels are currently being built). There is an equestrian centre, and a proposal for a golf course, too. Hotel blocks lining the beach offer accommodation within sight and sound of the sea, and many make an effort to keep their guests busy with cycles for hire, pedaloes, scuba-diving, boat trips and windsurfing facilities.

BELOW: Vila Baleira's simple parish church

To take advantage of all this, you must, of course, first get to the island: the 15-minute flight from Madeira is relatively expensive, but many will find it preferable to the alternative, which is a slow journey by catamaran or ferry across 37 km (23 miles) of choppy water. Visitors are usually very grateful to reach **Vila Baleira ❶** after being tossed about for up to three hours on the rough Atlantic waves.

Vila Baleira can easily be reached on foot from the harbour, although there are taxis and a public bus available. A more romantic way of travelling is by horse and carriage, also to be found in the settlement around the harbour (there's a handful of houses at the beach where you land, but it's not really big enough even to be called a village).

There are only a few buildings of interest in Vila Baleira, all close to **Largo do Pelourinho ❹**, the palm-lined square which fronts the Town Hall. One of the most interesting buildings is the restored parish church – **Nossa Senhora da Piedade ❸** – with its *azulejo*-tile pictures and its gleaming white walls. On the southern side of the church are the remains of the island's original Gothic chapel, one of the first places of worship to be built in the archipelago.

Did the great explorer really live in Porto Santo's Casa de Colombo?

Next to the church a narrow street leads to the **Casa de Colombo** (the "House of Columbus") **C**. This recently restored house is well worth a visit, but there is no hard-and-fast evidence to support the idea that Columbus actually lived in this house during his sojourn on the island.

So many theories and so many stories surround Columbus that you are entitled to feel confused. Some say he never came near Madeira or Porto Santo, while others claim that Porto Santo inspired his dream to explore the seas beyond the horizon: his adventurous spirit was fascinated by the strange tropical seeds and fruits that he found washed up on the island's shores *(see page 29)* and made him determined to find out whether they had drifted here eastwards from the fabled Spice Islands. Whatever the truth, studying the displays here and in the small Columbus library is one way of keeping your mind active if you feel the need for some mental exercise during your stay.

Getting around the island

After immersing yourself in the island's history, take a well-earned break at one of the cafés in the main square while you plan your next move.

If you'd like to book a boat trip around the island, there are travel agencies in the street running parallel to the beach (it can hardly be called a promenade). For those who wish to explore without joining an organised tour, there are two firms where you can hire cars: **Moinho Rent-a-Car** (13, Rua Dr Nuno Silvestre Teixeira) and **Atlantico** (Avenida Vieira e Castro). The alternatives are to travel by public bus, by taxi or – for the more adventurous – to rent a bicycle.

If you take a boat-trip, you will see some of the *ilhéus* – offshore islands – interesting because of their fantastical grottoes and weird rock formations.

BELOW: catching up on the gossip in Vila Baleira's main square.

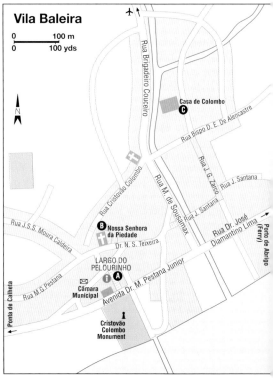

Vila Baleira

Many have poetic names such as the *Pedra do Sol* (Rock of the Sun) on *Ilhéu de Fora*, or the *Aranjas* (Oranges), which are orange-shaped calcareous formations on the *Ilhéu de Cima*.

The standard island tour offered by taxi drivers and tour operators takes you through **Portela ❷** and **Serra de Fora ❸**, where sulphurous yellow and ochre are the dominant colours, to **Serra de Dentro ❹**, the part of the island with the most water, and hence formerly its agricultural centre. The terraced hillsides here bear sad witness to the islanders' attempts to make a meagre living from the arid soil; nowadays the hillsides are deserted, and serve only as subjects for photographers. Apart from a few grazing cattle, goats and sheep, the area is completely uninhabited and shrouded in an almost eerie silence – although the ruined, abandoned farmhouses do provide an opportunity to study the characteristic architecture of the island.

As you'll notice, various attempts are being made to store rain water in **reservoirs** in some of the smaller eroded valleys. Together with reafforestation, these measures are intended to increase the fertility and soil stability of the island, and consequently improve the chances for agriculture.

Panoramic views

From here the tour continues to **Camacha ❺**, a tiny hamlet with two main claims to fame: the delicious barbecued chicken sold in local restaurants, and a picturesque traditional windmill, still in working order, although it has not actually been used since 1993.

Drinking the cold, mineral-rich spring water at **Fonte da Areia ❻** is said to guarantee eternal youth. The water bubbles out of the surrounding sandstone

Maps:
Area 236
City 238

Porto Santo's first governor, Bartolomeu Perestrelo, made the mistake of introducing rabbits to the island – within a few years the already sparse vegetation had been nibbled almost bare.

BELOW: the island's most treasured asset is its long sandy beach.

rocks, which wind and rain have eroded into bizarre natural sculptures. It's well worth making a day trip here with a picnic-basket (take the bus to Camacha and then walk). A small café-bar with covered benches and chairs provides refreshments and views of the rugged north coast, while a footpath leads down to the sea – a wonderful spot to fish, or just relax and enjoy the sound of the waves.

Our next stop is **Pico do Castelo** ❼, where, at an altitude of 438 metres (1,440 ft), you get a superb view of the whole island; rusty old cannons are all that's left of the fort that once stood here to protect the islanders from pirate attacks. You also get a close-up view of the most developed part of the island's infrastructure – the airport, whose 3,000 metre-long (9,850-ft) runway slices neatly north to south right down Porto Santo's middle.

The modern airport terminal looks too large for its purpose, and is still clearly waiting for the charter planes that local people hope will one day bring tourists in their thousands. For now, the airport is mainly used by the smaller planes which shuttle several times a day between Madeira and the island.

Heading east

The final stage of our tour takes you to **Pico das Flores** in the east, passing **Campo de Cima** and **Campo de Baixo** as well as a few windmills and perhaps the occasional donkey, once the island's principal form of transport. Pico das Flores offers sweeping views across the island from east to west. From here you can see the results of Porto Santo's reafforestation project, and, on a clear day, the outline of Madeira in the distance.

Eventually you arrive at Porto Santo's easternmost point – **Ponta da Calheta** ❽ – where the long, sandy beach breaks up into small bays, dominated

TIP

Fish is a good bet on Porto Santo. Look out for *fragateira* on local menus – a spicy fish stew made with octopus, prawns, *espada*, potatoes , onions and tomatoes.

BELOW: island windmills are an increasingly rare sight today.

by rocky outcrops; these provide shelter from the wind, making this a good choice for sunbathers. Two fish restaurants sit invitingly on the beach here; the menus are simple but the location is excellent. Come for lunch or an evening meal when you can relax and watch the sunset and gaze across to the **Ilhéu de Baixo**.

The island's other mountain peaks are ideal for exploring on foot. The highest is **Pico do Facho** (517 metres/1,696 ft), the "Peak of the Torch" – so-called because warning beacons were once lit here to alert islanders of impending attack by pirates.

Taking the cure

If all this sightseeing is too energetic for you, consider indulging in a little alternative therapy. Forget mud packs, ice-cold cucumber or aromatic oils – on Porto Santo the thing to do is to bury yourself from head to toe in sand. Just find a spot on the beach, dig a hollow, lie in it and ask an obliging friend to do the rest. Then wait patiently for the sands to work their magic. The people of Porto Santo are very proud of the healing powers attributed to their sand, and more than a few visitors can vouch for the fact that skin complaints, aggravated by Madeira's humid climate, have made a speedy recovery on coming here. Stomach, liver and intestinal problems are also said to benefit from drinking the island's natural spring water.

Perhaps that is where Porto Santo's real future lies – as a spa resort on the extreme western fringe of Europe. Perhaps one day this unspoilt holiday island will become a fully developed tourist resort; perhaps not. Just in case, anyone who values peace and quiet while on holiday would be wise to get to Porto Santo while it lasts. ❑

Map on page 236

Prickly pear thrives on Porto Santo, which lacks the lushness of Madeira.

BELOW: this dry island yields a surprisingly rich harvest.

THE ILHAS DESERTAS

*Separated from Madeira by a deep, drowned valley, and
populated only by goats, birds and seals,
these islands are steeped in legend*

Map on page 246

The Ilhas Desertas – the Desert Isles – lie southeast of Madeira, only 16 km (10 miles) away from Funchal. They are the long flat-topped islands that sit tantalisingly close on the horizon, visible most of the time from your hotel window or balcony. Sometimes they seem close enough to touch – an optical illusion that Madeirans have come to recognise as a warning of bad weather to come; the low air pressure combined with the southwesterly wind, which causes this illusion of proximity, is sure to bring rain and stormy seas.

The islands possess many moods. As one early traveller, W. H. Koebel, noted, "viewed from the mountain tops, their glamour is of an elusive order... they would seem to hang high aloft, poised between sea and sky." As the picture postcards testify, they are at their most beautiful in the late afternoon, when the last rays of the setting sun bathe them in colours ranging from grey-blue to pink and mother-of-pearl. And although they are uninhabited, the three islands – **Ilhéu Chão ❶**, which is flat and round like a cake, **Deserta Grande ❷** and **Búgio ❸** – have always been the subject of colourful legends.

The Desertas may look inviting enough but, unlike green and fertile Madeira, these islands are barren and inhospitable – to humans, that is (one creature that does feel very much at home here is the highly poisonous black wolf spider, *Lycosa ingens* – the largest in the archipelago). The lack of soil and fresh water means that the meagre vegetation struggles to survive, and the islands have stubbornly resisted all human attempts at colonisation. A community of goatherds was established in the 16th century, and although they managed successfully to defend their homeland against 80 British pirates in 1564, wild goats are the only legacy of their doomed attempt to settle these windswept and sun-scorched rocks.

Barren lands

Consequently, the Desertas' role in European history is distinctly limited. The native *oseille* lichen was at one time much in demand because a dye derived from it was highly prized in England and Flanders. At the turn of the century, Prince Albert of Monaco was one of several sportsmen who visited the region to shoot rabbits and wild goats. But perhaps the high point in the islands' history occurred in World War I, when a German submarine made use of their waters as a hiding place before emerging to torpedo the French battleship *Surprise*.

Geologically, the Ilhas Desertas are a continuation of Madeira's **Ponta de São Lourenço**, separated by a channel 50 metres (165 ft) or so deep. Like Madeira's southwesterly tip, the islands rise sheer from the sea, their towering orange and brown cliffs dashed by

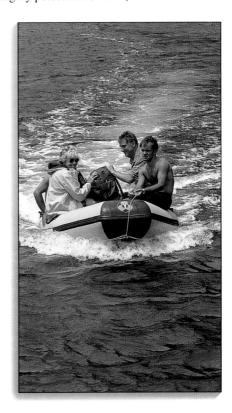

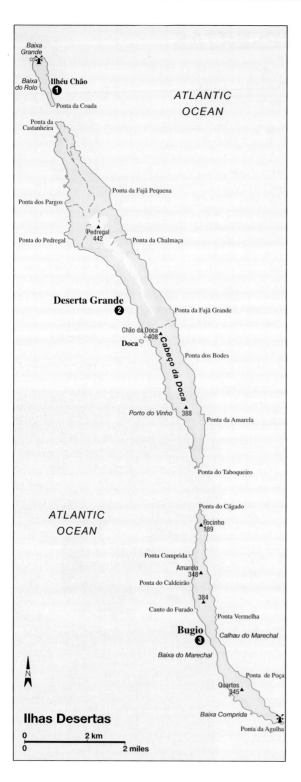

Ilhas Desertas

0 — 2 km

0 — 2 miles

rolling waves. There is nothing else here apart from the caves and weird rock formations and an endless rust-brown wilderness. There are few landing spots, but the narrow coves do support a small colony of monk seals *(Monachus monachus)* who spend most of their life at sea, returning to land only to give birth. They leave their pups during the day, returning nightly to feed them, until the pups are old enough to join their parents at sea.

The pups are an easy prey for fishermen who cull them to prevent depletion of their fish stocks. Officially they are a protected species and it is illegal to interfere with them, but old habits die hard. In an attempt to stop the slaughter, a biological observation station was set up on the islands in 1988. Its tasks include keeping a count of the pairs of monk seals and their young and monitoring the biological and ecological balance of the Desertas. The station is manned by two biologists, who work 14-day shifts.

Visiting the isles

In Funchal's marina, you'll see various tour operators advertising boat-trips to the Desertas. Excursions like these are a good opportunity to experience the eerie quality of these islands, which have remained unchanged for so many thousands of years. Landing is not permitted unless you have a licence (and these are only granted to *bona fide* scientific researchers), but boats are allowed within 10 metres (30 ft) of the shoreline. Sport fishing is also allowed in the waters around the Desertas, providing that it is within the context of day excursions.

Most of those who make the journey, however, are interested in observing wildlife rather than catching fish. Basking turtles, seals and dolphins can sometimes be seen, but the big attraction is the birdlife. The Desertas are a haven for birds, many of which prefer these uninhabited islands as a breeding spot to the busier haunts of man. Indigenous to the islands is the soft-plumaged petrel *(Pterodroma mollis deserta)*, and, if the weather is sufficiently still, you may be fortunate enough to hear the curious laughing call of the Atlantic shearwater.

Map on page 246

Remote neighbours

Even more remote are the **Ilhas Selvagens** (the Wild Islands), a tiny group of uninhabited rocky islets consisting of **Selvagem Grande** (the main island at 2.46 sq. km/0.95 sq. miles) and **Selvagem Pequena** (0.16 sq. km/0.23 sq. miles). Although geographically they are closer to the Canary Islands (they're just 165 km/103 miles north of Tenerife), they are nevertheless counted as part of the Madeiran archipelago and fall under the political control of the regional government. The Portuguese sailors who first claimed these islets and reefs for the Crown may not have realised this, but they were effectively extending Portuguese territorial waters to take in the 285 km (177 miles) of open sea that separate the Selvagens from Madeira.

Trips to visit the Ilhas Desertas can be booked at the marina in Funchal.

It was only in 1971 that this distant Portuguese outpost ceased to be the private property of the Madeiran banking family, Rocha Machado. Since 1976 sentries have been permanently stationed here, and relieved every two weeks. Biology students and scientists are occasionally granted permission to visit in order to study the rich flora and fauna – Günther Maul, founder of Funchal's natural science museum (the Museu Municipal; *see page 155*) carried out the first comprehensive survey of the island's wildlife as recently as 1963. The results of his work can be seen in the museum; happily, such was the wealth of flora and fauna that he discovered, that the government was persuaded to declare the islands a nature reserve.

BELOW: the wild Desertas are a haven for seabirds.

Just like the Desertas, the Selvagens are breeding grounds for shearwaters, a bird whose young once graced the dining tables of Madeiran and Canarian fishermen. Some 20,000 birds were caught here every year and salted and dried on the island before being taken back to Madeira. Now the birds have no predators, and the spectacular indigenous fauna of the "wild islands" has started to flourish again.

Science has so far failed, however, to resolve one of the region's enduring mysteries. Persistent legend has it that the legendary Captain Kidd buried his considerable pile of looted treasure somewhere on the Desertas. Many attempts have been made to find the hoard. Between 1848 and 1851 the English corvette *Rattler* was dispatched to the islands no less than four times with the blessing of the British Crown. Its particular mission was to locate the treasure of Lima Cathedral, which, if the reports of an escaped mariner were to be believed, the famous pirate had hidden here.

In the early 1920s the British Antarctic explorer Sir Ernest Shackleton (1874–1922) intended to continue the search on his way back from the South Pole, but he died there, taking the secret of the sunken treasure and all information concerning its whereabouts to his icy grave. The last serious expedition to find the treasure was mounted in the 1950s but, like all previous attempts, this was doomed to failure. To this day, the treasure waits to be found. ❏

INSIGHT GUIDES

Travel Tips

Insight FlexiMaps

Maps in Insight Guides are tailored to complement the text. But when you're on the road you sometimes need the big picture that only a large-scale map can provide. This new range of durable Insight Fleximaps has been designed to meet just that need.

Detailed, clear cartography
makes the comprehensive route and city maps easy to follow, highlights all the major tourist sites and provides valuable motoring information plus a full index.

Informative and easy to use
with additional text and photographs covering a destination's top 10 essential sites, plus useful addresses, facts about the destination and handy tips on getting around.

Laminated finish
allows you to mark your route on the map using a non-permanent marker pen, and wipe it off. It makes the maps more durable and easier to fold than traditional maps.

The world's most popular destinations
are covered by the 125 titles in the series – and new destinations are being added all the time. They include Alaska, Amsterdam, Bangkok, Barbados, Beijing, Brussels, Dallas/Fort Worth, Florence, Hong Kong, Ireland, Madrid, New York, Orlando, Peru, Prague, Rio, Rome, San Francisco, Sydney, Thailand, Turkey, Venice, and Vienna.

※ INSIGHT GUIDES
The world's largest collection of visual travel guides

CONTENTS

Getting Acquainted

The Place

Area: 741 sq km (286 sq miles)
57 km long/22 km wide
Capital: Funchal
Population: Approximately 260,000
inhabitants of which 120,000 live
in Funchal. The island of Madeira is
densely populated, with 440 people
per sq km. Porto Santo, however,
has only 103 people per sq km.

The Desertas (three islands) and
the Selvagens (two islands and a
series of tiny islets) are uninhabited
but for the scientists who staff the
various biological observation
stations here.
Language: Portuguese
Religion: Catholic
Time Zone: Central European Time
(CET), which is one hour ahead of
Greenwich Mean Time (GMT) in
winter, two hours ahead in summer.
Currency: The euro (written €).
Weights and Measures: Metric
Electricity: 220 volts, two-pin
plugs. During heavy winter rainfalls
and thunderstorms blackouts are
not unknown, while during the summer the water supply may occasionally be cut off. Fortunately, however,
all good hotels have reserve tanks
and generators at their disposal.
National flower: the Bird of
Paradise flower *(Strelitzia reginae)*.
International dialling code:
351 291 (no area code required).
Location: 700 km (435 miles) west
of the North African coast of
Morocco. 1,000 km (620 miles)
from Lisbon (1½ hr flight).

Geography

The archipelago has volcanic
origins. Madeira is actually the tip
of an enormous mountain range,
rising up from 4,000 metres
(13,100 ft) beneath the sea. The
total land area of the entire
archipelago is some 795.98 sq km
(303.58 sq miles), with the
geographical characteristics of each
island quite distinct from one
another. Mountainous and emerald-
green Madeira, whose highest
point, Pico Ruivo, is 1,861 metres
(6,100 ft) above sea-level, provides
a sharp contrast to the gently
rolling, almost barren landscape
of her neighbours. Porto Santo's
largest mountain, Pico do Facho,
for instance, is a mere 517 metres
(1,700 ft) high.

On Madeira – the main island –
there are no golden sandy beaches,
and very few black ones, either.
Almost everywhere, the coastline is
characterised by steep cliffs which
provide space in only a few areas
for small fishing ports. All bar one
of the tiny beaches are composed
of black basalt scree; only the
Prainha ("Little Beach") by the
Ponta de São Lourenço has dark
sand composed of fine lava ash.
However, fine golden sand can be
found in abundance along Porto
Santo's splendid 8-km (5-mile)
stretch of beach.

Climate

The climate on Madeira is
consistent and warm; the annual
average temperature varies
between 16–22°C (61–72°F),
with water temperatures between
16–20°C (61–68°F). Nevertheless,
the image of the main island as a
place of "eternal springtime" is
misleading. It rains a lot, particularly
from October to May, and it is rare
during the summer months to find
days without any cloud at all.

If you're looking for sunshine,
your best bet is to base yourself in
the capital. The humidity here is
bearable; at other places on the
main island it often reaches over
80 percent. The downside is that
the island's traffic pollution is at
its highest in Funchal.

Various micro-climates are
distinguishable on Madeira. A semi-
arid trade wind climate reigns along
the southern coast and on Porto
Santo, bringing a higher number
of annual sunshine hours.
Theoretically, you can expect
holiday weather the whole year
round here, although of course you
can never be 100 percent sure of
what you will encounter.

Downpours during September,
October, March and April can be
quite drenching, but generally do
not last very long. Cloudy days
are most common in June when
the *capacete* ("peaked cap") of
cloud covers the coast in the
morning and retreats in the late
afternoon. In high summer, the
leste, a dry wind from North Africa,
can push the temperature up into
the 90s.

Temperature/Rainfall

MONTH	RAIN (mm/ins)	TEMP (°C/°F)
January	100/4	18/64
February	90/3.5	19/66
March	70/2.7	20/68
April	45/1.7	21/70
May	25/0.9	22/72
June	10/0.4	24/75
July	2/0.08	25/77
August	3/0.12	26/79
September	25/0.9	25/77
October	75/3	24/72
November	105/4.1	22/72
December	75/3	19/66

Average yearly statistics for
Madeira (Funchal).

Economy

Exports include bananas, flowers,
embroidery, basketry and Madeira
wine, but Madeira's economy is to a
large degree dependent on tourism.
Currently 500,000 tourists visit the
archipelago annually.

Vegetables, wine grapes,
bananas, willow trees and sugar
cane are cultivated on the islands.
Subtropical fruits – including
passion fruit, mangoes and custard
apple – thrive, but aren't exported.
Fish and livestock are also destined
for domestic consumption.

Approximately 12.5 percent of the population is involved in agriculture, 28.5 percent in industry and 59 percent in services.

The minimum income is a low €275 per month. Prices are generally higher than in Portugal, and debts owed to the mainland are substantial.

Despite the revolution in 1974, Madeira has still not really been able to throw off the bonds of its old feudal structure.

Government

The Madeiran islands are collectively known as the *Regiao Autónoma da Madeira* (the Autonomous Region of Madeira). The regional parliament, composed of 59 elected members, has the power to make decisions regarding legislative issues which concern the islands, along with the regional budget. In matters of foreign policy and economics, however, Madeira is subject to decisions made by the Portuguese parliament in Lisbon.

The governing party is the PSD, the Social-Democratic Party. The Madeiran head of state is currently Dr Alberto João Jardim, a charismatic figure who has assured his party's victory since 1976; the PSD regularly polls around 70 percent of the electorate. The main opposition groups are the PS (socialist) party, the right-wing CDS, (Conservative) party and the UDP (Communist) party.

The Portuguese central government is represented on Madeira by a minister of the Republic; the regional government also dispatches five parliamentary representatives to Lisbon. On Porto Santo the regional government is represented by a single delegate.

Vilas (small towns) have their own *conselhos* or town councils, but their authority is limited, considering their geographical area. Porto Santo has its own council. Local politics can be quite heated where political factions hostile to the government, like the PS or the Communist Party, dominate these secondary governmental organs.

Planning the Trip

Entry Regulations

Madeira has no visa or health requirements for citizens of EU countries; other nationalities should contact their Portuguese consulate.

Madeira is part of the EU, but has separate duty-free status from Portugal and the rest of the union. Thus – despite the demise of duty-free throughout the rest of the EU – the allowances for duty-free goods are (per person aged over 17):
1 litre of spirits or 2 litres of table wine and 2 litres of sparkling or fortified wine; 75g of perfume; 200 cigarettes, 100 cigarillos, 50 cigars or 250g of tobacco.

Money Matters

Currency
The unit of currency on Madeira is the euro (€), which is divided into 100 cents. There are eight euro coins: 2 and 1 euros, then 50, 20, 10, 5, 2 and 1 cents. There are seven euro notes for 500, 200, 100, 50, 20, 10 and 5 euros.

Changing Money
Shop around for some of the best exchange rates before you go to Madeira – some organisations, including supermarket and retail groups have in-store *bureaux de change* offering better rates even than banks. On Maderia, banks offer the best rates of exchange, followed by hotels and commercial *bureaux de change*.

You will find banks and *bureaux de change* in the area around the Cathedral (Sé), at the main tourist information centre (Avenida Arriaga 18), and at the airport during regular business hours.

Portuguese Consulates

Australia
132, Ocean Street, Edgecliff, Sydney, NSW 2027
Tel: 02-3261844.
Canada
121, Richmond Street West, 7th Floor, Toronto, Ontario, M5H 2K1
Tel: 416-3608260.
New Zealand
85 Ford Street, Auckland
Tel: 309 1454.
United Kingdom
62, Brompton Road, 3rd Floor, London SW3 1BJ
Tel: 0207-581 8722. Visa information: Tel: 0891-600202.
United States
630, 5th Avenue, Suite 655, New York, NY 10111
Tel: 212-2464581.

Credit Cards
Credit cards are accepted in many restaurants and upmarket shops. With an ATM card you can withdraw money from your regular account at the various cash machines to be found on the island.

Banking Hours
Banks all have the same exchange rates. Business hours are Monday to Friday, 8.30am–2.45pm. Some banks are also open on Saturday from 9am–12.30pm.

What to Bring

Clothing
Regardless of when you are travelling, it is seldom extremely hot and never very cold. At any time of year, therefore, it's best to bring an assortment of "between-season" clothes, including waterproofs and a sweater. Summer daytime wear is invariably short sleeves and shorts. A pair of comfortable shoes for the cobbled streets of Funchal will come in handy, while a pair of sturdy hiking boots, rain gear, a sun hat and a torch will be needed is you want to go hiking in the mountains. If you forget anything, don't panic – shops in Funchal are reasonably well stocked.

Health Insurance

If you need to see a doctor while in Madeira, you will need to pay for the consultation. It is therefore recommended that you take out health insurance, so that any costs can be reimbursed on your return – as long as you can present your insurance company with a receipt.

EU citizens should fill in form E111, available from post offices at home, which will give certain health cover within the European Union. Once in Madeira, you should visit the Serviço de Migrantes, Centro de Saúde de Bom Jesús, Rua da Hortas 67 in Funchal (tel: 229161) to have the official form stamped and to obtain a medical insurance booklet valid everywhere in Portugal. The office is open 9.30am–noon and 2pm–4pm Monday to Friday.

In an emergency, head for the nearest Centros de Saúde (Health Centre). These permanently staffed centres are found in every town and are usually well signposted on roads into and around the town.

Getting There

BY AIR

The new runway at Madeira's Santa Caterina airport is now open and the newly extended airport now accepts large aircraft flying direct from North America and Europe. Even so, the high winds and storms that occasionally buffet the island in January and February can result in the airport being closed at short notice, in which case flights are diverted to nearby Porto Santo, to the Canary Islands or even back to Lisbon. In such circumstances, the airline company usually makes temporary accommodation arrangements for passengers.

British Airways (see website, www.british-airways.com) has direct scheduled flights to Funchal from Gatwick, London and also flies to major destinations on the Portuguese mainland.Air Portugal (TAP – www.tap-airportugal.pt) has two flights a week direct from Heathrow and daily flights via Lisbon.

Charter flights are the cheapest

Public Holidays

January New Year's Day (1)
February Shrove Tuesday/Ash Wednesday (dates vary))
March/April Good Friday, Easter Monday (dates vary), Day of the Revolution (25)
May 1 Labour Day (first Monday), Spring Bank Holiday (last Monday)
June Corpus Christi (date varies), National Day (10)
July Regional Day (1)
August Feast of the Assumption (15), Funchal Day (21)
October Republic Day (5)
November All Saints' Day (1)
December Christmas Day (25), Boxing Day (26)

No-one works on Shrove Tuesday, Ash Wednesday or other national holidays, or on Sundays.

and often the quickest flights to Madeira, taking roughly four hours from northern Europe. Some of the largest holiday companies have their own charter airlines and sell-off spare seats. Some of these airlines, like Monarch, Air 2000, Caledonian and Airtours, fly direct to Funchal from Manchester in the north of England, as well as from London airports.

Return fare prices vary considerably depending on the time of year you go. Don't rely on getting a last-minute flight booking or bargain to Funchal because flights are often fully booked.

Consult your travel agent, TV information services or newspapers for more details; the Internet is another good source of information on flight availability and cheap tickets.

One of the best tour agents specialising in Madeira is **Destination Portugal** (www.destination-portugal.co.uk).

BY SHIP

Surprisingly, there are no regular passenger ferry services to Madeira, and the freight-carrying ships from Lisbon no longer take passengers. However, Funchal

harbour is a famous anchorage for cruise ships, some of which may take on passengers from Europe who don't want to stay on board for the entire cruise.

Tourist Information Abroad

Tourist Offices Abroad

Canada
60 Bloor Street West, Suite 1005, Toronto, Ontario, M4W, 3B8.
Tel: 416-921 7376.
Eire
54 Dawson Street, Dublin 2
Tel: (353) 1 670 9133
South Africa
4th floor, Sunnyside Ridge, Sunnyside Drive, Parktown, PO Box 2473 Houghton, 2173 Johannesburg.
Tel: (2711) 484 3487.
United Kingdom
2nd Floor, 22–25a Sackville Street, London, W1X 1DE.
Tel: 020-7494 1441.
United States
590 Fifth Avenue, 4th floor, New York, NY 10036-4785.
Tel: 212-719 3985/719-4091.

Tour Operators

Abercrombie and Kent (Europe)
Sloane Square House, Holbein Place, London SW1W 8NS.
Tel: 0845 070 0610
www.abercrombiekent.co.uk
Avro
Vantage House, 1 Weir Road, London SW19 8UR.
Tel: 020-8715 1910
British Airways Holidays
Astral Towers, Betts Way, London Road, Crawley, West Sussex RH10 2XA.
Tel: 01293-723 100.
Caravela Tours
38/44 Gillingham Street, London SW1V 1HU.
Tel: 020-7630 9223.
www.caravela.co.uk
Castaways
2–10 Cross Road, Tadworth, Surrey KT20 5UJ.
Tel: 01737-812255.
www.castaways.co.uk
Classic Collection Holidays

Wiston House, 1 Wiston Avenue,
Worthing, BN14 7QL.
Tel: 01903-823088.
Cosmos Holidays
Wren Court, London Road,
Bromley, Kent BR1 1DE.
Tel: 020–464 3444.
www.cosmos-holidays.co.uk
CV Travel
43 Cadogan Street,
London SW3 2PR.
Tel: 020-7591 2841.
www.ct.trravel.net
Destination Portugal
Madeira House, 37 Corn Street,
Witney, OX28 6BW.
Tel: 01993-773269.
www.destination-portugal.co.uk
The Magic of Portugal
227 Shepherd's Bush Road,
London W6 7AS
Tel: 020-8741 1181.
Mundi Color Holidays
276 Vauxhall Bridge Road,
London SW1V 1BE.
Tel: 020-7828 6021.
Parkway
Parkway Business Centre 300
Princess Road
Manchester M14 7QU
Tel: 0161 232 6464
www.mytravel.com
Saga Holidays
The Saga Building, Enbrook Park,
Folkestone, Kent CT20 3SE.
Tel: 0800-056 5880.
www.sagaholidays.co.uk
Style Holidays
Coomb House, 7 St Johns Road,
Middlesex TW7 6NA.
Tel: 0870 444 4404
www.style-holidays.co.uk
Sunvil Holidays
Sunvil House, 7/8 Upper Square,
Old Isleworth, Middlesex TW7 7BJ.
Tel: 020-8568 4499.
Thomson Holidays
Greater London House, Hampstead
Road, London NW1 7SD.
Tel: 020-7387 8451.
www.thomsonholidays.com
Traveller's Way
Hewell Lane, Bromsgrove, B60 1LP.
Tel: 01527 578000.
www.travellersway.co.uk
Voyages Jules Verne
21 Dorset Square, London NW1 6QG.
Tel: 020-7616 1000.
www.vjv.com

Practical Tips

Tourist Information Offices in Madeira

The biggest tourist information
offices are in Funchal and on Porto
Santo, but there are information
offices in the smaller centres too:
Funchal (Secretaria Regional do
Turismo) Avenida Arriaga 18
Tel: 229057.
Câmara de Lobos
Lobos Town Hall, Largo da
República.
Tel: 942108.
Caniço
Port d'Oliveira, Caniço de Bairo.
No tel.
Machico
Forte Nossa Senhora do Amparo.
Tel: 962289.
Porto Moniz
Tel: 852 594.
Porto Santo
Avenida Henrique Vieira e Castro.
Tel: 982361.
Ribeira Brava
Forte de São Bento.
Tel: 951675.
Santa Caterina Airport
Tel: 524933.
Santana
Sitio do Serrado.
Tel: 572992.
You can contact the **Portuguese
Chamber of Commerce** (ACIF) at
Edificio D. Henrique, Avenida do
Infante, Funchal (tel: 230137).

Media

Newspapers
There are two local daily papers:
Jornal da Madeira and *Diário de
Notícias do Funchal*, which prints a
daily 4-page news summary in
English, plus listings and weather
reports. All Portuguese newspapers
published on the continent are also

available, as are English
newspapers (with a day's delay).

TV and Radio
The regional TV channel screens
good films in the original language
(with Portuguese subtitles), usually
on Wednesdays, Fridays and
Saturdays. All the upmarket hotels
offer satellite TV.
Local radio stations broadcast
reasonable music programmes as
well as a radio service aimed at
tourists (in various languages –
details are listed in the *Diário de
Notícias do Funchal*). The BBC
World Service can be received on
shortwave at the following times
(GMT):

8am–4.15pm	17705 kHz
8am–8.30pm	15070 kHz
4pm–11.15pm	12095 kHz
6am–9.15am	9410 kHz
6pm–11.15pm	9410 kHz

Postal Services

There are post offices – *correios* –
all over Madeira and Porto Santo,
but as a tourist you'll probably fare
best in the **Main Post Office** on
Funchal's Avenida do Zarco, where
there are English-speaking staff.
Open: weekdays 8.30am–8pm,
Saturdays 9am–12.30pm.
Telephone calls can be made here
until 10 pm, and it also offers telex
and fax services. Two collections –
late mornings and afternoons – are
made from island post boxes.
There is a special philatelic shop
in Funchal's main post office,
selling commemorative Madeiran
stamps. There is also a stamp and
coin shop for serious collectors in
the Marina Shopping Centre, at the
Hotel Zone at the end of the
Avenida Arriega.

Telecommunications

In the opening pages of local
telephone directories you will find a
list of international dialling codes
and emergency numbers.

Long-distance Calls
These are best made with *credifone*
cards rather than from coin-operated

telephones. Telephone booths that accept these cards are marked, and not difficult to find. Phone cards are available at the post office and at many news kiosks as well. Night rates for long-distance calls are effective from midnight until 8am.

Mobile phones

With good roaming international connections, mobile phones can be much cheaper than some local services – be sure to check the rates beforehand though.

Business Hours

Most businesses are open weekdays 9am–1pm and 3pm–7pm, and Saturday from 9am–1pm. Shopping hours on Saturday are extended in the weeks leading up to Christmas. Office hours generally correspond to those elsewhere in Europe.

See *Money Matters (page 251)* for banking hours.

Medical Services

Madeira has plenty of chemists even in the smaller towns, and on Porto Santo as well. There is always one which is open 24 hours a day; the current schedule is posted on every chemist's door. Many medications only available with a prescription in other countries are sold on Madeira over the counter, and pharmacists are good at diagnosing ailments and recommending solutions. English-speaking visitors should head for

Emergency Numbers

HOSPITALS
Hospital Cruz Carvalho
Funchal, Tel: 742111.
Hospital dos Marmeleiros
Funchal. Tel: 782933

Fire, Ambulance and Police:
call 112

For non-emergencies there is a main police station in Funchal, at Largo de São João (tel: 222022).

the centrally-located **Botica Inglesa** pharmacy, on Rua da Câmara Pestana 23–25 (tel: 220158).

Many hotels will arrange for their respective hotel doctors to visit, but this can be quite expensive. Note that consultation fees must normally be paid on the spot. See page 248 for information on health insurance.

In an emergency go directly to Funchal's nearest hospital casualty department (outside Funchal, go to one of the Centros de Saúde, or Health Centres).

For minor aches and pains the **Centro Médico da Sé**, directly next to the cathedral at Rua das Murças 42 (tel: 230127), is recommended as English is spoken.

Dentists

If you need a dentist, Dr J. Sousa is located at:
Infante Shopping Centre
Avenida do Infante
Tel: 231277.
An emergency dental service is also available (tel: 998 998731).

Security & Crime

Madeira is generally a very safe place. There are no really dangerous trouble spots and Funchal is not a threatening city, even late at night. Of course, use your common sense: watch your personal belongings and use a safe if your hotel offers security.

All emergency services can be called by dialling 112. If you have your passport stolen, you should contact your consulate.

Lost property

Polícia de Pierdidos and Achados, Larginho de São João, Funchal.
Tel: 208200.

Consulates

United Kingdom
Avenida de Zarco 2,
9000 Funchal.
Tel: 221221.
The UK Embassy handles queries from Irish, Australian, New Zealand and South African nationals.

United States
Avenida Luís de Camões
Edificio Infante Bloco B,
Apartamento B-4,
4th Floor, 9000 Funchal.
Tel: 743429.

Travelling with Kids

Madeira is better suited to grown-ups than younger children. There is only one tiny sandy beach – at Prainha in the east of the island – and the few places where it is possible to swim in the sea off the rocks can prove dangerous. However, Madeirans are very good with kids, and many of the hotels offer special child-minding and listening-in facilities.

Nor are provisions for babies a problem. In the larger hotels, for example, special balcony safety nets can be provided to protect smaller children.

Activities for youngsters, however, are generally limited to splashing about in the swimming pool. For a good runaround, try either the Santa Caterina Park in Funchal's Avenida do Infante, or the grounds of the Quinta Magnolia in Rue Dr Pita. Madeirans also take their children to play on the open grasslands at Bica da Cana, on the Paul da Serra plateau.

Travellers with Disabilities

With its steep hills and rough tracks, Madeira is not an easy place to negotiate if you have mobility problems. However, the newer hotels have good ramp access and spacious lifts.

Etiquette

Great importance is attached to proper etiquette in Madeira. Among friends the "social kiss" is customary – one on the left cheek, one on the right – but not between men. Generally, men shake hands with one another, particularly in formal business situations.

Hotels each have their own particular etiquette. In Funchal the

Religious Services

English language services for the following denominations can be attended:

Anglican
Holy Trinity,
Rua do Quebra Costas 18
Tel: 220674
11am every Sunday

Baptist
Rua Cidade de Honolulu 9.
6pm every Sunday

Catholic
Igreja da Penha, Rua do Carvalho Araújo (behind the Savoy Hotel).
10.30am every Sunday

emphasis is on being well-dressed; to urban Madeirans, the image you present is very important.

Topless sunbathing is frowned upon on public beaches, but is the norm in hotel swimming pools and is also tolerated at the main Lido Sol complex.

Being invited to somebody's home carries great social significance and usually happens only within the context of the family. Most social contacts take place in cafés; no Madeiran stays happily at home for long.

Tipping

Tipping is not generally expected on Madeira. It is normal, however, to reward good service with a small tip at your hotel, for the porter who sees to your luggage or the person who regularly cleans your room. Wages are not high in Madeira, so every little helps.

Getting Around

On Arrival

Transport from the airport to Funchal takes 25 minutes by taxi, and costs around €20. The bus is very cheap but irregular; the journey into town takes about 45 minutes.

Public Transport

BY BUS

Bus services on Madeira are excellent, clean and inexpensive, though they are designed for the needs of commuters and so do not always run at times that are convenient for visitors. This might mean an early rise because services are relatively infrequent between 10.30am and 3.30pm.

Arming yourself with an up-to-date bus timetable is vital for planning walks and day trips. Copies of the 56-page booklet can be purchased at the tourist office at Avenida Arriada 18.

Essentially, there are two different types of bus: those that operate within Funchal and the suburbs (orange livery, run by Horários do Funchal), and those that provide long-distance services (five different bus operators, all with different bus stops: Madeirans usually refer to "Town Bus No. 12" if it's a local service, and just "No. 12" if it's a long-distance service.

All buses depart from stands strung out along Avenida do Mar, stretching from the São Lourenço palace at the eastern end to the Monte cable car station in the Zona Velha. This is the best place to catch the buses because there are ticket booths with helpful staff right

next to the bus stops. Some bus services pass through the hotel zone, however, so it is worth checking with your hotel concierge whether there is a bus stop nearby.

You must buy a ticket in advance if getting on at Avenida do Mar, but you can buy a ticket from the driver if you board elsewhere. Note that tickets bought on the bus are more expensive than those bought in advance from kiosks. Once you get the hang of the system, you might want to buy a stock of tickets from the bus station kiosks in advance and use them as required. If you plan to make more than 15 journeys a week by bus, it can be cheaper to buy a seven-day pass

Tickets are priced according to the number of zones you will pass through and they have to be inserted into the cancelling machine alongside the driver when you get on the bus.

BY AIR

During the spring and summer, there are several flights a day between Madeira and Porto Santo. The price for the 15-minute flight is relatively expensive, but worth it to avoid the ferry crossing, which can be rough, even in summer. Bookings can be made at all travel agencies and through TAP, the national Portuguese airline, who have an office (tel: 239200) at Avenida das Comunidades Madeireises 10 in Funchal.

BY BOAT

Crossing to Porto Santo by the car ferry *Lobo Ma Rinha* is less expensive than flying, but it takes about 2 hours and 40 minutes. The boat makes the trip once a day with the exception of Tuesdays. For more information contact the car ferry office at Rua Praia 8, Funchal (tel: 226511) or enquire directly at the harbour.

During the summer the government-owned yacht *Pirata Azul* makes irregular voyages to the

Ilhas Desertas. Details may be obtained from the sales kiosks, or from hotel concierges and travel agents.

Driving

Madeira is very mountainous and roads are characterised by constant hairpin bends – not wonderful for those who suffer from vertigo or car sickness.

However, undoubtedly the best way to get to know Madeira and Porto Santo is by car, even though it is fairly expensive to hire one on both islands. Drivers must be over 21 with at least one year's driving experience. Credit cards are

Taxis

Standard tariffs have been established for the main tourist destinations (e.g. Monte, the Botanical Gardens); these prices also include waiting times. Each taxi driver carries a corresponding list, which should be consulted if misunderstandings arise. Tariffs for other destinations are at least partially negotiable, although general guidelines have been laid down (for example, a complete island tour costs about €80). Short journeys within Funchal are metered. During the daytime, Tariff 1 is applicable; at night (after 10pm) and at weekends, Tariff 2 is used. The minimum fare is €1.5.

Useful Taxi Numbers:
Funchal
Avenida Arriaga
Tel: 220911/222500
Largo do Municipio
Tel: 222000
Avenida do Mar
Tel: 224588
Caniço
Tel: 934522
Monte
Tel: 782158
Santana
Tel: 572540
Porto Santo
Tel: 982334

accepted. At some car rental agencies you can also hire a driver.

When you compare hire-car prices, be sure that you include all the extras. Many car-rental companies advertise very low headline rates but often bury various additional tax and insurance charges in the small print.

It is essential to take out damage waiver insurance (which costs about €35), since otherwise a bump or a scratch – a common occurrence in Maderia – can cost you an automatic €450.

Car rental

The following addresses are all in Funchal.
Atlas
Avenida do Infante 29.
Tel: 223100
Avis
Santa Caterina Airport.
Tel: 524392
Brava
Caminho do Amparo 2.
Tel: 764400
Europcar
Santa Caterina Airport.
Tel: 765116
Hertz
Santa Caterina Airport.
Tel: 524360
O Moinho
Estrada Monumental.
Tel: 762123
Nunes Rent-A-Car
Rua Ivens 13b, Funchal.
Tel 213130

A good place to try on Porto Santo is **O Moinho** (Rua Dr Nuno Silvestre Teixeira 13, tel: 982403), which rents out Mini-Mokes at reasonable daily or weekly rates.

The **Automobile Club** can be reached through Club Sports da Madeira, Avenida Arriaga 43, tel: 231190.

Driving Tips

Madeira may be a paradise for rally drivers, but it can be quite harrowing for the average motorist. It's not unusual to hear someone honk approaching a sharp curve or have them overtake you in a daredevil manoeuvre. Yet although

most Madeiran drivers appear to take more notice of the prevailing conditions than of the traffic signs, it's worth driving carefully and being considerate. Hitchhiking is not encouraged.

Don't forget traffic drives on the right. Seat belts have to be worn. Speed limits vary from 60 kmph (38mph) to 80 kmph (50mph), 100 kmph (62mph) and 120 kmph (75 mph), depending on the area. Drink-drive laws are very strict, and random checks are frequently carried out as part of a campaign to stamp down on drunken driving.

Parking

Traffic is heavy and parking spaces are hard to find in central Funchal. Parking is available by the Marina shopping complex, along the coast and out of the centre. It costs around €2 for 2 hours. The minimum parking fine is €250.

Outside Funchal parking is relatively easy and uncomplicated if you take a hire car out for sightseeing, or park somewhere to take a *levada* walk. There are also plenty of *miradouros* (look-out points) where the roadside verges have been extended to accommodate vehicles. Cars are generally safe, even when left in remote places.

Holiday villas beyond indulgence.

BALEARICS ~ CARIBBEAN ~ FRANCE ~ GREECE ~ ITALY ~ MAURITIUS
MOROCCO ~ PORTUGAL ~ SCOTLAND ~ SPAIN

If you enjoy the really good things in life, we offer the highest quality holiday villas with the utmost privacy, style and true luxury. You'll find each with maid service and most have swimming pools.

For 18 years, we've gone to great lengths to select the very best villas at all of our locations around the world.

Contact us for a brochure on the destination of your choice and experience what most only dream of.

INTERNATIONAL
CHAPTERS

Toll Free: 1 866 493 8340
International Chapters, 47-51 St. John's Wood High Street, London NW8 7NJ. Telephone: +44(0)20 7722 0722
email: info@villa-rentals.com www.villa-rentals.com

INSIGHT GUIDES

The classic series that puts you in the picture

Alaska	Dublin	**M**adeira	Rome
Amazon Wildlife	**E**ast African Wildlife	Madrid	Russia
American Southwest	Eastern Europe	Malaysia	**S**t Petersburg
Amsterdam	Ecuador	Mallorca & Ibiza	San Francisco
Argentina	Edinburgh	Malta	Sardinia
Arizona & Grand Canyon	Egypt	Mauritius, Réunion	Scandinavia
Asia, East	England	& Seychelles	Scotland
Asia, Southeast	**F**inland	Melbourne	Seattle
Australia	Florence	Mexico	Sicily
Austria	Florida	Miami	Singapore
Bahamas	France	Montreal	South Africa
Bali	France, Southwest	Morocco	South America
Baltic States	French Riviera	Moscow	Spain
Bangkok	**G**ambia & Senegal	**N**amibia	Spain, Northern
Barbados	Germany	Nepal	Spain, Southern
Barcelona	Glasgow	Netherlands	Sri Lanka
Beijing	Gran Canaria	New England	Sweden
Belgium	Great Britain	New Orleans	Switzerland
Belize	Great Railway Journeys	New York City	Sydney
Berlin	of Europe	New York State	Syria & Lebanon
Bermuda	Greece	New Zealand	**T**aiwan
Boston	Greek Islands	Nile	Tenerife
Brazil	Guatemala, Belize	Normandy	Texas
Brittany	& Yucatán	Norway	Thailand
Brussels	**H**awaii	**O**man & The UAE	Tokyo
Buenos Aires	Hong Kong	Oxford	Trinidad & Tobago
Burgundy	Hungary	**P**acific Northwest	Tunisia
Burma (Myanmar)	**I**celand	Pakistan	Turkey
Cairo	India	Paris	Tuscany
California	India, South	Peru	**U**mbria
California, Southern	Indonesia	Philadelphia	USA: On The Road
Canada	Ireland	Philippines	USA: Western States
Caribbean	Israel	Poland	US National Parks: West
Channel Islands	Istanbul	Portugal	**V**enezuela
Chicago	Italy	Prague	Venice
Chile	Italy, Northern	Provence	Vienna
China	Italy, Southern	Puerto Rico	Vietnam
Continental Europe	**J**amaica	**R**ajasthan	**W**ales
Corsica	Japan	Rio de Janeiro	
Costa Rica	Jerusalem		
Crete	Jordan		
Cuba	**K**enya		
Cyprus	Korea		
Czech & Slovak Republics	**L**aos & Cambodia		
Delhi, Jaipur & Agra	Lisbon		
Denmark	London		
Dominican Rep. & Haiti	Los Angeles		

 INSIGHT GUIDES

The world's largest collection of visual travel guides & maps

Where to Stay

Hotels and Pensions

Thanks to its celebrated illuminations and New Year fireworks display – not to mention the balmy weather – Madeira is enormously popular at Christmas and New Year. Hotels generally charge their highest rates for these two weeks, and often insist that you buy tickets to their gala Christmas and New Year dinners as a condition of booking. Book well in advance if you want to bag a room during this period – indeed, during any of the school holiday periods.

By contrast, rates out of season plummet. Some tour operators in Britain offer six-month winter holiday packages (1 October to 31 March) for an all-in price averaging around £5 per day including flights. Madeira's winter temperatures rarely drop below 18°C (64°F), and attractive out of season bargains (including substantial discounts at the luxurious Reid's Palace Hotel) are regularly advertised in the British press.

Prices

As elsewhere, prices of hotels on Madeira equate to the quality of the accommodation and the location. Luxury accommodation in 5- or 4-star hotels within ten minutes' walk of Funchal's city centre costs from around €150–300 a night for a double room, although you may have to pay extra for a sea view.

You'll pay around €75–125 a night for mid-range accommodation in one of the 3-star hotels or aparthotels lining the Estrada Monumental (about 30 minutes' walk away from central Funchal). Although taxis are relatively easy to get during the day, the competition is fiercer at night, when everyone wants to head out for their evening meal. The better hotels, and those furthest out of the town, offer free mini-bus shuttle services. But, in fact, there are plenty of shops and restaurants within the hotel district itself which cater to tourists, although they have less character than the downtown shops and restaurants.

Cheap Accommodation

The two-star city-centre pensions cost around €50–75 per night. The setting may not be ideal (you could find yourself above a bar or restaurant on a busy street), but the prices are reasonable, and the facilities ideal for budget travellers.

The concept of Bed & Breakfast doesn't really exist on Madeira, though there are one-star pensions offering cheap accommodation (about €25–50 per night) with breakfast included in the price (*see budget-price hotels listed below*).

Outside Funchal

If you want to avoid the bustle of Funchal, there are plenty of resort complexes and hotels strung out along the southern coast. To the north and inland, the choice is not that wide, but walkers will find two *pousadas* deliberately located in isolated rural situations. You should book several days in advance for these, especially if you want to stay over a weekend.

One island property magnate has also stated his intention to convert a chain of rural *quintas* (mansions) into small characterful hotels. These are unlikely to be cheap but they do open up the prospect that it will one day be possible to walk round the island, or tour by car, staying somewhere different every night.

Hotel Listings

The hotels below are listed by price category (starting with the most expensive), and then in alphabetical order within each category. We start with the hotels in the capital, followed by a selection of the best hotels outside Funchal.

FUNCHAL

Expensive (€€€)

Baía Azul
Estrada Monumental
Tel: 766260. Fax: 764245
This new first-class hotel has 215 double rooms, the majority with balcony and sea-view. Excellent modern facilities include a squash court, fitness room, sauna, 400-person conference space, bars and coffee shop. There is a regular courtesy bus to the centre of Funchal.

Pestana Carlton Madeira
Largo António Nobre
Tel: 239500. Fax: 227284
This modern 375-room hotel competes with the Casino Park in offering guests a wide range of sports facilities along with plenty of evening entertainment. As a result, many guests appear to spend their entire holiday within the confines of the hotel.

Price Guide

Approximate prices for a double room with bathroom, usually including breakfast, are:

€€€ €150–300
€€ €75–150
€ €75 and below

Pestana Carlton Park
Rua Imperatriz Dona Amélia
Tel: 233111. Fax: 232076
This brutally modern 400-room hotel and conference centre includes a circular casino complex which looks very much like Oscar Niemeyer's famous "Crown of Thorns" cathedral in Brasilia. The hotel puts on a range of dance and cabaret shows, some featuring a far-from-racy version of the can-can.

Cliff Bay Resort Hotel
Estrada Monumental 147
Tel: 707700. Fax: 762525
This five-star hotel overlooking the ocean has 201 rooms and is known for its "gastronomic nights". Regular shellfish buffets to the accompaniment of Portuguese folk music make for atmospheric dining.

Reid's Palace
Estrada Monumental 139
Tel: 717171. Fax: 717177
Occupying an elevated position on the cliffs just west of Funchal city centre, the legendary Reid's Palace Hotel enjoys an enviable view of the harbour and the half-shell of hills which cup Madeira's capital. If you like a traditional atmosphere, impeccable service and dressing up for dinner, Reid's is the place to come (many of the best rooms have recently been refurbished), and for one of the world's top hotels, it can be remarkably inexpensive if you choose an out-of-season package.

Quinta Perestrelo
Rua do Dr Pita 3
Tel: 763720. Fax: 763777
A fine old mansion now converted into a 68-bedroom hotel, with period character and modern comforts. There is a small pool and a pretty garden terrace.

Savoy Resort
Avenida do Infante
Tel: 222031. Fax: 223103
After Reid's, this is the smartest of Madeira's hotels, and the newly completed resort area means that it has some of the best sports and leisure facilities on the island. There is a large indoor swimming pool and another pool complex, set on a large terrace overlooking the ocean. Sea bathing is also available from a finger of rock thrusting out into the Atlantic. The beautiful gardens are used for evening barbecues and folklore evenings. Each of the 350 rooms in the old hotel has recently been refurbished, and there is an equal number of new rooms in the resort area on the seafront.

Moderate (€€)
Eden Mar
Rua do Gorgulho 2
Tel: 762221. Fax: 761966
One of the best hotels in the mid-price bracket with facilities comparable to the more luxurious hotels. The attraction of this hotel is its proximity to the big Lido Sol complex, with its Olympic-size swimming pool, children's pool and restaurants. The hotel also has a

smaller pool set in a palm-fringed garden, plus squash courts and a gym. Nearly all rooms have a kitchenette, satellite TV and air-conditioning.

Hotel do Centro
Rua do Carmo 20–22
Tel: 200510. Fax: 233915
This smart new hotel is situated in the city centre, with some great views from the top floor rooms over the sea.

Monte Carlo
Calçada da Saúde 10
Tel: 226131. Fax: 226134
This small and friendly hotel with its grand baroque façade was once a private house and is full of character. As it's located to the north of the town, near the Quintas das Cruzes museum, it takes a stiff uphill walk to reach it, but by way of compensation there are sweeping views from the hotel pool and terraces across the city to the sea.

Quinta da Bela Vista
Rua do Avista Navios 4
Tel: 764144. Fax: 765090
This atmospheric, antique-filled hotel, is set in well-tended gardens. It is one of the few fine old mansions in this part of Funchal that has managed to escape being demolished and replaced with a tower block.

Windsor
Rua das Hortas 4-C
Tel: 233081. Fax: 233080
A friendly small hotel in the city centre, away from the rather sanitised tourist zone. The (rooftop) pool is smaller than most, but the rooms are spacious and there is a large garage for guests' cars.

Inexpensive (€)
Monaco
Rua das Hortas 14
Tel: 230191. Fax: 233080
Comfortable small hotel set in the bustle of Funchal city centre's tightly-packed warren of streets.

Pension Astoria
Rua João Gago 10–14
Tel: 223820. Fax: 227229
Modern, clean pension, centrally located near the cathedral.

Quinta da Penha de Franca
Rua Penha de France 2
Tel: 204650. Fax: 229261

Price Guide

Approximate prices for a double room with bathroom, usually including breakfast, are:

€€€ €150–300
€€ €75–150
€ €75 and below

Homely hotel dwarfed by the nearby Savoy, not far from the city centre.

Residencial Santa Clara
Calçada do Pico 16b
Tel: 742194. Fax: 743280
It's a steep climb to this picturesque old mansion with its small pool, but the reward is marvellous views over the city. There's a modern annexe nearby, too.

OUTSIDE FUNCHAL

Expensive (€€€)
Casa Velha do Palheiro
Palheiro Golfe, São Gonçalo
Tel: 794901. Fax: 794925
Perfect for golf lovers, this elegant hotel sits alongside the island's most scenic golf course. Converted from the wealthy Conde de Carvalhal's 19th-century hunting lodge, the hotel has a country-house atmosphere, a gourmet restaurant that is considered one of the best on Madeira, extensive gardens, tennis courts and a swimming pool.

Quinta do Furão
Achado do Gramacho, Santana
Tel: 570100Fax: 573560
This luxury hotel on the north coast is set amongst vineyards (visitors are encouraged to get involved in the harvest in the late summer and early autumn). Unashamedly targeted at affluent travellers, the hotel has 39 large and stylishly decorated rooms and a restaurant serving international cuisine.

Quinta do Lorde
Sítio da Piedade, Caniçal
Tel: 960200. Fax: 960202
A good choice if you want peace and quiet, this smart, comfortable hotel is set on the Ponta de São Lourenço and has great sea views.

Quinta Splendida
Sítio da Vargem, Caniço
Tel: 930400. Fax: 930401
Modern hotel complex set in the beautiful grounds of a grand old *quinta*. Good facilities, including sauna, jacuzzi and swimming pool.

Roca Mar
Caniço de Baixo
Tel: 934334. Fax: 934044
The most luxurious of the hotels in the vicinity of Caniço, and very popular with German visitors. It offers a good range of activities, from the large sea-water swimming pool to boat trips and diving lessons. Courtesy coaches shuttle guests back and forth to Funchal, or you can opt for the hotel's own restaurants and evening entertainment programme of *fado* music, discos and folklore.

Royal Orchid Hotel
Caniço de Baixo
Tel: 934600. Fax: 934700
Smart new hotel with good facilities. All rooms have kitchenettes, most also have balconies and sea views Heated pool, gym and sauna, too.

Moderate (€€)

Estalagem do Santo
Casais Próximos,
Santo da Serra
Tel: 552595. Fax: 552596
New hotel in a modern *quinta*-style building. Friendly management.

Auto da Barca
Praceta 25 de Abril, Machico
Tel: 965330. Fax: 965563
Family-run hotel with all the mod cons you'd expect for the price.

Bravamar
Ribiera Brava
Tel: 952220. Fax: 951122
Modest establishment which makes a good base for exploring the west of the island. The town bus station is only a short step away, and you have comfortable rooms and swimming pool to return to after a days' walking in the hills.

Cabanas de São Jorge
Sítio da Baira da Quinta, Santana
Tel: 576291 Fax: 576100
Sleep in rondhovels (round houses) modelled on South African village huts, set in flower-filled gardens or stay in more conventional rooms with extensive ocean views. Located 8km (5 miles) west of Santana, the complex makes a peaceful base for exploring the island's north coast.

Residencial Calhau
Porto Moniz
Tel: 853104. Fax: 853443
Located on the wind and wave-battered coast in Madeira's northernmost village, this upmarket hotel offers panoramic views from its perch just above the resort's famous seawater bathing pools. Decent food, too, and the dining-room has a nice terrace overlooking the sea.

Dom Pedro Garajau
Sítio da Quinta,
Garajau
Tel: 934421. Fax: 932454
Pleasant if nondescript modern chain hotel in this modern seaside town. All rooms have balconies

Estalegem do Mar
Juncos – Fajã da Areia, São Vicente
Tel: 842218. Fax: 840019

In an attempt to attract visitors away from Funchal, São Vicente villagers have invested heavily in their hotels and restaurants, and this smart establishment right on the water's edge offers a surprising degree of sophistication for such a remote spot. There's a tennis court, a jacuzzi, while all rooms have sea views.

Eira do Serrado
Eira do Serrado, Curral das Freiras
Tel: 710060 Tel: 710061
Perched on the rim of the mountain that drops sheer down to the village of Curral das Freiras, this new hotel has, arguably, the best views in Madeira. Restaurant and bedroom windows enjoy romantic views of the peaks of the island's central massif.

Estalagem Onda Azul
Calheta
Tel: 823230
Located almost on the beach, close enough for you to be lulled to sleep by the sound of the ocean. With just 11 rooms, this is a favourite with visitors on walking tours in the west of the island. The restaurant, naturally, specialises in fresh fish.

Estalagem Relógio
Camacha
Tel: 922777. Fax: 922415
Wonderful views down to the sea across a broad valley. Clean, bright décor and efficient staff.

Inn and Art
Rua Robert Baden Powell R61/62,
Caniço do Baixo
Tel: 938200. Fax: 938219
This friendly, small hotel is tucked amongst flower-filled gardens on

Budget Hotels

Estrela
Calheta
Tel: 824518. Fax: 824481
Clean, spacious apartments, set on a hill looking down over town and out to sea.

Residencial Machico
Praceta 25 de Abril, Machico
Tel: 966511
Overlooks a bustling square in the centre of town. Rooms have TV and en-suite bathrooms.

O Cortado
Sítio do Cortado, Santana
Tel: 572240. Fax: 574538
Set in lovely countryside on the eastern outskirts of Santana, this modest hotel is clean and down-to-earth.

O Escondidinho das Canas
Pico António Fernandes, Santana
Tel: 572319
This classic Santana thatched cottage sleeps four.

O Salguerio
Sítio do Poças, Porto Moniz
Tel: 850080. Fax: 850089
A simply furnished guesthouse set in a good location not far from the sea.

Residencial Santo António
Rua Cónego César de Oliveira,
Santa Cruz
Tel: 524198. Fax: 524264
Friendly pension handily placed in the town centre.

the clifftops at Caniçal and is fronted by an art gallery with works for sale. Every room is different, with comfortable beds and big showers. Breakfast buffets are superb and the well-presented evening menu includes that rarity on Madeira, decent vegetarian food. Discounts are available for guests who book in for a week and pay in advance and a free car is included in the package. The hotel also has several self-catering villas and apartments in the village that can be rented by the week.

Jardim Atlântico
Lombo da Rocha,
Prazeres
Tel: 822200. Fax: 822522
This well-run resort hotel perched on the clifftops is very popular with German visitors. All rooms are complete with mini kitchens.

Hotel Jardim do Mar
Sítio da Piedade,
Jardim do Mar
Tel: 823616. Fax: 823617
The only hotel in this delightful seaside village. Friendly management.

O Rancho Madeirense
Pico das Pedras,
Santana
Tel: 572022. Fax: 572222
A group of rustic chalets which make a fine walker's base. Each sleeps two to four, and comes equipped with a kitchenette.

Orca Praia
Prainha do Arieiro,
São Martinho
Tel: 763322. Fax: 763311
Smart modern building set in steps down a cliff-face, in a village that's fast becoming an outer suburb of Funchal. All rooms have views out to sea.

Pousada do Pico Arieiro
Pico do Arieiro
Tel: 230110. Fax: 228611
This 18-room *pousada* is located just below the summit of the Pico do Arieiro, Madeira's third highest mountain. Most guests are hikers planning an early start along the footpath that links this peak to Madeira's highest, some four hours' walk away. Even if you do not want to walk, it is worth spending a

Price Guide

Approximate prices for a double room with bathroom, usually including breakfast, are:

€€€ €150–300
€€ €75–150
€ €75 and below

night here for the silence of the mountains, the dazzling clarity of the stars in the night sky and, if you are an early riser, the stunning colours of the dawn sunlight on the volcanic rocks of the peak.

Quinta da Capela
Sitio do Folhadal,
Porto da Cruz
Tel: 562491
Pleasant guest house in a converted 18th-century *quinta* overlooking the town.

Residencial São Bento
Rua 1 de Dezembro,
Ribeira Brava
Tel: 951506. Fax: 951505
Smart, comfortable hotel with some good views.

Hotel San Roque
Sítio Chão,
Cedro Gordo
Tel: 575249. Fax: 575534
Good views from the upper rooms down onto Penha da Águia and the sea. Good facilities, including a swimming pool.

Solar de Boaventura
Sítio do Serrão,
Boaventura
Tel: 863888. Fax: 863877
This is an old farmhouse now tastefully converted into a comfortable guesthouse. Good food, too.

Pousada dos Vinháticos
Serra de Água
Tel: 952344. Fax: 952540
This 12-room, rather spartan *pousada* is popular with walkers, thanks to its splendid setting on the Encumeada Pass amidst acres of protected natural woodland. The restaurant bustles with coach parties during the day, but the evening brings relative peace. Suitably, it specialises in country dishes such as stewed rabbit.

Holiday Flats

Most of the tour operators that feature Madeira (*see pages 248–9*) offer self-catering accommodation, either in aparthotels (where you share the facilities of the main hotel, but have your own small kitchen and dining suite), or flats in converted townhouses.

If you're based in the UK, have a look at the classified section of the Royal Horticultural Society magazine, *The Gardener*, which often has adverts for accommodation on the island. You could also try the classified ads in *The Lady* and in national newspapers with substantial travel supplements, such as the Saturday editions of *The Telegraph* and *The Independent,* or the *Sunday Times.*

Campgrounds

Madeira's only official campsite, the tiny **Parque de Campismo** (tel: 853447) is in Porto Moniz on the north-western coast. Porto Santo has one official campsite, too, off Rua Goulart Madeiros, in Vila Baleira (tel: 982361). Camping is permitted in the Parque Ecológico do Funchal as long as you have a permit from the forest wardens (details at Funchal's Department of Agriculture, tel: 204200). Permit numbers are restricted and priority is given to local students. Basic facilities of standpipes and barbecue pits are supplied, but there are no showers or toilets.

Where to Eat

What to Eat

On Madeira, you can eat well fairly inexpensively. The cuisine is simple and hearty, and includes specialities such as *espetada*, succulent cubes of marinated beef roasted over a wood fire. *Carne vinho alhos* – pork marinated in wine and garlic and braised – is another very popular dish, which is traditionally served at Christmas

From the wide range of desserts you are likely to encounter on the island, *pudim* – a fruit-flavoured custard – is well worth mentioning. *Bolo de mel*, a dark rich fruitcake made with molasses and spices was once served only at Christmas. Nowadays, however, it is popular all year round and is a much appreciated gift to take when you go visiting. It keeps for months, too.

Picnics

Chão Dos Louros, at Bica Da Cana on the Paul da Serra Plateau, is one of the best and busiest picnic spots on the island, particularly at weekends. But the Madeirans are great picknickers and you will notice lots of stopping-off places as you explore the island, many with barbecue-pits where you can grill an *espetada* or two.

If you are shopping for picnic ingredients, choose from the bustle of the **Mercado dos Lavradores**, with its wonderful array of bread, fresh fruit and salads and shops selling cheese and charcuterie, or cross the road to the well-stocked supermarket in the basement of the Anadia Shoping Complex

For a full description of Madeiran food and wine, see pages 123–5.

Choosing a Restaurant

Madeira has hundreds of bars and restaurants, most of which serve at least snacks. The smartest restaurants traditionally serve French or "international" cuisine, but with the vogue for regional cusine, more and more are offering dishes or entire menus inspired by regional cooking. Traditional dishes are also served in more casual restaurants.

Restaurant Listings

Restaurants are listed in alphabetical order by area within the capital. Those outside Funchal are listed alphabetically by town.

FUNCHAL

Old Funchal (Zona Velha)
Arsénio's
Rua da Santa Maria 169.
Tel: 224007.
Lively and casual seafood eaterie, very popular with tour parties as it regularly stages *fado* performances in the evenings. **€€**

Jaquet
Rua de Santa Maria 5. Tel: 225344.
No menu – instead, Senhor Luis will tell you what to eat in this little fish restaurant by the market. In addition to creating mouth-watering fish specialities, his mother cooks up delicious oregano chips. Prices, however, do not exactly correspond to the exceedingly simple decor. **€€**

O Jango
Rua de Santa Maria 166
Tel: 221280.
This small family-run place serving delicious local specialities (including fabulously fesh fish) is one of the best of the Old Town restaurants. Arrive early to avoid having to queue. **€**

Ipanema
Rua Dom Carlos I, 62. Tel: 225070
Smart hangout for Funchal trendies, serving Brazilian grilled steak, or chilli-flavoured fish dishes. **€€**

City Centre
Fim do Século
Rua da Carriera 144. Tel: 224476.
Good, solid menu, swift and friendly service and an intimate atmosphere. **€€**

Londres
Rua da Carriera 64. Tel: 235329.
Cheerful and cosy place for a quick bite to eat, usually packed with locals at lunchtime. **€€**

Mar Azul
Marina. Tel: 230079.
Simple but tasty menu, ranging from grilled meats to seafood, including fresh lobster. **€€**

Hotel Zone
A Rampa
Avenida do Infante. Tel: 235275.
Across the road from the Savoy, this smart, popular establishment specialises in Italian cuisine. **€€**

Casa Velha
Rua Imperatriz Dona Amélia 69.
Tel: 205600.
Regarded as one of Madeira's top gourmet restaurants, with a *faux*-rustic setting. **€€€**

Hong Kong
Olimpo Shopping Centre, Avenido do Infante. Tel: 228181.
A reasonable bet if you develop a sudden yen for Chinese food. **€**

Les Faunes
Reid's Hotel.
Tel: 717171 ext 7011.
Haute cuisine in elegant surroundings is what you'd expect from this legendary olde-worlde hotel. Evening dress is not compulsory – as it is in the hotel dining-room. **€€€**

Santa Catarina
Avenida do Infante 22.
Snack bar serving good, light meals; be sure to try their delicious fruit juices. **€**

Villa Cliff
Estrada Monumental 139.
Tel: 763725.
With great sea views from its clifftop setting, this light, airy restaurant serves good Italian food. €€

OUTSIDE FUNCHAL

A Nossa Aldeia
Sítio dos Casais Próximos, Santo da Serra. Tel: 552142.
Cheap-'n-cheerful joint in a rustic setting, serving a range of substantial dishes from hamburgers to *espetada*. €

Café Relógio
Camacha. Tel: 922114.
In the same building as the island's largest wicker souvenir shop. Local food, live jazz and both dancing on Friday and Saturday, and marvellous views. €€

Casa de Portela
Portela. Tel: 966169.
Chalet-style bar and restaurant serving straightforward Madeiran dishes. The *espetada* is excellent, as is the home-made cider. €

Casa do Abrigo do Poiso
Poiso, on the EN103 between Funchal and Faial. Tel: 782259.
Cosy place with an open fireplace and plenty of hearty regional specialities on the menu. €€

Churchill's Place
Câmara de Lobos. Tel: 944336.
Built close to the spot where Churchill liked to sit and paint, this upmarket little place has some unusual salads on the menu, along with the normal range of grilled fish and meat dishes. €€–€€€

Dom Pepe
Piornais, Sao Martinho.
Tel: 763240.
Seafood, fresh fish and the famous

Pichana meat are some of the dishes on offer at this pleasant restaurant on the western outskirts of Funchal. €€

Escondidinho
Machico. Tel: 965442.
Large, bustling establishment dishing up tasty, hearty local dishes, along with grilled meats and fish. €€

Ferro Velho
São Vicente. Tel: 842763.
Unpretentious bar-cum-restaurant in the centre of the village. €

Giuseppe Verdi
Garajau. Tel: 934663.
Pleasant pasta restaurant just outside town on the way to Caniço de Baixo. €€

Izidro
Caniço. Tel: 934342.
Highly rated local restaurant near the church serving fine home cooking. Especially good for fresh fish. €

Nun's Valley
Curral das Freiras. Tel: 712177.
The place to come for chestnut soup and other local specialities. €€

O Boieiro
Caniço. Tel: 934332.
Tables are fixed inside old bullock-carts at this jolly restaurant, which makes it a big hit with the coach-tour parties. The food's good but simple, offering a range of grilled meats and fish. €€

O Virgílio
São Vicente. Tel: 842467.
Beachfront bar-cum-restaurant very popular with the locals, thanks to its tasty home cooking. €€

Quinta do Furão
Santana. Tel: 570100.
Upmarket establishment owned by the Madeira Wine Company with a good wine list and great views. €€

Riba Mar
Câmara de Lobos. Tel: 942113.
Choose from an extensive selection of fish dishes at this family-run restaurant overlooking the sea. €€

São Cristóvão
Caramanchão, nr Machico.
Tel: 962444.
In a village just outside Machico, and a fine place to come for regional specialities such as rabbit and goat stew. €€

Gay Cafés

The **Theatre Café**, next door to Funchal's municipal theatre on Avenida Arriaga, is the island's most relaxed hangout for gays and lesbians.

Solar de Boaventura
Boaventura. Tel: 863888.
This small village restaurant with its open log fire serves hearty regional dishes, cooked with care – try the braised pork. €€

Solpoente
Ponta do Sol. Tel: 765424.
Housed in a former lighthouse with views over a pebble beach, Solpoente does good-value meals (prawns, salad and chips for about €9). €€

Victor's Bar
Ribeiro Frio. Tel: 575898.
Trout's the speciality at this cosy log-cabin with its open fire. €€

Cafés

Café Apolo, Rua Dr António Almeida, Funchal. Tel: 220099.
A great rival of the Café Funchal opposite. Good for people-watching.
Café Funchal, Rua Dr António Almeida, Funchal. Tel: 234600.
One of Funchal's most popular meeting-spots, this pleasant café is packed day and night with locals exchanging gossip.
Golden Gate, Avenida Arriaga 25, Funchal. Tel: 220053.
An old colonial café-restaurant near the main tourist office, with wicker chairs, ceiling fans and a nice upper terrace from which to watch the world go by. Good-value light meals range from toasted sandwiches to fish'n'chips; delicious cakes, too.
Hortensia Gardens Tea House
Caminho dos Pretos. Tel: 792179.
Close to the Jasmine Tea House, this café is set in lovely gardens.
Jasmine Tea House
Caminho dos Pretos. Tel 792796.
Just outside Funchal, and the perfect place to end a walk along the Levada dos Tornos or a visit to the Palheiro gardens. It is English-owned, hence the heavenly cakes and cream scones on the menu.

Culture

Architecture

The most architecturally impressive sites on the island are in Funchal: don't miss the Cathedral, the Colégio Church, the Santa Clara Convent and the Corpo Santo Chapel. None of these maintains regular visiting hours, however, and only the Santa Clara Convent offers guided tours.

Funchal's fortress of São Lourenço can only be visited if you book in advance, since it contains government offices. The same rules applie to the Old Customs House (the Alfândega Velha), which nowadays is the seat of the regional parliament. The fortress of São Tiago now houses a worthwhile Museum of Modern Art and the Peak Fortress is open during daylight hours, with a one-room display on the fort's history.

The rose-coloured Quinta Vigia, which is undoubtedly one of the grandest villas in Funchal, is now the official residence of Madeira's head of government, and only accessible when no formal reception is being held there. The luxuriant gardens are nonetheless well worth a stroll (open during working hours). Also try to have a look at the magnificent inner courtyard of the Town Hall.

Films

Three of Funchal's cinemas are particularly recommended: the **Cine-Max** in the Marina shopping centre (Avenida Arriaga), the **Cine Anadia** in Anadia shopping centre (Rue do Anardia); and the **Cine Santa Maria** in the old town, near the market.

Outside Funchal the parish churches at Santa Cruz, Ribeira Brava, Calheta and Monte are all worth seeing. Ribeiro Brava's São Bento, in particular, has fine 16th-century sculpture and a 16th-century Flemish *Nativity* above the altar.

Full descriptions of all the above buildings are given in the Places section of this book.

Memorials

As you walk through Funchal, look out for the bronze statues by Madeira's most famous sculptor, Francisco Franco: the **Airmen's Memorial** by the harbour, the "**Sower**" in Santa Catarina Park and the huge **Zarco Memorial** in the Avenida do Zarco.

The island's most important religious monument is the statue of the **Senhora da Paz** ("Our Lady of Peace"), located in Terreiro da Luta, above Monte. A small bust of the **Pope** beside the Regional Parliament in Funchal recalls a visit of John Paul II to Madeira.

Music, Theatre, Dance

Classical music concerts, theatre and ballet performances are extremely rare on the island. If they do take place, they are usually held in conjunction with festivals and are not always widely publicised. If you don't speak Portuguese and therefore can't decipher the daily newspapers, ask for details of what's happening when and where at Funchal's main tourist office .

Teatro Municipal Baltazar Dias
Avenida Arriaga
Tel: 220416.
This beautiful Belle Epoque theatre hosts visiting musicians, dance companies and theatre troupes. It is sometimes used as a cinema for art film festivals, too.

Open-air concerts

These are sometimes staged by local bands in the ampitheatre in the Municipal Gardens. The programme is usually displayed on a board on the Avenida Arriaga.

Nightlife

Where to Go

Madeira doesn't have a very sophisticated or pacy nightlife. As a result, several major hotels put on special tourist "shows" and cabarets two or three nights a week; these are open to allcomers.

For a taste of something more authentically Madeiran, head for the cafés of Funchal's Old Town or the Yacht Harbour. And don't miss a performance of **fado** music, a plaintive sound, which has its origins in the backstreets of Lisbon. The best place to experience it is at **Arsénio's Restaurant**, Rua de Santa Maria (tel: 224007), or round the corner at the hole-in-the-wall bar called **Marcelino Pão e Vinho** (literally "Marcellino's Bread and Wine") at Travessa das Torres (open 8pm to 4am daily).

Bars

Funchal
Berilights, corner of Estrada Monumental and Rua do Gorgulhol. Good music and peppy decor make this a promising choice for the young and young-at-heart.
Number Two, Rua do Favila (next to the Carlton Hotel). This is a pub proud of its British character.
Salsa Latina, Rua Imperatriz D. Amélia. An excellent local band (sometimes guests, too), does its best to keep the atmosphere pulsing. Good place for a gander at Funchal's yuppies in all their multi-generational glory.
Savoy Hotel: Avenida do Infante. Tel: 2223103. The Galáxia bar here is pleasant, if a trifle conservative.

Outside Funchal
Village Pub, Caniço. The town's hottest hangout. Pub ambience.

Ship's Bar, Caniço. German residents and tourists pack out this popular bar in the hotel district.

Vista Alegre, Curral das Freiras. Try the house speciality, homemade cherry liqueur.

Escondidinho, Machico This disco-pub is where the younger generation tend to congregate.

Nightclubs

Pestana Carlton Park
Rua Imperatriz Dona Amélia
Tel: 233111.
This has one of the smartest nightclubs on the island. Guests are also offered a well-rounded show programme and cabaret three nights a week, while the Casino da Madeira in the grounds has bingo and blackjack.

Pestana Carlton Madeira
Largo António Nobre. Tel: 239500.
The nightclub here is almost as swish as the Casino Park, and offers regular shows/cabarets, too.

In Zona Velha, the old city, a few down-to-earth local haunts you might want to check out include:

Mambo, Rampa D. Manuel.

Jaguar, Rua 5 de Outobro.

Royal, Rua 31 de Janeiro.

Kalifa, Rua Conde Carvalhal.

Discos

Don't spend too much time outside Funchal looking for clubs: all the following are in the capital city.

Copacabana Club
Rua Imperatriz Dona Amélia
Tel: 233111
This smart, spacious hangout is in the gounds of one of Madeira's poshest hotels. Don't expect the latest beats from Ibiza or Ayia Napia, though: think 70s disco instead.

Vespas
Avenida Sá Carneiro 60
Tel: 231202
Less formal than the Copacabana. Popular with a slightly younger crowd.

Duas Torres Hotel
Estrada Monumental.
TekL 762061
The club in this hotel is always packed with locals.

Festivals

Calendar of Events

Madeirans celebrate many festivals throughout the year, some primarily organized for tourists and others deeply rooted in religion and folklore. Many of the celebrations are the feast days of saints. The most important religious holiday takes place on 15 August in Monte in honour of Our Lady of Madeira.

For further information and exact dates of moveable feasts, contact the tourist office.

January
Santo Amaro
Santa Cruz (5th)
São Sebastião
Caniçal, Câmara de Lobos (20th).

February
São Brás
Arco da Calheta (3rd).
Festa dos Compadres (Godfathers' Carnival)
Santana and other towns across the island (moveable feast).
Carnival
Weekend prior to Ash Wednesday. Huge festival in Funchal with themed floats and mayhem.

April
Festa da Flôr
Flower Festival, Funchal (mid- to late April). Another excuse for street parades and floats weighed down with flowers.
Esperito Santo
Whitsuntide. Camacha (moveable feast, sometimes falls in May).

May
Nossa Senhora de Fátima
Funchal (13th May).

June
Festival of Classical Music
Funchal.
Santo António
Santo da Serra (13th).
São João
Various locations including São João, S. Martinho, Câmara de Lobos, Lombada, Ponta do Sol, Fajã da Ovelha, etc (24th).
São Pedro
Câmara de Lobos, Ponta do Pargo, Ribeira Brava (29th).
Festa das Tosquias
Sheep-Shearing Festival. Santana, Paúl da Serra (end of the month).

July
Festa do Senhor
Santa Cruz (moveable feast).
Santa Maria Madalena
Porto Moniz, Madalena do Mar (moveable feast).
Santa Ana
Santana (22nd)
"24 Horas a Bailar"
A 24-hour dance, Santana, held at weekends, mid- to late July.
Feira Agro-Pecuária
Agricultural Fair and Festival, Porto Moniz.

August
Nossa Senhora do Monte
Monte (15th).
São Laurenço
Camacha (14/15th).
São Francisco Xavier
Calheta (last Sunday in the month).

September
Nossa Senhora dos Remédios
Quinta Grande (first Sunday).
Festa do Vinho Madeira
Wine Festival. Estreito de Câmara de Lobos, Funchal (third Sunday).
Festa do Pêro
Apple Festival. Ponta do Pargo (mid- to late September).

October
Festa do Rosàrio
São Vicente (first Sunday).
Nossa Sehnora do Livramento
Ponta do Sol (8/9th).
Festa do Senhor dos Milagres
Machico (Sun at end of month).
Festival de Bandas
Ribeira Brava.

Festa da Macã
Camacha.

November

Festa da Castanha
Chestnut Festival. Curral das
Freiras (1st).
S. Martinho
S. Martinho, etc (moveable feast).
Santo André Avelino,
Canhas (30th).

December

Nossa Senhora da Conceição,
Ribeira Brava, Câmara de Lobos,
Machico (8th).
Festival of Lights
From the 8th. Sees the streets
of Funchal lit up with imaginative
displays and buildings outlined
with white bulbs.
New Year's Eve
Madeira's firework display, with
boat cruises in the harbour, is
internationally famous.
Funchal (31st).

The Great Outdoors

Spectator Sports

Football

Madeira's premier team, Club
Sport Maritimo, is currently in
the Portuguese First Division. The
Nacional and União teams also play
in the National League.

Matches take place on alternate
Sunday afternoons at the Barreiros
stadium in Funchal, near the hotel
zone. Dates and times of matches
are published in the local
newspapers. Alternatively,. just ask
your hotel concierge or any taxi
driver for details.

Information

Direção Regional dos Desportos,
Rua da Carreira 43 (Pátio)
Tel: 233561/62.
This office can provide information
on local sport events, including
international tournaments (tennis,
swimming, cycling, bridge, rallies,
etc). It also has a list of Madeira's
numerous sports clubs.

Many of the big hotels organize
local and even international
sporting championships, too.

Participant Sports

DEEP-SEA FISHING

Big game fishing is well
established, with swordfish, marlin
and shark are just some of the fish
to be won. To organize a trip, try
contacting one of the following:
Turipesca
Funchal Yacht Harbour. Tel: 231063
Open 9.30am–4.30pm daily.
Costa do Sol
Funchal Yacht Harbour. Tel: 224390
Anguilla Lapeira
Porto Santo. Tel: 983479 (pm only).

DIVING

Snorkelling and diving are both
popular during the main Easter to
October holiday season. The
Madeira Carlton, Savoy and Cliff
Bay hotels in Funchal alll have
diving clubs with equipment to hire.
Otherwise, you can ask at your
hotel reception for details of schools
nearby. Outside Funchal, you can
contact one of the following:
Galomar
Caniço de Baixo
Tel: 932410.
Here, you can join up with groups
heading off to explore Madeira's
underwater national parks.
Diving equipment, cutters and a
decompression chamber are at
your disposal, and courses are
also available.
Atalaia
Roca Mar
Caniço de Baixo
Tel: 933334.
Equipment and courses offered. If
it's more convenient, you can get in
touch with this club through the
Hotel Pedro in Machico.
Urs Moser Diving Center
Porto Santo
el: 982162.
This centre is is only open from
early May to late October. Diving
equipment, boat hire and courses are
available, with excursions for both
beginners and experienced divers.

FITNESS TRAINING

If you aren't the outdoor type, you
may like to investigate Madeira's
gym facilities. Nearly all the larger
hotels on the island offer exercise
programmes. Some recommended
gyms in Funchal are:
Symetrix
the Monumental Commercial Centre
Tel: 766179.
This public gym has good facilities,
including a fully-equipped gym,
aerobic and yoga classes, sauna
and massage.
Quinta Magnolia
Rua do Dr Pita
Tel: 764598.
Once the British Country Club, this

is now open to all comers. Has a fitness trail which winds through delightful gardens. Open summer 8.30am–7pm; winter 8.30am–5pm; entrance fee.
The Casino Park Hotel
Rua Imperatriz D. Amélia
Tel: 233111.
Has a particularly good fitness centre, which you can use for a fee.

GOLF

The mountainous terrain of Madeira means that this is not a great island for golfing. The courses that do exist, however, tend to be in lovely locations.
Lessons are also available, and clubs can be rented or bought.
Santo da Serra Golf Course
Tel: 552345.
Also known as the Campo de Golfe), sits high up on a plateau at Santo da Serra village, 25 km (15 miles) outside Funchal. The oldest course on the island, it hosts the PGA European Tour's Madeira Open. It is marvellously scenic (distance 6,039 metres, par 72) with inspirational views back up the mountains and out over the Atlantic below. It also has a driving range, putting green and a pitch-and-putt area. Buggies are readily available.
Palheiro Golf
Tel: 792116. www.madeira-golf.com
Opened in 1993, and is only 15 minutes' drive east of Funchal. Classic Madeiran hills, ridges and deep valleys have all been incorporated into the terrain to produce a dramatically interesting course, with stunning views. Course distance is 6,015 metres, par 71. Buggies are available for hire, and there is also a driving range and putting green.

HORSE RIDING

The Hotel Estrelícia (Caminho Velho da Ajuda, tel: 765131) acts as the agent for the Centro de Hipismo da Madeira (tel: 792582)and can also organize transportation out to the riding club (*hipismo* in Portuguese).

Sightseeing Tours

If you want to explore the remoter parts of the island, jeep safaris are available through the following companies:
Intertours. Tel: 228344
Costa do Sol
Marina do Funchal. Tel: 238538.
Mini-Cruise Safari Company
Tel: 0931 9864485.

An equestrian centre has also been opened on Porto Santo; for information, contact Funchal's tourist office.

SAILING

To date, it has not been possible to hire sailing boats without crews. *Albatroz and Mont Carmel,* sailing yachts moored in the yacht harbour at Funchal, are both available for trips. Enquire directly on board, or at any of the small agencies located in the yacht harbour. Other places to contact are:
Aquasports, at Funchal's Lido swimming pool complex, Rua do Gorgulho, which hires out sailing dinghies.
Eurofun (tel: 0936-5011440), which organizes trips on the *Turquesa* Yacht.
Santa Maria de Columba: a splendid new replica of Christopher Columbus's boat, built in Câmara de Lobos. The galleon makes regular trips along the coast of Madeira. Contact Marina do Funchal, tel: 220327.
Aquanautica organizes yacht and water sports. Tel: 0931-9914257

SWIMMING

Large hotels such as the Savoy and the Carlton have swimming pools, along with access (via a pier) to sea bathing areas, but entrance fees for non-residents are generally high. Public swimming pool charges are more reasonable.
All the swimming pools listed below are open 9am–6pm all year

round; hours are extended during the summer months.

Funchal
Lido
Rua do Gorgulho (below Hotel Eden Mar). The largest lido complex on Madeira, with an Olympic-sized pool and a children's pool, plus bars and restaurants. Lounge chairs and sun umbrellas cost extra. At weekends it can get unbearably crowded, but it's usually pleasantly quiet during the week. Open daily; small entrance fee.
Quinta Magnólia
Rua do Dr Pita, tel: 764598. This freshwater heated swimming pool is set in the middle of gorgeous gardens. It is popular with school-children and is especially suitable for families with kids. Open summer 8.30am–7pm; winter 8.30am–5pm; entrance fee.
Clube Naval do Funchal
Estrada Monumental. For a minimal entrance fee you can use the sea access and bathe off the rocks here, as well as make use of the club rooms. Various watersports are also available.
Complexo Balnear da Barreirinha
Old Town, near São Tiago fortress. This small lido complex is almost exclusively frequented by locals.
Clube de Turismo
Estrada Monumental. This smart beach club has access to the sea via a lift.

Outside Funchal
Beach-Club Albatroz
Sitio da Terça, Santa Cruz, A quiet private beach club in the grounds of an old *quinta*.
Galo
Caniço de Baixo (located next to the Galomar hotel). Access to the beach is via a path through the cliffs. A really nice place to relax – it would be easy to spend the entire day here.
Dom Pedro Garajau Indoor Swimming Pool, Garajau. Good for children and senior citizens.
Sea Water Swimming Pools, Porto Moniz. An especially beautiful location. It is claimed that swimming here is beneficial for your health.

BEACHES

If you're not averse to pebbly beaches, you'll find a string of them in the small seaside towns along the south coast. As for sand, there is a small black sand beach at Prainha, near Caniçal. The best beach in Madeira, however, is the much larger golden sandy beach on Porto Santo.

TENNIS

Tennis has become akin to a national sport on Madeira, so courts are numerous. All the larger hotels have their own, and the staff should also be able to put you in contact with coaches.

The tennis courts at **Quinta Magnólia** (Rua do Dr Pita, Funchal; tel: 764598) are in a very beautiful setting, and the fees are reasonable. There are squash courts, too. Open summer 8.30am–7pm; winter 8.30am–5pm; entrance fee.

WINDSURFING

Boards can be rented from most good hotels, including the Hotel Porto Santo, along with (on Madeira) Reid's, the Casino Park Hotel, the Carlton and the Savoy.

You can also try Aquasports at the main Lido swimming complex in Funchal, and at Nautileste on Machico beach.

Alugabarc on Porto Santo is Madeira's only windsurfing school and is located right on the beach.

Walking

For a detailed description of walks on the island, see pages 211–230.

Transport

Buses The local buses are surprisingly easy to use and can take you to the most easily accessible starting points. If you choose to travel around by bus, you should get a copy of the bus timetable from the main tourist office in Funchal. This is an invaluable aid for serious walkers.

Taxis Journeys by taxi can be expensive, particularly to parts of the island with the most infrequent bus services. But hiring a taxi or a self-drive car for the day is almost always going to be more productive than waiting around for the buses.

The main taxi services are concentrated on the Avenue Arriaga in the capital, or call **Antral**, the Madeira Taxi Association (tel: 766620), which publishes a list of set prices to various parts of the island, which is also available from the main tourist office.

See also Getting Around.

Organized Walks

These can be very good value and also informative; they are particularly worth joining to reach the more inaccessible parts of the island.

Natura (Rua Dos Murcos, Funchal, tel: 236015, www.madeirawalks.com) offers a good programme of "easy walks for all ages", as well as more difficult mountain walks along the *levadas* and *veradas,* plus botanical and birdwatching expeditions. The company leads small groups with trained guides and using air conditioned transport. Tasty picnics are provided, too.

Walking Equipment

For most island walks, boots are far better than shoes or trainers. A small rucksack will carry all you need and keep your hands free for balancing, holding on and gesticulating in amazement at the views. A sunhat, a wet-weather top, a small torch (for tunnels), and a bottle of water are other essential items, as is a camera with an abundance of film.

Parks/Nature Reserves

Funchal and Monte
Jardim Botânico
Caminho do Meio, Funchal
Tel: 211200.
Open: daily 9am–6pm; entrance fee.
Jardim Orquídea
Rua Pita da Silva, (directly below the Botanical Gardens)
Tel: 238444. www.madeiraorchid.com
An orchid garden with 30,000 plants of 300 species. Open daily, 9am–6pm; entrance fee.
Jardim de São Francisco
Avenida Arriaga, across from the theatre. A little gem. Open daily, free.
Parque de Santa Catarina
Avenida do Infante.
Has great views down over the harbour, plus a snackbar, a disused chapel and a couple of statues. Open daily; free.
Quinta das Cruzes
Calçado do Pico 1.
The peaceful Archaeology Park surrounding the mansion is well worth a visit. Open daily 10am–6pm.
Quinta Magnólia
Rua do Dr Pita, Funchal
Tel: 764598.
Well-equipped sports complex set in beautiful gardens. Open summer 8.30am–7pm; winter 8.30am–5pm; entrance fee.
Quinta do Palheiro Ferreiro
(Blandy's Garden), Funchal.
Tel: 793044.
The most famous garden on the island. Open Mon–Fri 10am–12.30pm; entrance fee.
Quinta Vigia
Avenida do Infante (Presidential Palace). Open weekdays 9am–5pm, unless an official reception is being held here.
Jardim do Monte Palace
Monte. Tel: 782339.
A vast park with an oriental section, an *azulejo* collection and elaborately terraced gardens. Open Mon–Fri 9am–6pm; entrance fee.

Outside Funchal
Santo da Serra Park
Santo da Serra. Open daily; free.
Ribeiro Frio Nature Park
Open daily; free.
São Vincente Nature Park
A small park just outside the town displaying indigenous plants.

Shopping

Where to Shop

You can get a good overview of the kind of handicrafts produced on the island from the **Casa do Turista** souvenir shop on Rua do Conselheiro, located just off the seafront.

Some of the best souvenirs are handmade embroidered goods. You should buy directly from the embroidery factories if you want a good price; try **Patricio & Gouveira**, Rua do Visconde de Anadia 33.

For basketry, your best bet is the salerooms of the Café Relógio, in Camacha, although there are also a few outlets in Funchal, for example **Sousa & Gonçalves** at Rua do Castanheiro 47.

Bookshops & Libraries

Two bookshops offer a selection of foreign language literature: the **English Bookshop**, Rua da Carreira 43 (Pátio) and the **Livraria Esperança**, on Rua dos Ferreiros 119.

The best library is the **Direção Regional Assuntos Culturais** (DRAC) in Rua dos Ferreiros. Other public libraries include the **Calouste Gulbenkian**, located in Avenida Arriaga, and the library in the **Palácio São Pedro**, Rua da Mouraria 31 (historical archives). There are also a few smaller branches situated throughout various parts of the city. The **Barbeito** library, on Avenida Arriaga 48, has a selection of books about Columbus. A new foreign languages library is housed in the Quinta Magnolia, Rua do Dr Pita.

The best place to buy flowers is at the main Funchal market (**Mercado dos Lavradores**), but they can also be purchased at the airport. Flower sellers will advise you on the rules governing the export/import of cut flowers and plants, but essentially the rule is that the import of plant material is permitted, so long as it is free from soil. This means that bulbs can be imported, and the island's several orchid specialists will supply you with rooted stock in a protective get that prevents dehydration until you can plant the orchid at home.

Wine

You can taste Madeira wine without any obligation to buy in the tasting rooms of well-known vintners such as Barbeitos and Oliveira. Others are to be found in the Avenida Arriaga, the Rua dos Ferreiros and the Estrada Monumental.

The **Madeira Wine Company**, (Avenida Arriaga 28) offers guided tours around its premises on: Monday to Friday 10.30am and 3pm, Saturday 11am.

Clothes

Woollen hats with ear-flaps and pompoms, boots and other items of Madeiran folk costume are sold at street markets and in the usual tourist shops. A good street for finding all these items handily laid out for view is **Rua dos Mucas** in the city centre.

Good quality Portuguese shoes are stocked at **Cloé**, **Godiva** and **Artecouro**, in the city centre (around the cathedral) and in the larger shopping centres. Artecouro also manufactures other kinds of leather goods, though these sell for only slightly less here than they do elsewhere. Younger visitors may want to suss out the Hera brand of shoes, available at **Mattas** (Rua dos Ferreiros).

HYPERMARKETS

Hipermercados offer a wide range of food and goods. In Funchal, try the Anadia supermarket complex, opposite the covered market. Also, **Pingo Doce** has several outlets, with a particularly big store just off the Estrada Monumental in Funchal. There is a good choice of food, and wines and beers are very good value. Other companies to look out for are **Hiper Sa** and **Modelo**.

Outside Funchal, good hypermarkets can be found in Caniço and Ribeira Brava.

All shopping centres are open from 10am–10 or 11pm, and large supermarkets until 9 or 10pm.

Language

Pronunciation

Madeira's national language is Portuguese, and although a general knowledge of Spanish is always useful, the vowel sounds are not the same. The following are a few pronunciation examples which indicate special cases:

Se faz favor (please), is pronounced "se fash favor". A "z" except before a vowel is pronounced "sh".

A simple "r" is rolled only once and not several times, as is common in other Latin languages. The double "rr", found in *carro* (car) for example, is "rolled". An "o" found at the end of a word is spoken as "u", therefore *carro* is pronounced "carru".

Generally speaking a "c" when it precedes a, o and u is pronounced "k", for instance in the word *a conta* (the bill). This holds true unless it is accompanied by a cedilla, as in *açucar* (sugar), which is pronounced "assukar". If the "ç" falls in front of an e or i, it is pronounced as "s", for example *çedo* (early) is pronounced "sedu". The "j" of *jardim* (garden) is soft and corresponds to the "g" in the English word genie.

The odd plural endings "ães" and "ões", like the Portuguese ending "cão", are nasalised.

Language Lessons

For information regarding Portuguese lessons enquire at hotels or at the language school **Academia de Linguas da Madeira**, Rua Ribeirinho de Baixo 33. Tel: 231069.

Don't forget that *obrigado*, or *obrigada* for a female speaker, means thank you, *bom dia* means good day (morning), and *boa tarde* means good afternoon.

Useful Words/Phrases

Please *por favor/faz*
Thank you *obrigado/a*
Yes/no *sim/não*
Excuse me *desculpe/com licença*
Waiter, please... *faz favor... chefe!*
How much is it? *Quanto custa isto?*
Where are the *Onde é a* **restrooms?** *casa de banho?*
Can you tell me...? *Podeme dizer...?*
where/when/why *donde/quando/porquê*
Can you please *Ajude-me,* **help me?** *por favor.*
I'm lost *Perdi-me.*
What does that mean? I don't understand *O que significa isto? Não compréndo.*
Where is the... consulate? *Onde fica o consulado...?*

PLACE NAMES	PRONUNCIATION
Achada da Serra	*Ashada d'a Séra*
Calheta	*Calyéta*
Caniçal	*Canissal*
Câmara de Lobos	*Camara de Lobsh*
Estanquinhos	*Eshtangkingush*
Funchal	*Funshal*
Jardim de Serra	*Shardin d'a Séra*
Jardim Municipal	*Shardin Municipál*
Palheiro	*Palyéru*
Paúl da Serra	*Powl d'a Séra*
Pico dos Barcelos	*Piku dush Barkelush*
Portela	*Portéla*
Porto Moniz	*Portu Monish*
Porto Santo	*Portu Santu*
Pico do Arieiro	*Piku du Ariéru*
Ribeiro Frio	*Ribéru Fríu*
Santa Cruz	*Santa Croosh*
São Lourenço	*Siaou Lorenssu*
Seixal	*Sé-ishal*
Vinháticos	*Vinhatikush*

Further Reading

Flora

Da Costa, António and Franquinho, Luis de O: *Madeira, Plants and Flowers* (Francisco Ribeiro). Handy reference guide to local flora, with plenty of illustrations that walkers will find invaluable.
Vieira, Rui: *Flowers of Madeira* (Francisco Ribeiro). Another useful guide, but with fewer illustrations.

History

Liddell, Alex: *Madeira* (Faber and Faber). Though ostensibly a book about Madeira wine, this is as much about the history of the island and so makes excellent background reading.

Walks

John and Pat Underwood: *Landscapes of Madeira* (Sunflower Press). The walker's bible, full of well-researched *levada* walks.

Books and Magazines

Funchal's TURISMO stocks a good range of guides and maps of Madeira. Maps are handed out free of charge here, as is the monthly tourist English-language magazine *Madeira Island Bulletin*, and the brochure *Hello Madeira*. The bus schedule *Madeira By Bus* is kept up-to-date and can also be obtained here for a small charge.

Some tourist literature can also be found at the reception areas of good hotels, and some street kiosks.

Other Insight Guides

Insight Guides
A number of *Insight Guides* cover this region, each with the same fine photography and detailed text. Titles include *Insight Guide Portugal* and *Insight Guide Lisbon*.

Insight Pocket Guides
Insight Pocket Guides are written
by host authors who have devised
special itineraries to help you get
the most from a short stay. Titles
include Algarve and Lisbon.

Insight Compact Guides
The handy mini-encylopaedia
Compact Guides give you facts
at your fingertips and are ideal for
on-the-spot use. Text, pictures and
maps are carefully cross-referenced
for maximum convenience. Titles
include Portugal, Lisbon, Algarve
and Madeira.

Feedback

We do our best to ensure the information in our books is as accurate and
up-to-date as possible. The books are updated on a regular basis, using
local contacts, who painstakingly add, amend and correct as required.
However, some mistakes and omissions are inevitable and we are
ultimately reliant on our readers to put us in the picture.

We would welcome your feedback on any details related to your
experiences using the book "on the road". Maybe we recommended a hotel
that you liked (or another that you didn't), as well as interesting new
attractions, or facts and figures you have found out about the country itself.
The more details you can give us (particularly with regard to addresses,
e-mails and telephone numbers), the better.

We will acknowledge all contributions, and we'll
offer an Insight Guide to the best letters received.
Please write to us at:
> **Insight Guides**
> **PO Box 7910**
> **London SE1 1WE**
> **United Kingdom**

Or send e-mail to: **insight@apaguide.demon.co.uk**

ART & PHOTO CREDITS

AKG London 50
Archives Leonore Ander 58, 79R, 129, 184, 210
Tony Arruza 21, 22, 31, 56L, 56R, 57, 61, 63
Nick Bayntun 98, 191, 194/195, 218, 220
British Museum London 27
Casa Museu Frederico de Freitas 45, 52
Dieter Clarius 43
Deimer/Monachus 105, 106, 107, 109
Empresa Pública dos Jornais, Noticias e Capital 56R, 57, 62
Foul Anchor Archives 40
Glyn Genin spine, back cover left, top right, bottom centre, back flap top, 2B, 5B, 19, 24, 63R, 69, 71, 146, 149L, 152, 161T, 165, 167T, 169, 169T, 181, 182/183, 193, 201, 202T, 217, 220T, 229, 234, 235, 237, 237T, 238, 241T, 242/243, 244, 245, 247T
Bob Gibbons/Oxford Scientific Films 219
Thomas Grimm/Abacus 79L, 81, 196, 222R, 247
Terry Harris back cover centre right, 4/5, 99, 123, 131, 211, 231
Günther Heubl 79R, 215, 230
Jayawardene Photo Library 2/3, 10/11, 68, 188
Michael Jenner front flap top, 1, 160, 179
Paul Murphy 88, 104
Museu da Marinha, Belém 56L

Museu Nacional de Arte Antiga, Lisbon 21
New York Public Library 36/37
Gerhard H. Oberzill 6/7, 12/13, 20, 53, 66/67, 75, 86, 116, 119, 125, 127, 138/139, 142/143, 204, 224, 226, 232/233
Miguel Perestrelo 128L, 239
G.P. Reichelt 18, 16/17, 26, 28, 30, 47, 55, 60, 64/65, 72/73, 74, 77, 87, 89, 93, 94, 95, 100/101, 102, 113, 114, 120/121, 122, 130, 134/135, 136/137, 150, 161, 162/163, 227, 240
Victor Miguel Sousa 23
Scholastic Magazines Inc. 32, 33, 34/35
Vicente Museum of Photography Funchal 46, 51, 54
Bill Wassman 92, 103, 117, 149R, 225
Weidenfels Archives/British Library 44
Wilmington Society of the Fine Arts 38, 39
Phil Wood front flap bottom, 4B, 8/9, 25, 41, 42, 59, 63L, 70, 76, 78, 80, 84/85, 96, 97, 108, 110/111, 112, 124L, 124R, 126, 128R, 147, 148, 149T, 151, 151T, 153, 153T, 154, 155, 156, 157, 164, 167, 168L, 168R, 170/171, 172, 173, 175, 176, 177, 177T, 178, 178T, 189L, 189T, 190, 191T, 192, 197, 200, 200T, 202, 203, 205, 208/209, 214, 214T, 216, 219T, 221, 222L, 223, 227T, 228, 238T, 241

Picture Spreads

Pages 82/83: *Top row left to right*: Glyn Genin, Bob Gibbons/OSF, Mike Slater/OSF, Glyn Genin, Heather Angel. *Centre row*: Glyn Genin. *Bottom row left to right*: Nigel J. Dennis/NHPA, Glyn Genin, J.K. Burras/OSF, Glyn Genin.
Pages 132/133: *Top row*: All Photography by Miguel Perestrelo. *Centre row*: Paul Murphy. *Bottom row left to right*: Glyn Genin, Glyn Genin, Miguel Perestrelo, Nick Bayntun.
Pages 158/159: *Top row left to right*: J Highet/Hutchison Library, Glyn Genin, Phil Wood, J Highet/Hutchison Library. *Bottom row left to right*: Michael Jenner, Gerhard H. Oberzill, Phil Wood.
Pages 206/207: *Top row left to right*: Jayawardene Photo Library, Jayawardene Photo Library, Heather Angel, Glyn Genin. *Centre row*: Michael Jenner. *Bottom row left to right*: Glyn Genin, Glyn Genin, Jayawardene Photo Library, Trip/J Highet.
Pages 212/213: *Clockwise from top left*: Nick Bayntun, Terry Harris, Phil Wood, Glyn Genin; *the rest*: Phil Wood

Map Production Colin Earl
© 2002 Apa Publications GmbH & Co.
Verlag KG (Singapore branch)

Cartographic Editor **Zoë Goodwin**
Production **Stuart A Everitt**
Design Consultants
Carlotta Junger, Graham Mitchener
Picture Research **Hilary Genin**

Index

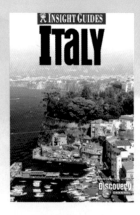